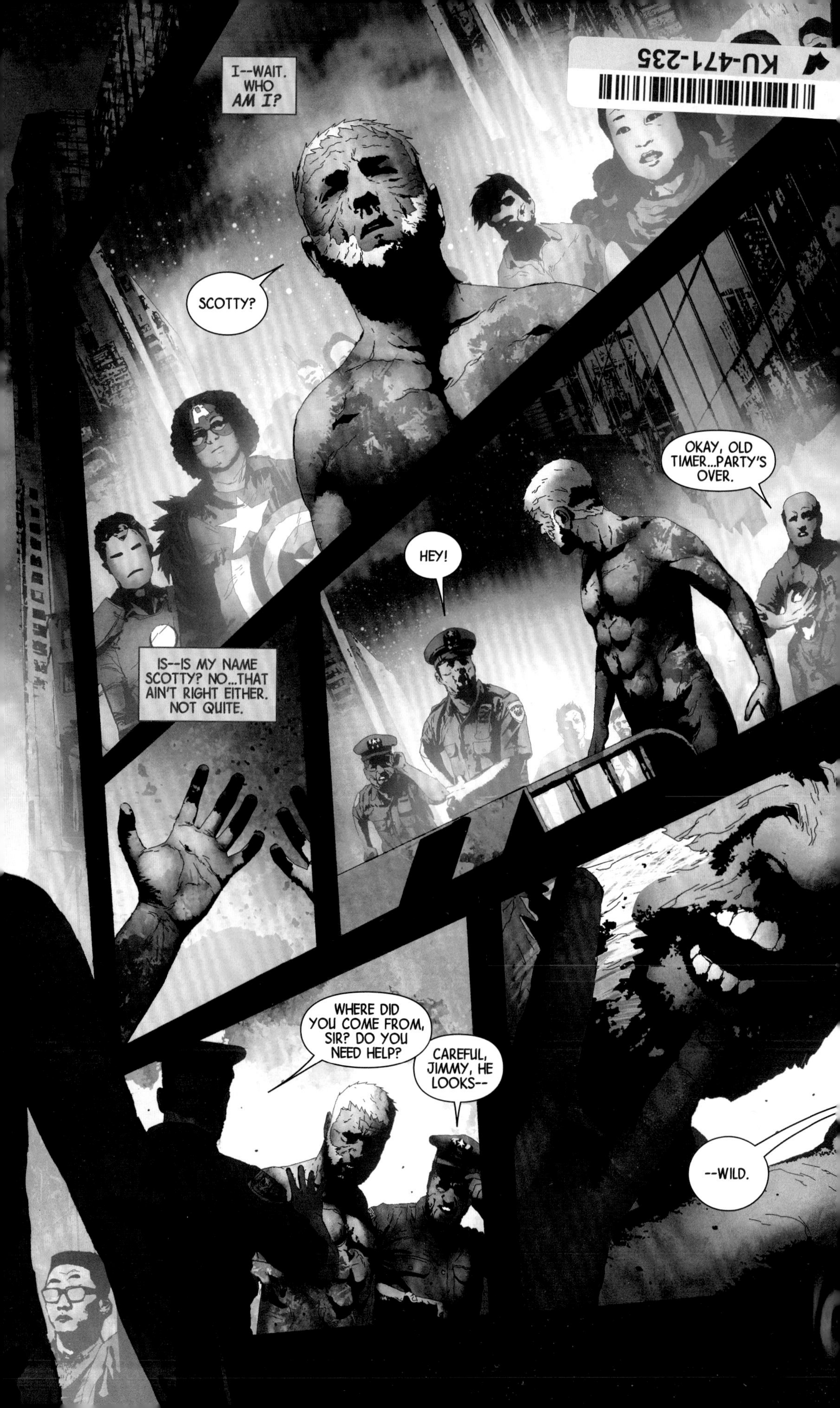
I--WAIT. WHO AM I?
SCOTTY?
IS--IS MY NAME SCOTTY? NO...THAT AIN'T RIGHT EITHER. NOT QUITE.
HEY!
OKAY, OLD TIMER...PARTY'S OVER.
WHERE DID YOU COME FROM, SIR? DO YOU NEED HELP?
CAREFUL, JIMMY, HE LOOKS--
--WILD.

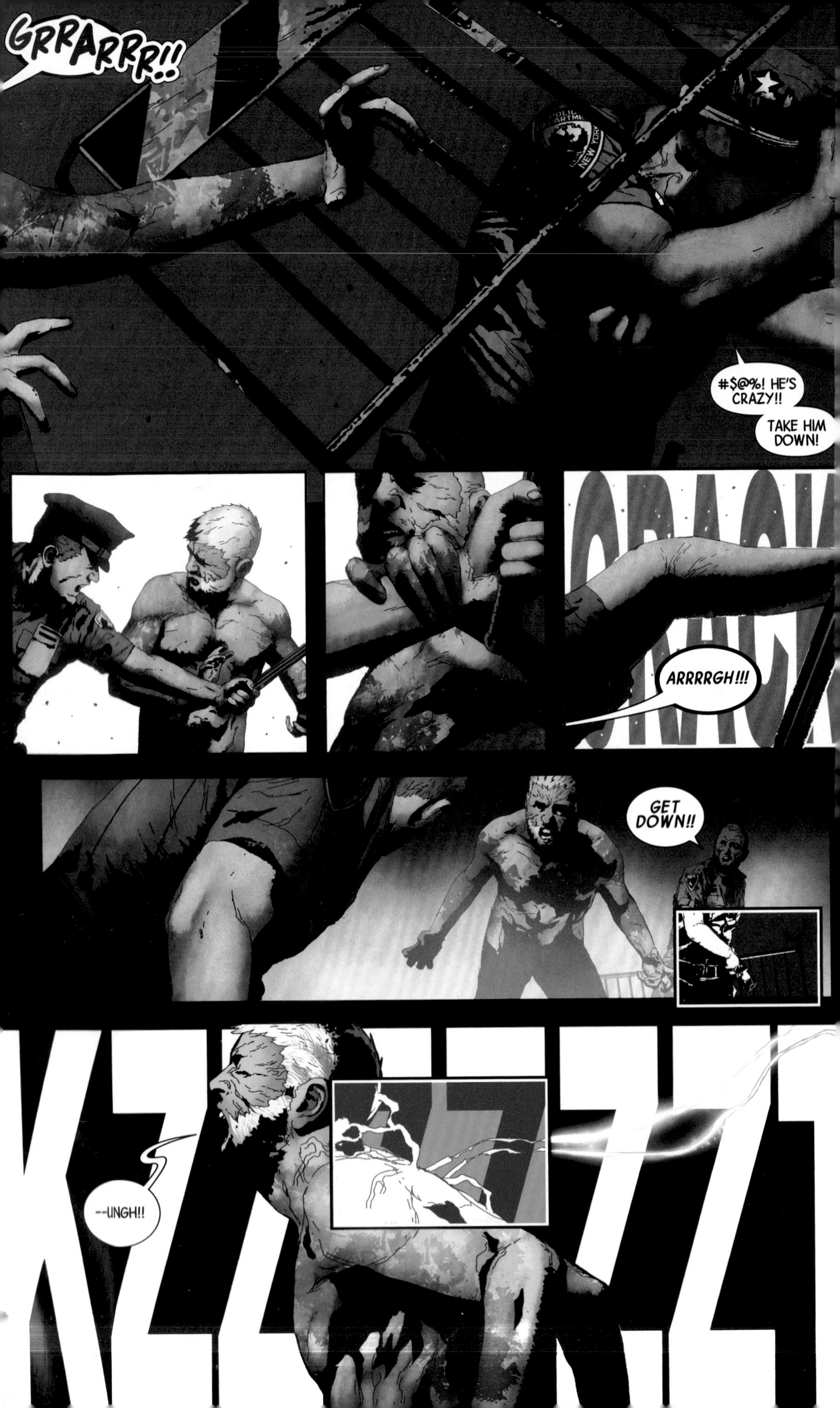
GRRARRRR!!
#$@%! HE'S CRAZY!!
TAKE HIM DOWN!
CRACK
ARRRRGH!!!
GET DOWN!!
KZZZZZT
--UNGH!!

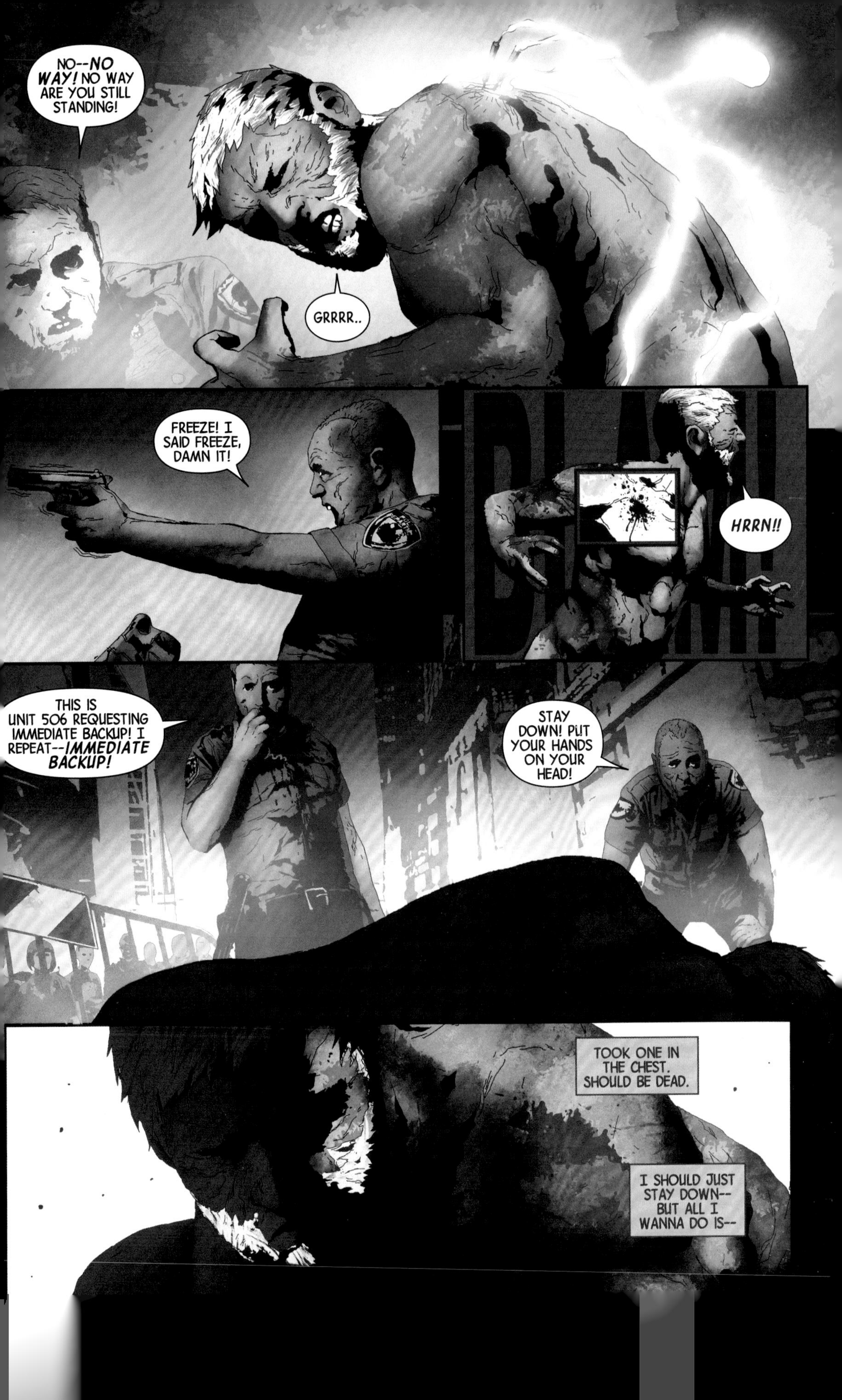
NO--NO WAY! NO WAY ARE YOU STILL STANDING!
GRRRR..
FREEZE! I SAID FREEZE, DAMN IT!
BLAM!
HRRN!!
THIS IS UNIT 506 REQUESTING IMMEDIATE BACKUP! I REPEAT--IMMEDIATE BACKUP!
STAY DOWN! PUT YOUR HANDS ON YOUR HEAD!
TOOK ONE IN THE CHEST. SHOULD BE DEAD.
I SHOULD JUST STAY DOWN-- BUT ALL I WANNA DO IS--

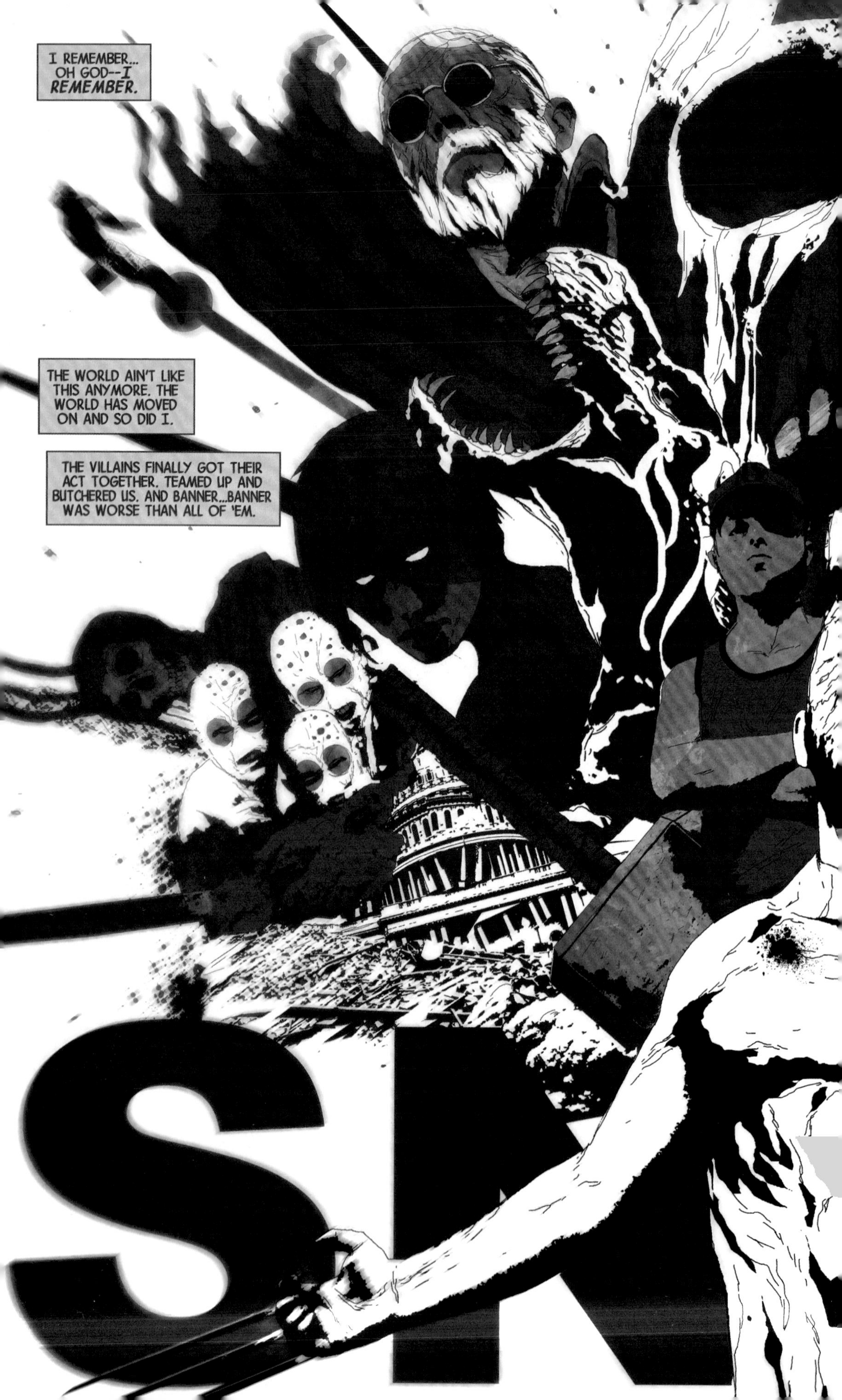

I REMEMBER... OH GOD--I REMEMBER.
THE WORLD AIN'T LIKE THIS ANYMORE. THE WORLD HAS MOVED ON AND SO DID I.
THE VILLAINS FINALLY GOT THEIR ACT TOGETHER. TEAMED UP AND BUTCHERED US. AND BANNER...BANNER WAS WORSE THAN ALL OF 'EM.

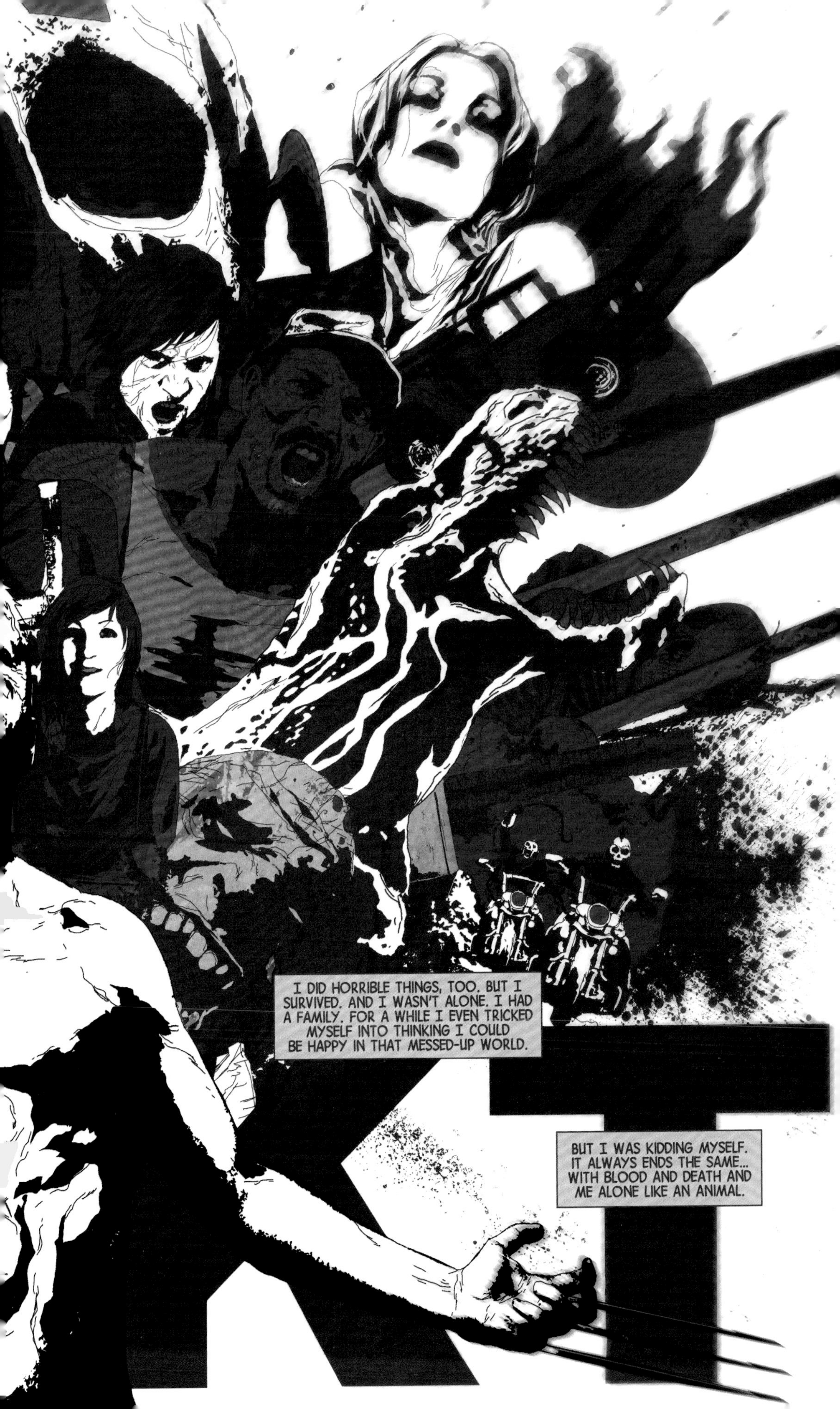
I DID HORRIBLE THINGS, TOO. BUT I SURVIVED. AND I WASN'T ALONE. I HAD A FAMILY. FOR A WHILE I EVEN TRICKED MYSELF INTO THINKING I COULD BE HAPPY IN THAT MESSED-UP WORLD.
BUT I WAS KIDDING MYSELF. IT ALWAYS ENDS THE SAME... WITH BLOOD AND DEATH AND ME ALONE LIKE AN ANIMAL.

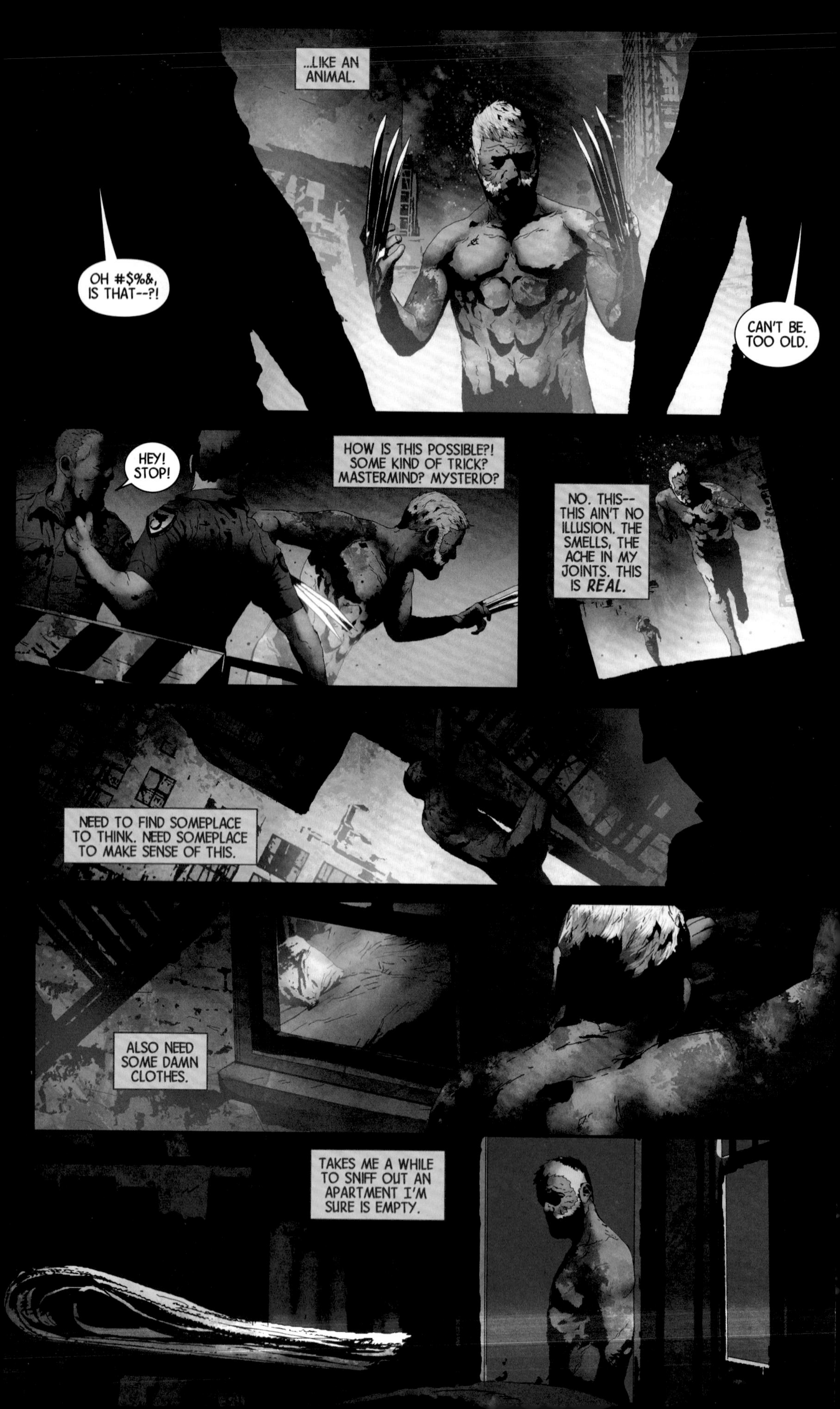
...LIKE AN ANIMAL.
OH #$%&, IS THAT--?!
CAN'T BE. TOO OLD.
HEY! STOP!
HOW IS THIS POSSIBLE?! SOME KIND OF TRICK? MASTERMIND? MYSTERIO?
NO. THIS-- THIS AIN'T NO ILLUSION. THE SMELLS, THE ACHE IN MY JOINTS. THIS IS REAL.
NEED TO FIND SOMEPLACE TO THINK. NEED SOMEPLACE TO MAKE SENSE OF THIS.
ALSO NEED SOME DAMN CLOTHES.
TAKES ME A WHILE TO SNIFF OUT AN APARTMENT I'M SURE IS EMPTY.

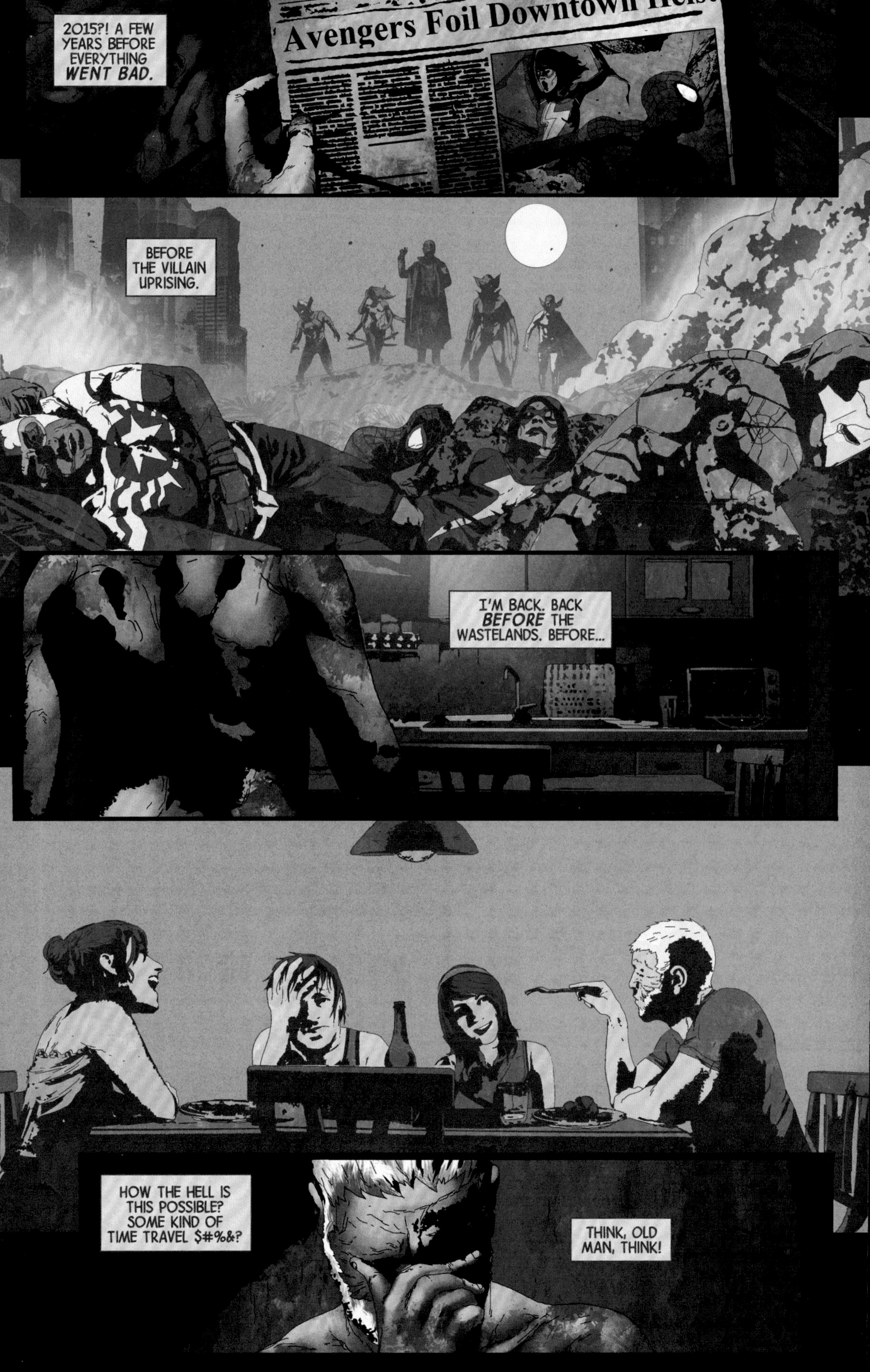

2015?! A FEW YEARS BEFORE EVERYTHING WENT BAD.
Avengers Foil Downtown Heis
BEFORE THE VILLAIN UPRISING.
I'M BACK. BACK BEFORE THE WASTELANDS. BEFORE...
HOW THE HELL IS THIS POSSIBLE? SOME KIND OF TIME TRAVEL $#%&?
THINK, OLD MAN, THINK!

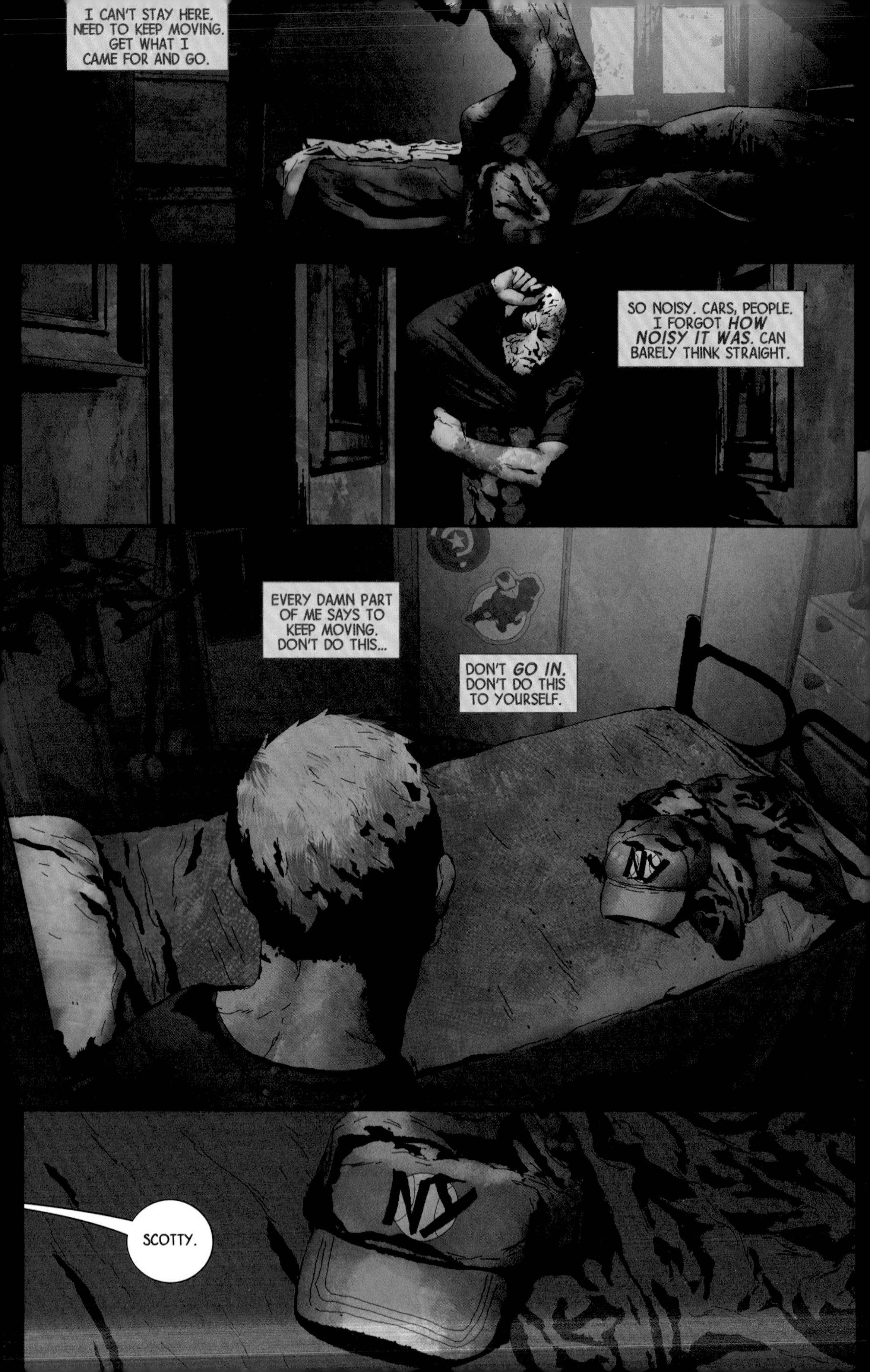
I CAN'T STAY HERE. NEED TO KEEP MOVING. GET WHAT I CAME FOR AND GO.
SO NOISY. CARS, PEOPLE. I FORGOT HOW NOISY IT WAS. CAN BARELY THINK STRAIGHT.
EVERY DAMN PART OF ME SAYS TO KEEP MOVING. DON'T DO THIS...
DON'T GO IN. DON'T DO THIS TO YOURSELF.
NY
NY
SCOTTY.

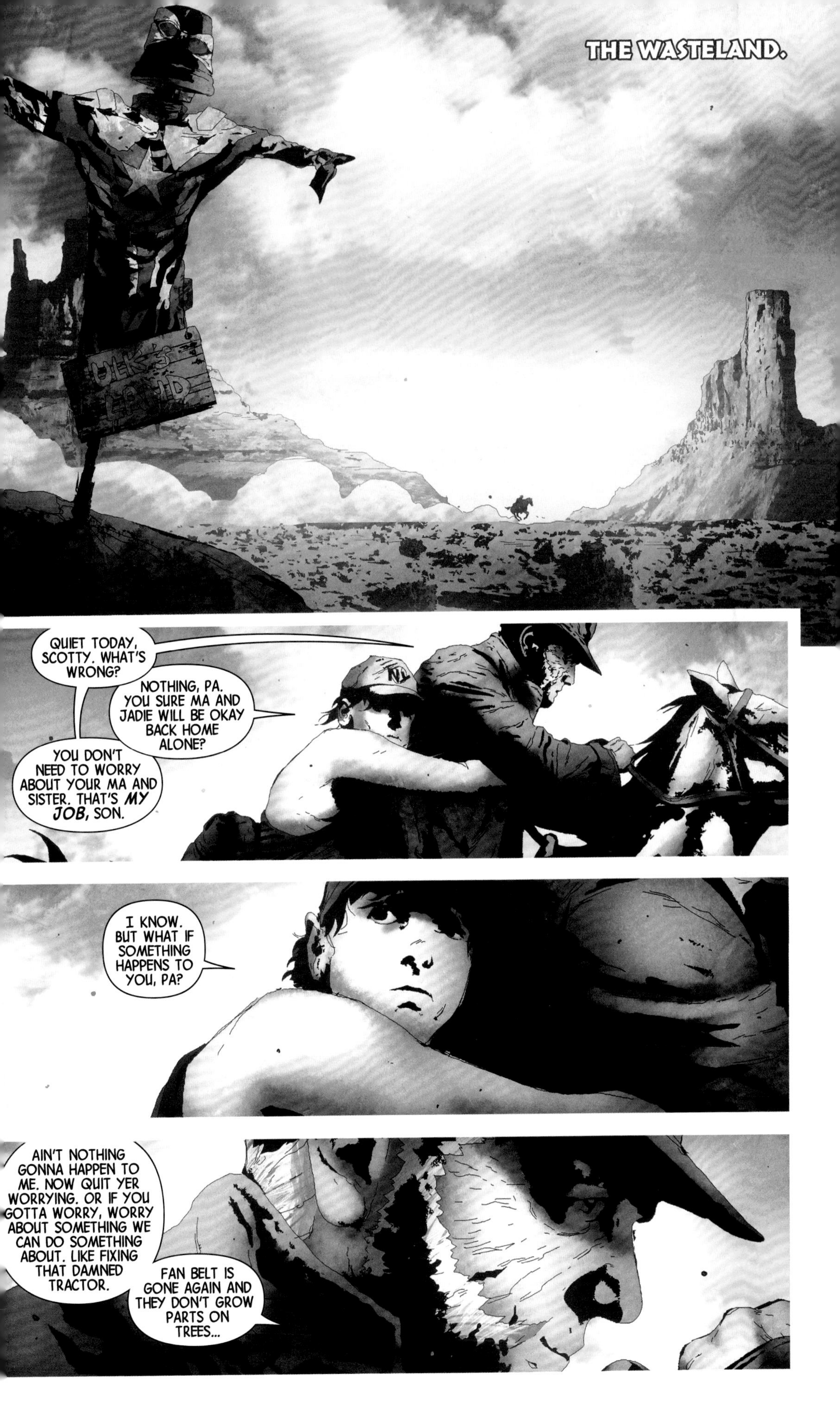
THE WASTELAND.
QUIET TODAY, SCOTTY. WHAT'S WRONG?
NOTHING, PA. YOU SURE MA AND JADIE WILL BE OKAY BACK HOME ALONE?
YOU DON'T NEED TO WORRY ABOUT YOUR MA AND SISTER. THAT'S *MY JOB*, SON.
I KNOW. BUT WHAT IF SOMETHING HAPPENS TO YOU, PA?
AIN'T NOTHING GONNA HAPPEN TO ME. NOW QUIT YER WORRYING. OR IF YOU GOTTA WORRY, WORRY ABOUT SOMETHING WE CAN DO SOMETHING ABOUT. LIKE FIXING THAT DAMNED TRACTOR.
FAN BELT IS GONE AGAIN AND THEY DON'T GROW PARTS ON TREES...

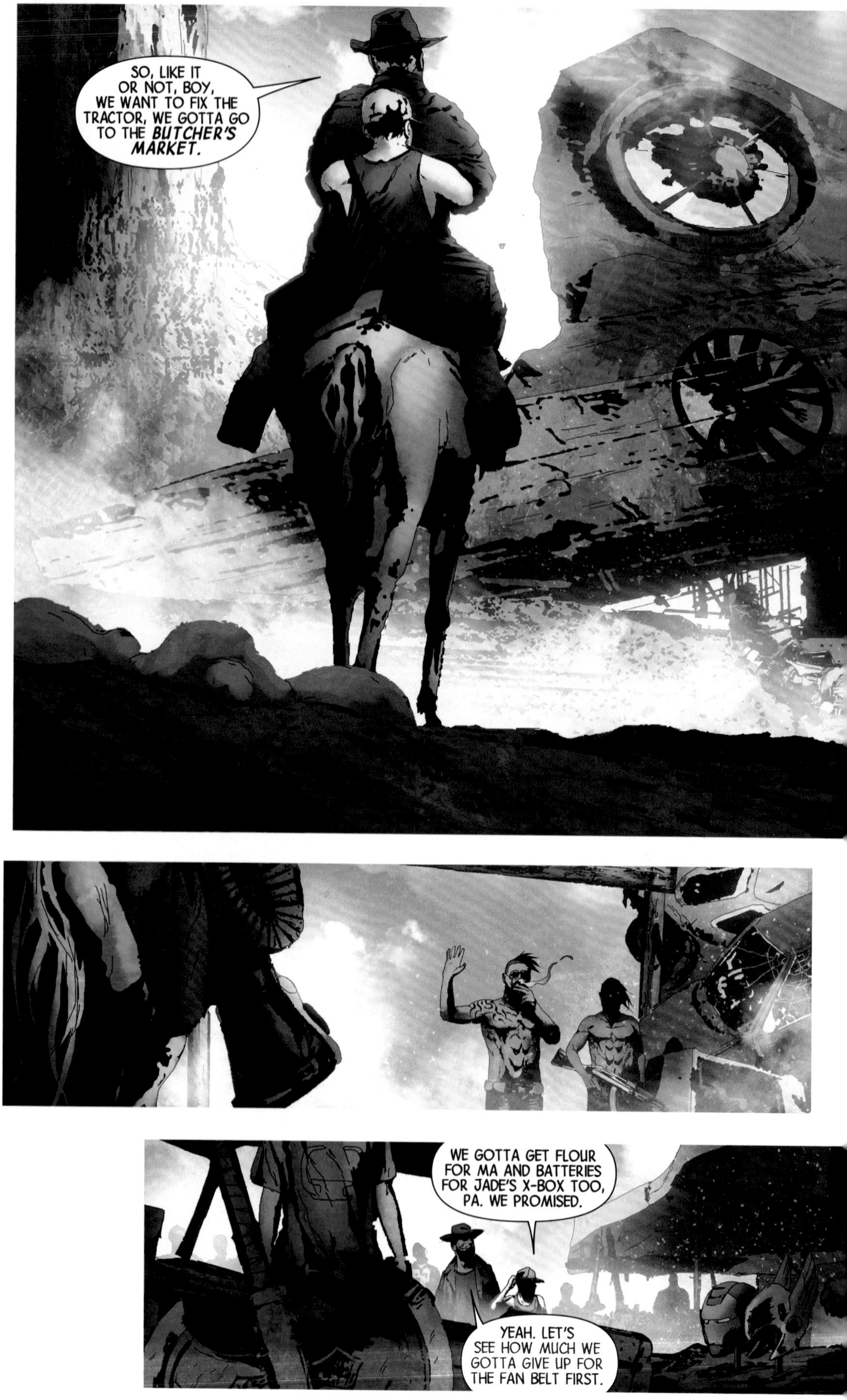
SO, LIKE IT OR NOT, BOY, WE WANT TO FIX THE TRACTOR, WE GOTTA GO TO THE BUTCHER'S MARKET.
WE GOTTA GET FLOUR FOR MA AND BATTERIES FOR JADE'S X-BOX TOO, PA. WE PROMISED.
YEAH. LET'S SEE HOW MUCH WE GOTTA GIVE UP FOR THE FAN BELT FIRST.

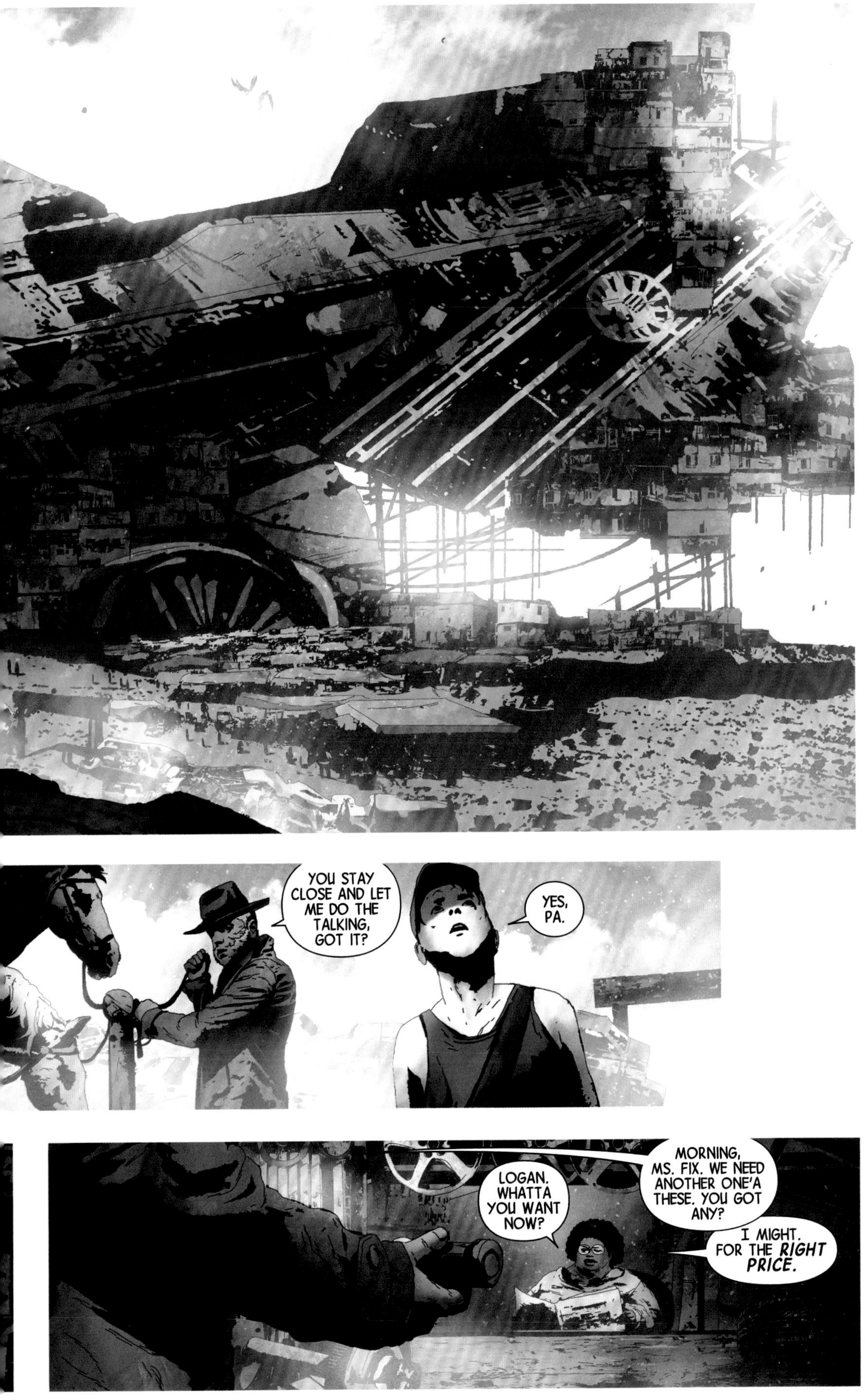

YOU STAY CLOSE AND LET ME DO THE TALKING, GOT IT?
YES, PA.
MORNING, MS. FIX. WE NEED ANOTHER ONE'A THESE. YOU GOT ANY?
LOGAN. WHATTA YOU WANT NOW?
I MIGHT. FOR THE RIGHT PRICE.

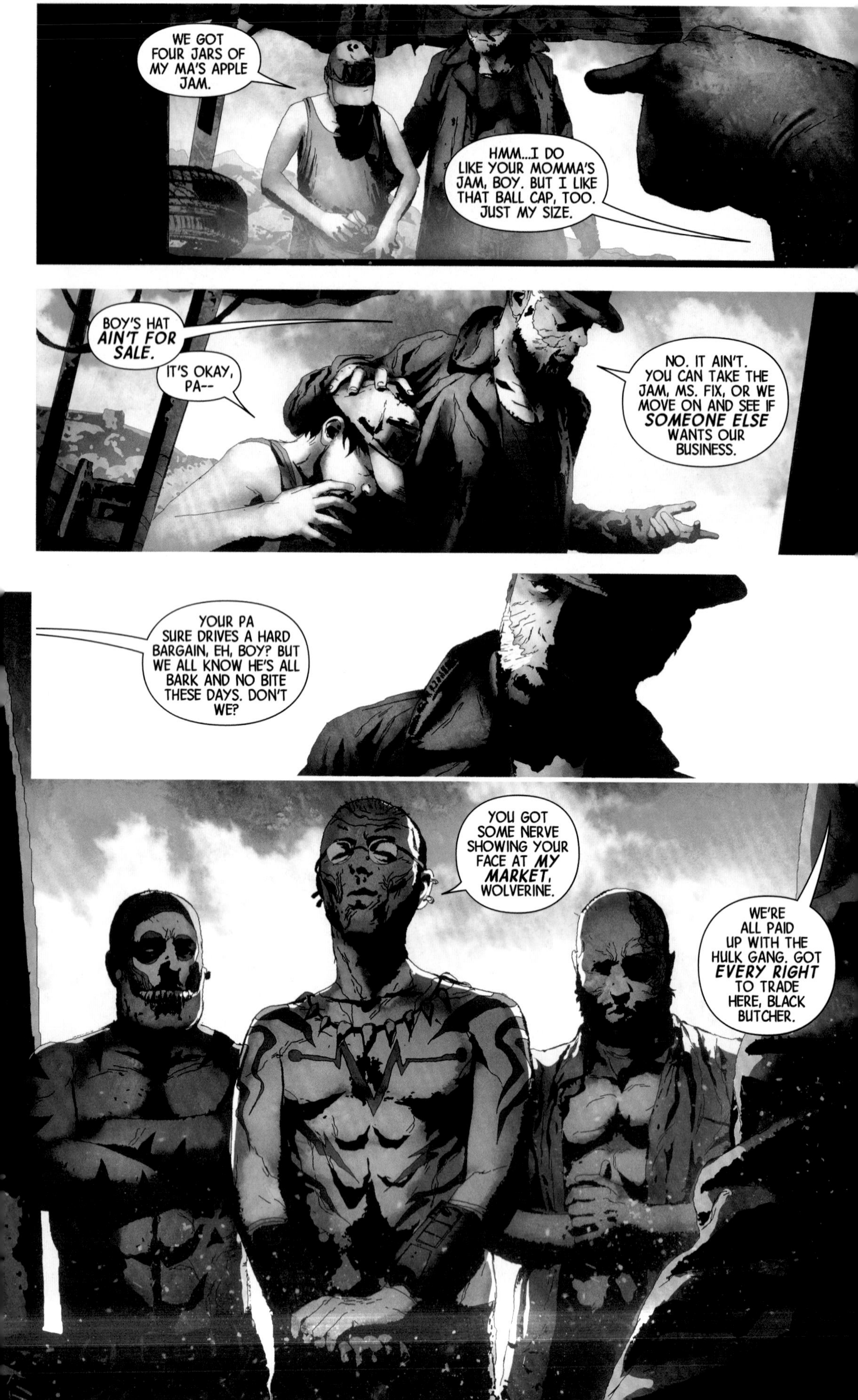

WE GOT FOUR JARS OF MY MA'S APPLE JAM.
HMM...I DO LIKE YOUR MOMMA'S JAM, BOY. BUT I LIKE THAT BALL CAP, TOO. JUST MY SIZE.
BOY'S HAT AIN'T FOR SALE.
IT'S OKAY, PA--
NO. IT AIN'T. YOU CAN TAKE THE JAM, MS. FIX, OR WE MOVE ON AND SEE IF SOMEONE ELSE WANTS OUR BUSINESS.
YOUR PA SURE DRIVES A HARD BARGAIN, EH, BOY? BUT WE ALL KNOW HE'S ALL BARK AND NO BITE THESE DAYS. DON'T WE?
YOU GOT SOME NERVE SHOWING YOUR FACE AT MY MARKET, WOLVERINE.
WE'RE ALL PAID UP WITH THE HULK GANG. GOT EVERY RIGHT TO TRADE HERE, BLACK BUTCHER.

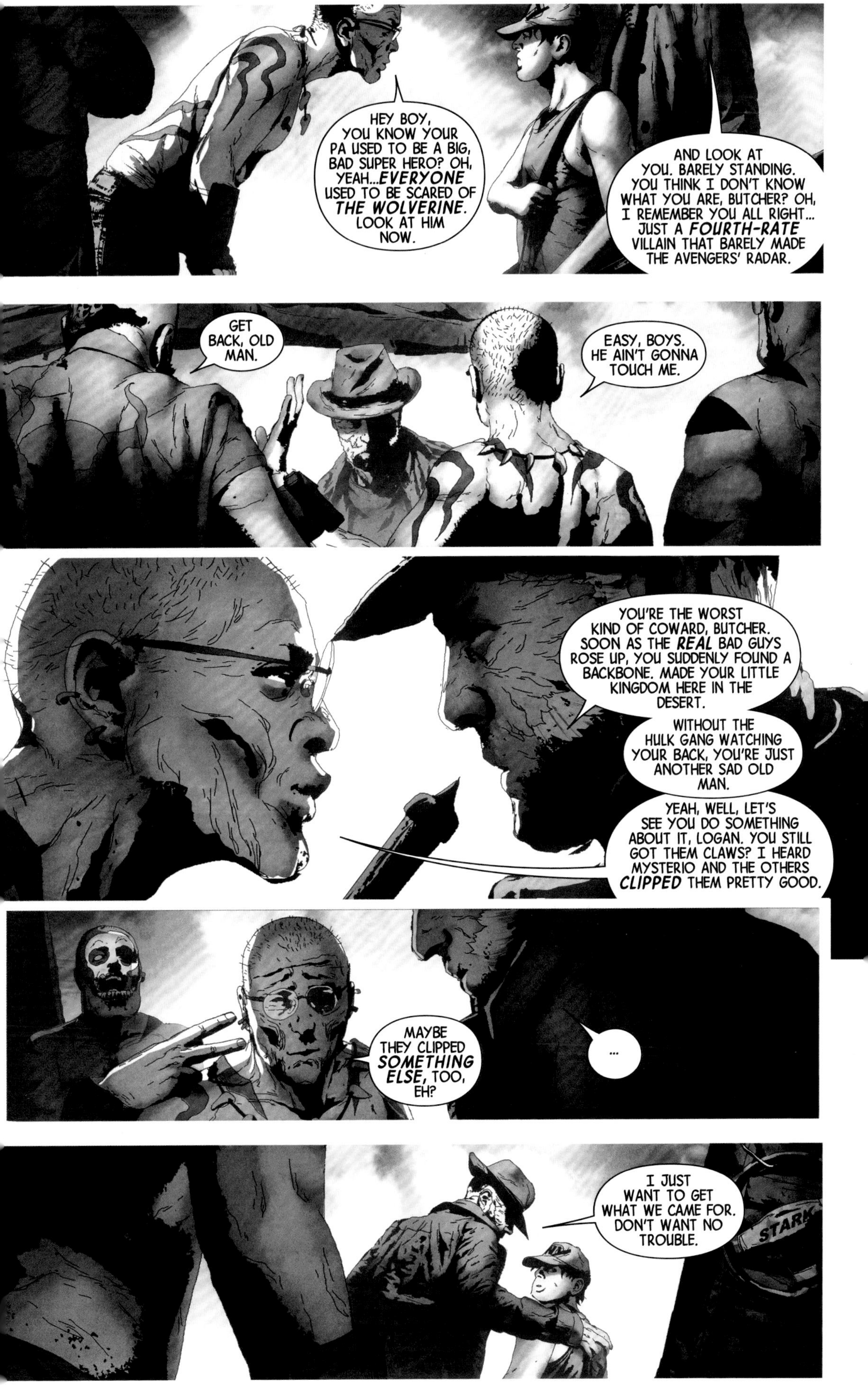
HEY BOY, YOU KNOW YOUR PA USED TO BE A BIG, BAD SUPER HERO? OH, YEAH...EVERYONE USED TO BE SCARED OF THE WOLVERINE. LOOK AT HIM NOW.
AND LOOK AT YOU. BARELY STANDING. YOU THINK I DON'T KNOW WHAT YOU ARE, BUTCHER? OH, I REMEMBER YOU ALL RIGHT... JUST A FOURTH-RATE VILLAIN THAT BARELY MADE THE AVENGERS' RADAR.
GET BACK, OLD MAN.
EASY, BOYS. HE AIN'T GONNA TOUCH ME.
YOU'RE THE WORST KIND OF COWARD, BUTCHER. SOON AS THE REAL BAD GUYS ROSE UP, YOU SUDDENLY FOUND A BACKBONE. MADE YOUR LITTLE KINGDOM HERE IN THE DESERT.
WITHOUT THE HULK GANG WATCHING YOUR BACK, YOU'RE JUST ANOTHER SAD OLD MAN.
YEAH, WELL, LET'S SEE YOU DO SOMETHING ABOUT IT, LOGAN. YOU STILL GOT THEM CLAWS? I HEARD MYSTERIO AND THE OTHERS CLIPPED THEM PRETTY GOOD.
MAYBE THEY CLIPPED SOMETHING ELSE, TOO, EH?
...
I JUST WANT TO GET WHAT WE CAME FOR. DON'T WANT NO TROUBLE.
STARK

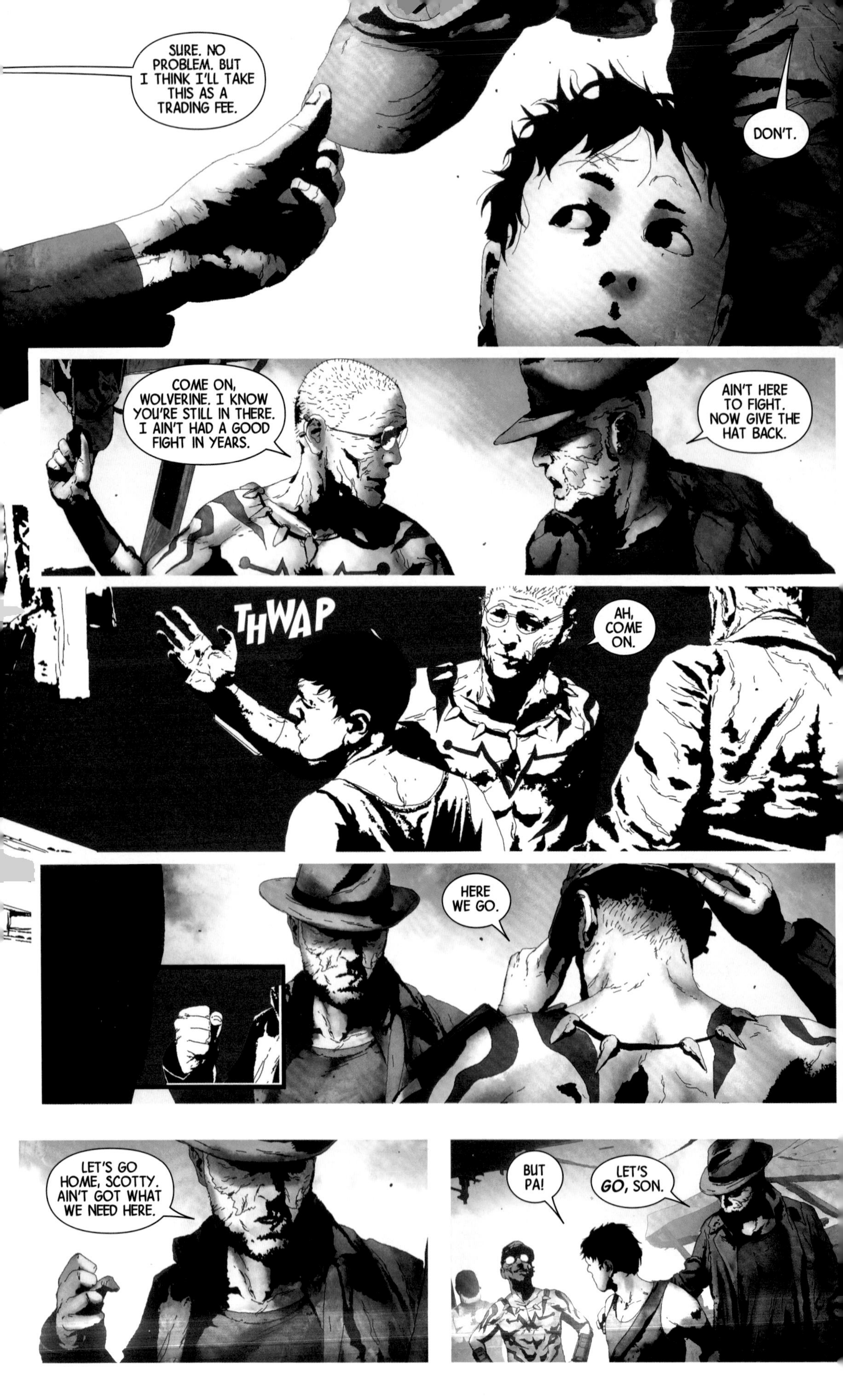
SURE. NO PROBLEM. BUT I THINK I'LL TAKE THIS AS A TRADING FEE.
DON'T.
COME ON, WOLVERINE. I KNOW YOU'RE STILL IN THERE. I AIN'T HAD A GOOD FIGHT IN YEARS.
AIN'T HERE TO FIGHT. NOW GIVE THE HAT BACK.
THWAP
AH, COME ON.
HERE WE GO.
LET'S GO HOME, SCOTTY. AIN'T GOT WHAT WE NEED HERE.
BUT PA!
LET'S GO, SON.

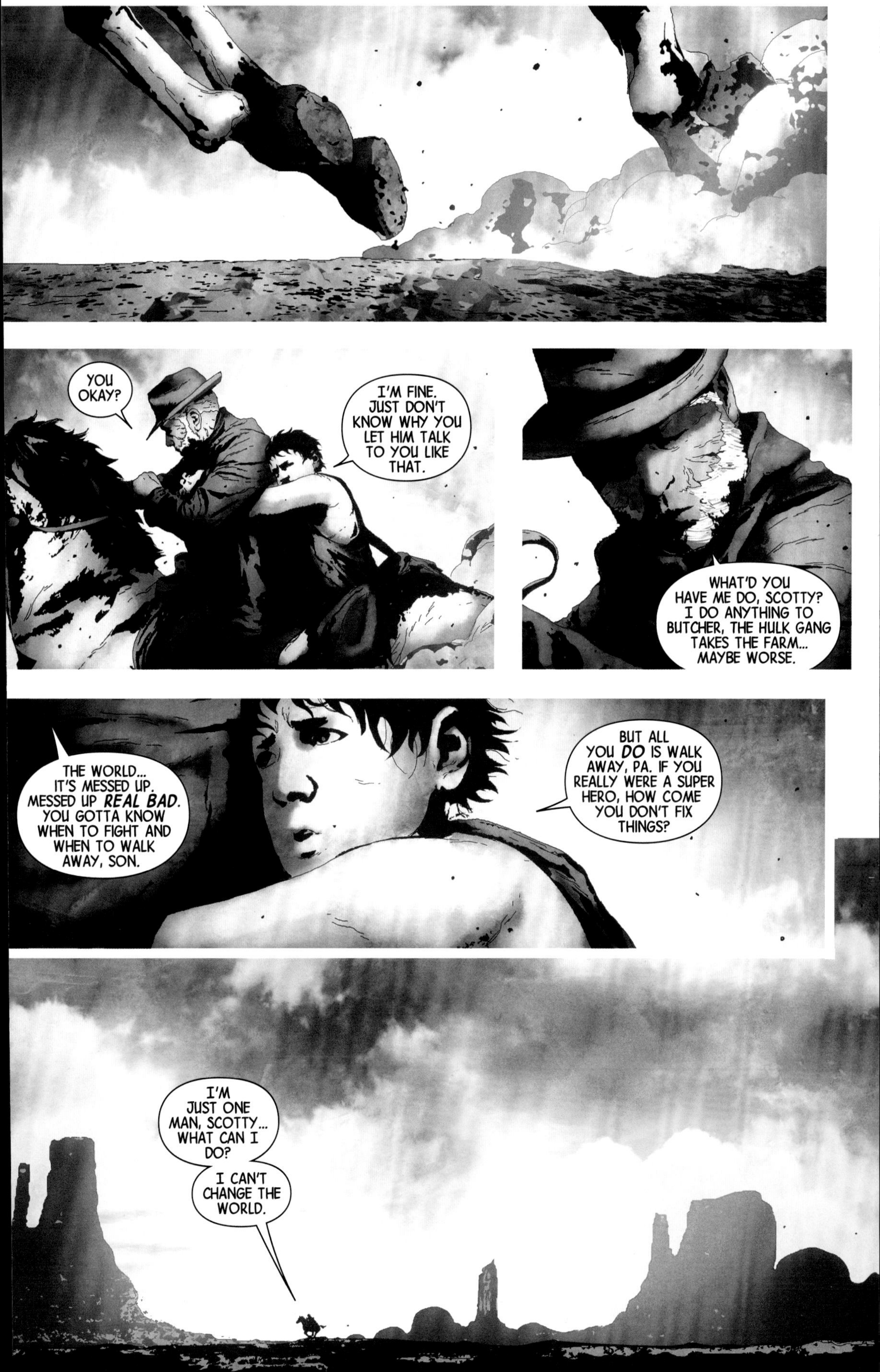
YOU OKAY?
I'M FINE. JUST DON'T KNOW WHY YOU LET HIM TALK TO YOU LIKE THAT.
WHAT'D YOU HAVE ME DO, SCOTTY? I DO ANYTHING TO BUTCHER, THE HULK GANG TAKES THE FARM... MAYBE WORSE.
THE WORLD... IT'S MESSED UP. MESSED UP REAL BAD. YOU GOTTA KNOW WHEN TO FIGHT AND WHEN TO WALK AWAY, SON.
BUT ALL YOU DO IS WALK AWAY, PA. IF YOU REALLY WERE A SUPER HERO, HOW COME YOU DON'T FIX THINGS?
I'M JUST ONE MAN, SCOTTY... WHAT CAN I DO?
I CAN'T CHANGE THE WORLD.

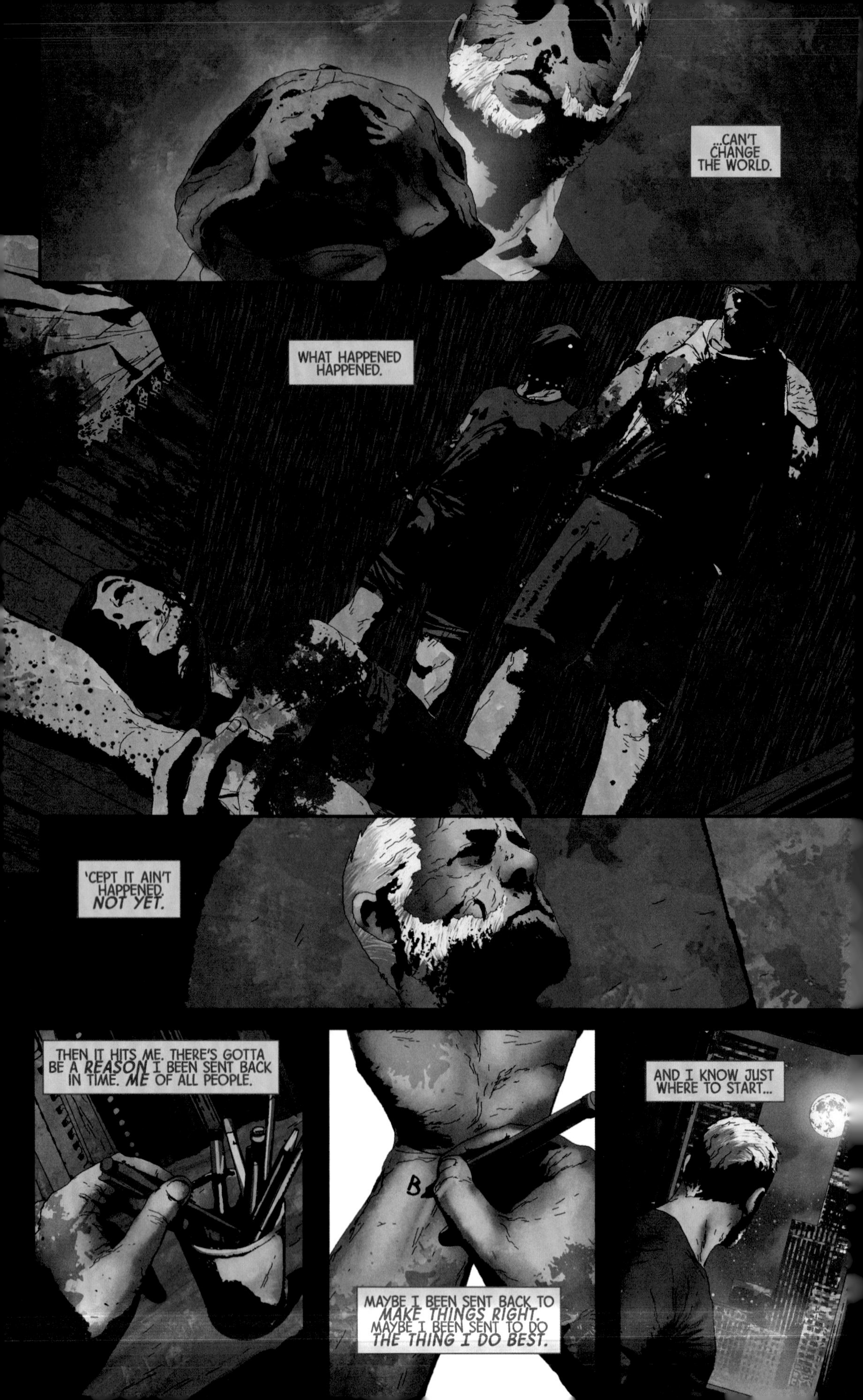
...CAN'T CHANGE THE WORLD.
WHAT HAPPENED HAPPENED.
'CEPT IT AIN'T HAPPENED. NOT YET.
THEN IT HITS ME. THERE'S GOTTA BE A REASON I BEEN SENT BACK IN TIME. ME OF ALL PEOPLE.
B
MAYBE I BEEN SENT BACK TO MAKE THINGS RIGHT. MAYBE I BEEN SENT TO DO THE THING I DO BEST.
AND I KNOW JUST WHERE TO START...

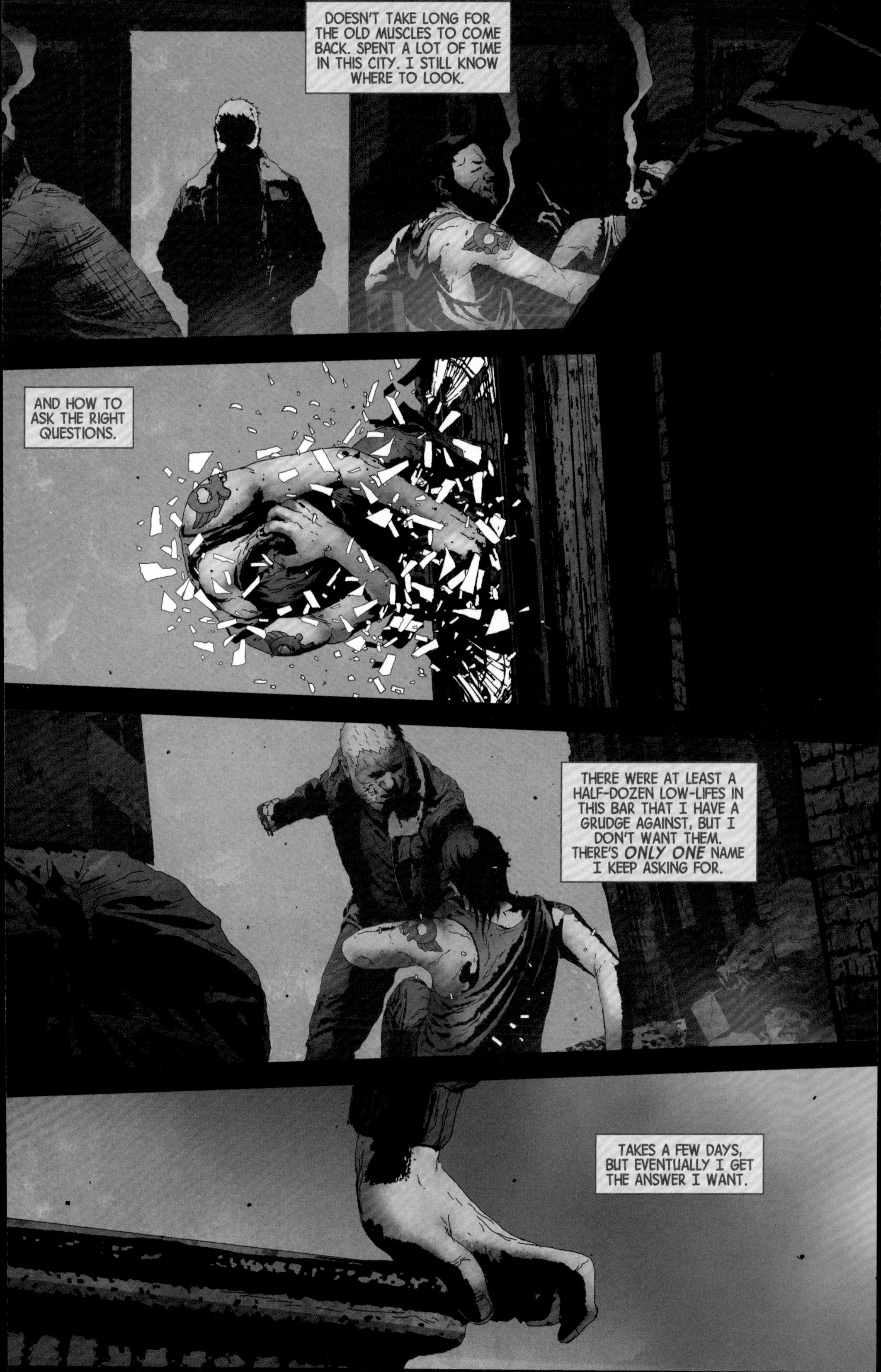
DOESN'T TAKE LONG FOR THE OLD MUSCLES TO COME BACK. SPENT A LOT OF TIME IN THIS CITY. I STILL KNOW WHERE TO LOOK.
AND HOW TO ASK THE RIGHT QUESTIONS.
THERE WERE AT LEAST A HALF-DOZEN LOW-LIFES IN THIS BAR THAT I HAVE A GRUDGE AGAINST, BUT I DON'T WANT THEM. THERE'S *ONLY ONE* NAME I KEEP ASKING FOR.
TAKES A FEW DAYS, BUT EVENTUALLY I GET THE ANSWER I WANT.

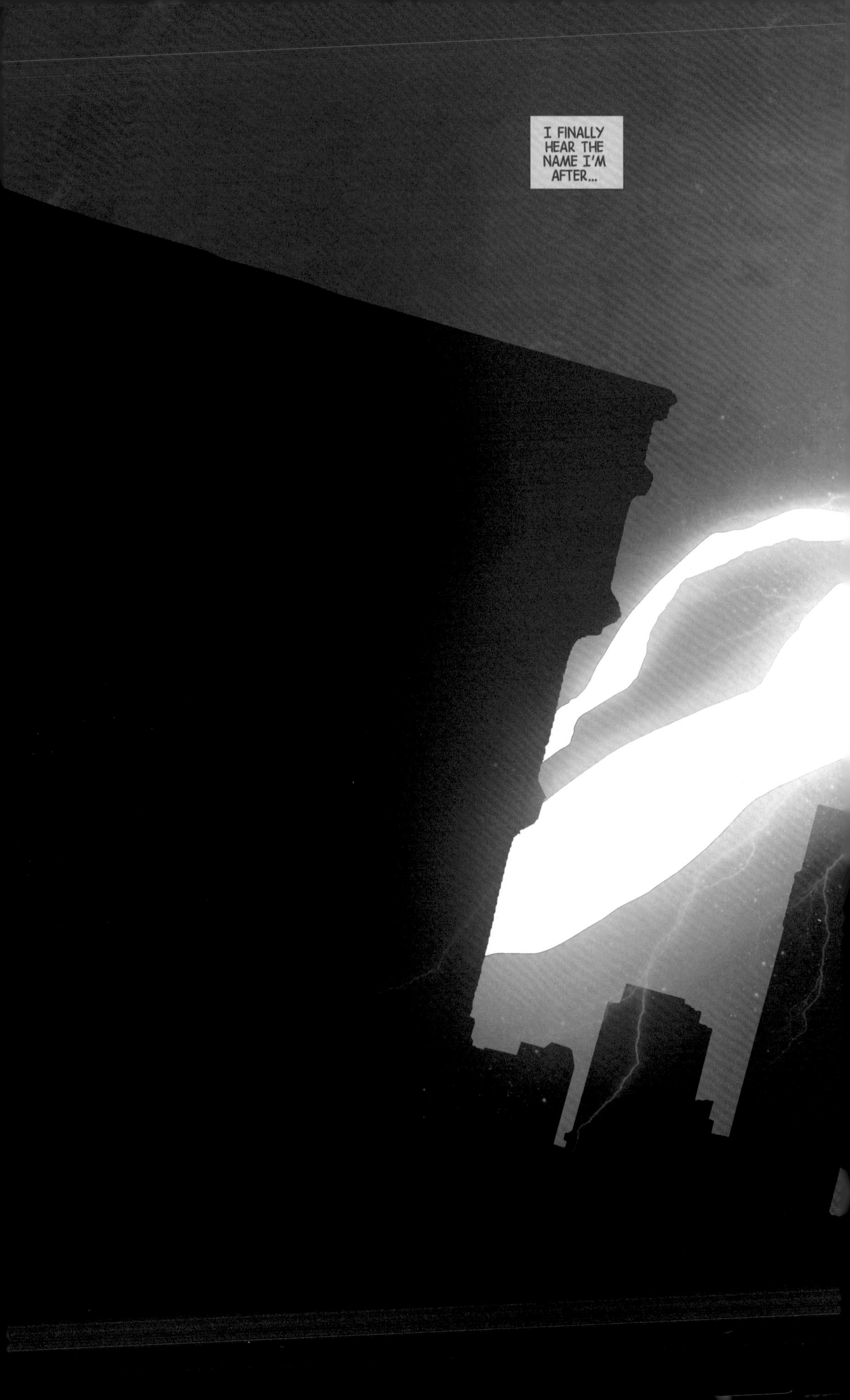
I FINALLY HEAR THE NAME I'M AFTER...

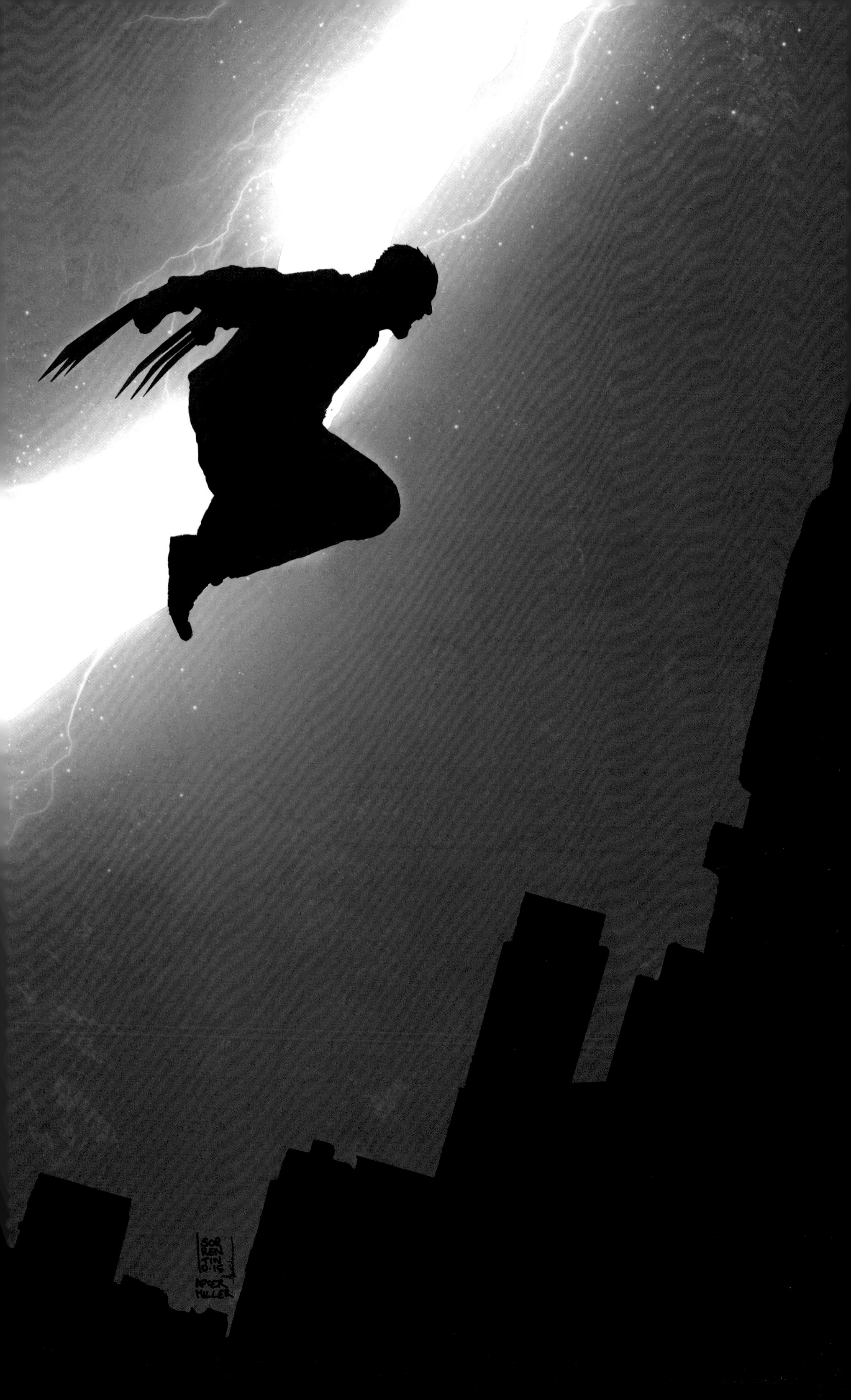
SOR
REN
TIN
AFTER MILLER

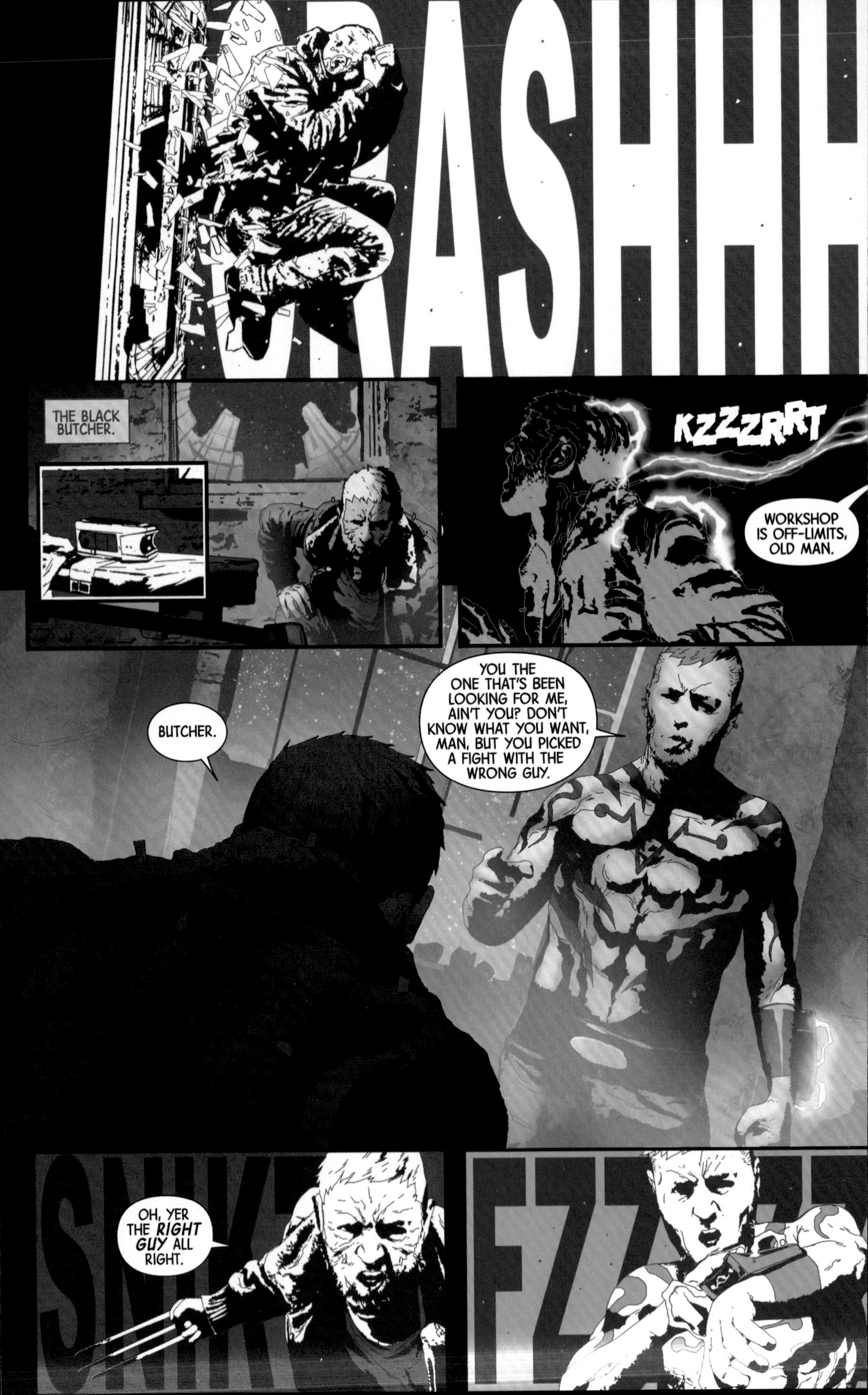
CRASHHH
THE BLACK BUTCHER.
KZZZRRT
WORKSHOP IS OFF-LIMITS, OLD MAN.
BUTCHER.
YOU THE ONE THAT'S BEEN LOOKING FOR ME, AIN'T YOU? DON'T KNOW WHAT YOU WANT, MAN, BUT YOU PICKED A FIGHT WITH THE WRONG GUY.
OH, YER THE *RIGHT GUY* ALL RIGHT.

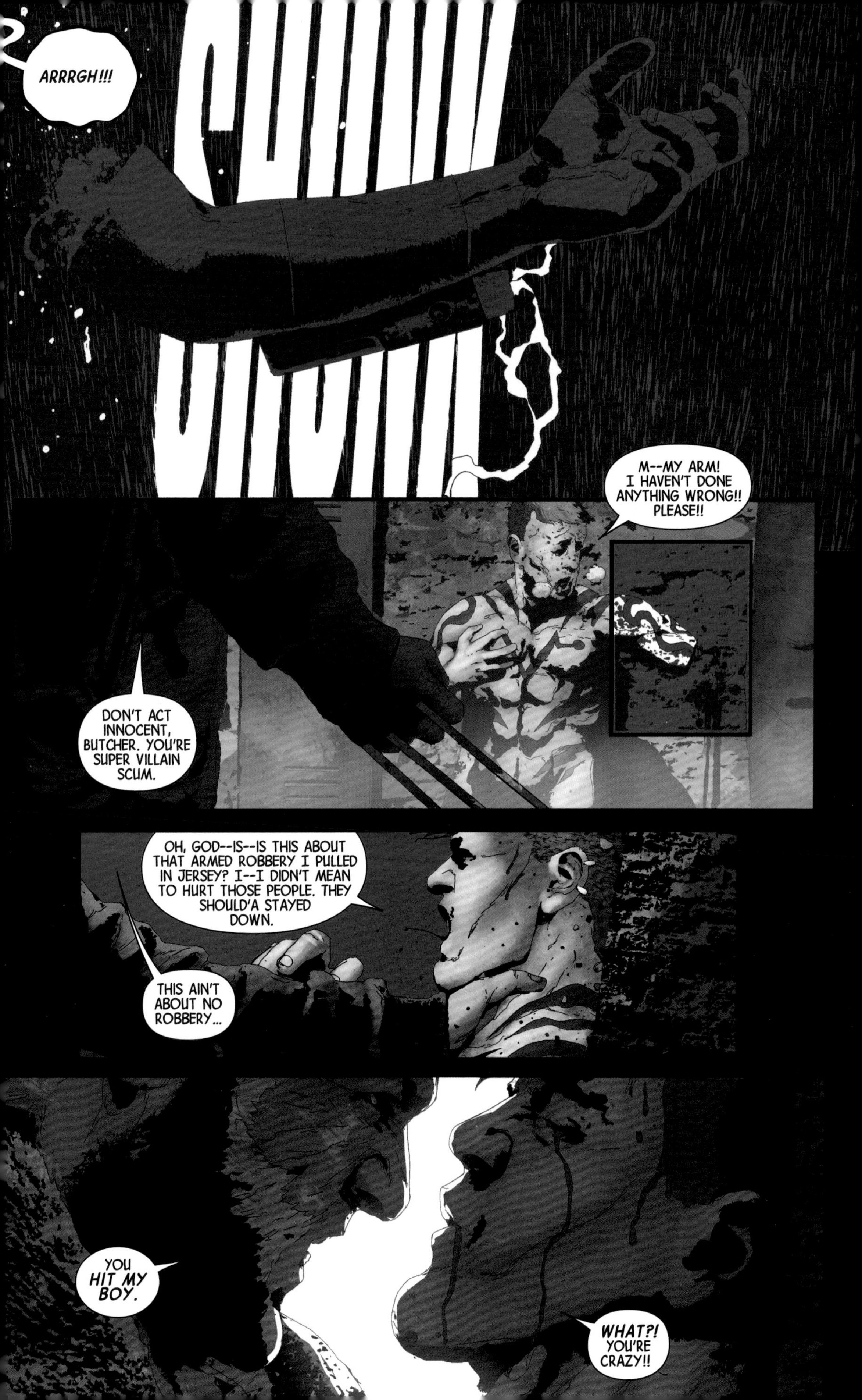
ARRRGH!!!
M--MY ARM! I HAVEN'T DONE ANYTHING WRONG!! PLEASE!!
DON'T ACT INNOCENT, BUTCHER. YOU'RE SUPER VILLAIN SCUM.
OH, GOD--IS--IS THIS ABOUT THAT ARMED ROBBERY I PULLED IN JERSEY? I--I DIDN'T MEAN TO HURT THOSE PEOPLE. THEY SHOULD'A STAYED DOWN.
THIS AIN'T ABOUT NO ROBBERY...
YOU HIT MY BOY.
WHAT?! YOU'RE CRAZY!!

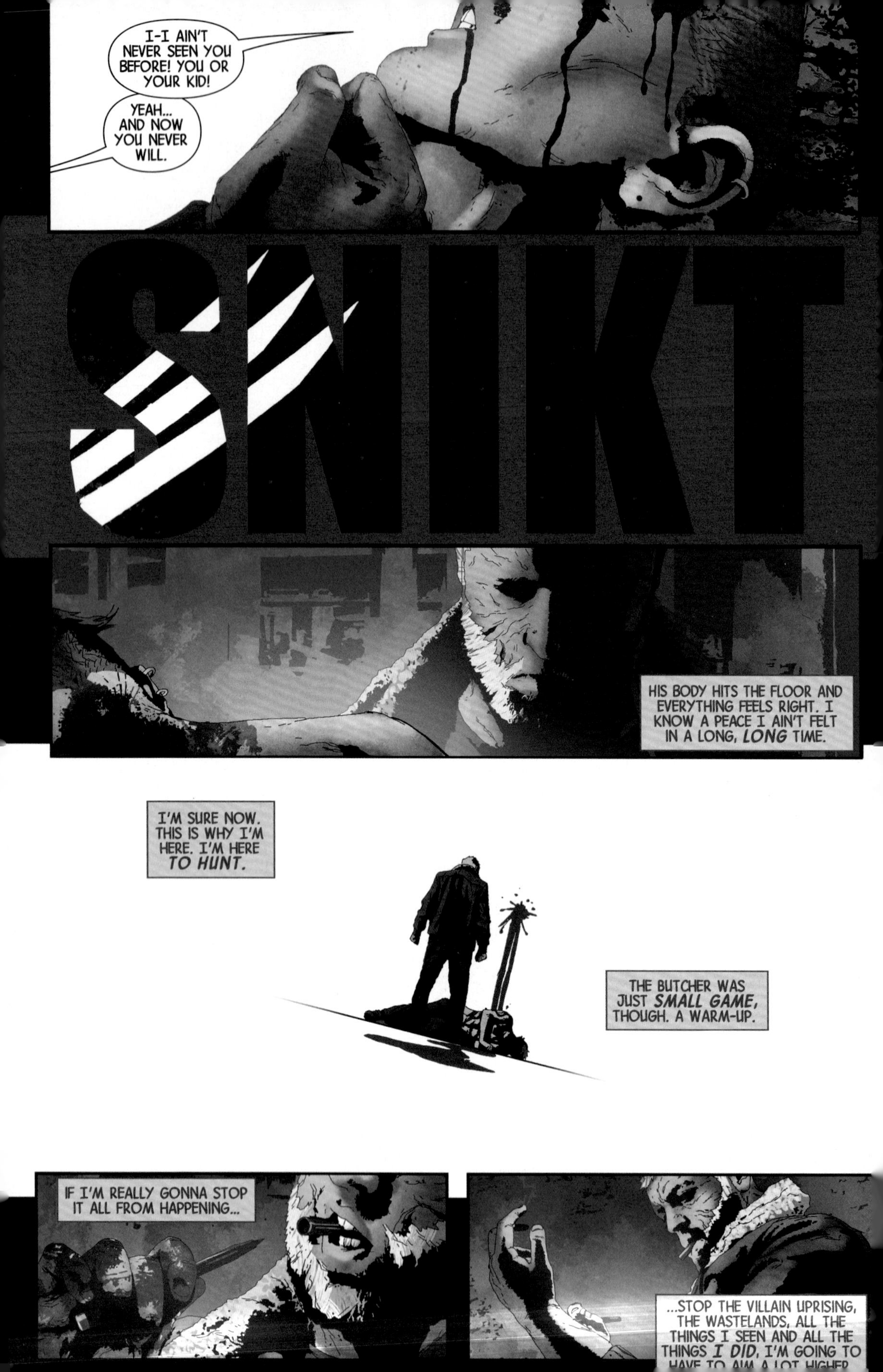
I-I AIN'T NEVER SEEN YOU BEFORE! YOU OR YOUR KID!
YEAH... AND NOW YOU NEVER WILL.
SNIKT
HIS BODY HITS THE FLOOR AND EVERYTHING FEELS RIGHT. I KNOW A PEACE I AIN'T FELT IN A LONG, LONG TIME.
I'M SURE NOW. THIS IS WHY I'M HERE. I'M HERE TO HUNT.
THE BUTCHER WAS JUST SMALL GAME, THOUGH. A WARM-UP.
IF I'M REALLY GONNA STOP IT ALL FROM HAPPENING...
...STOP THE VILLAIN UPRISING, THE WASTELANDS, ALL THE THINGS I SEEN AND ALL THE THINGS I DID, I'M GOING TO

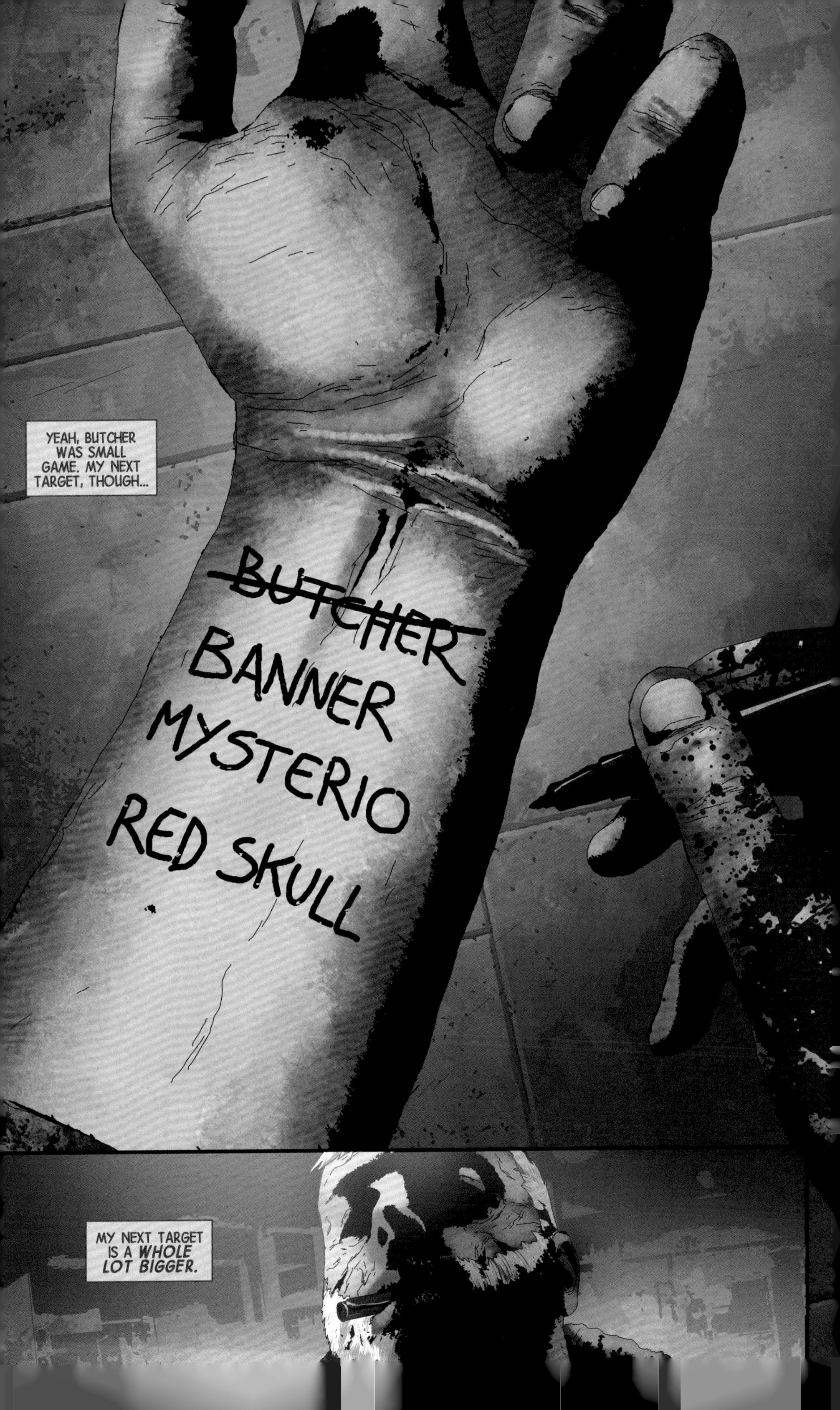
YEAH, BUTCHER WAS SMALL GAME. MY NEXT TARGET, THOUGH...
BUTCHER
BANNER
MYSTERIO
RED SKULL
MY NEXT TARGET IS A *WHOLE LOT BIGGER.*

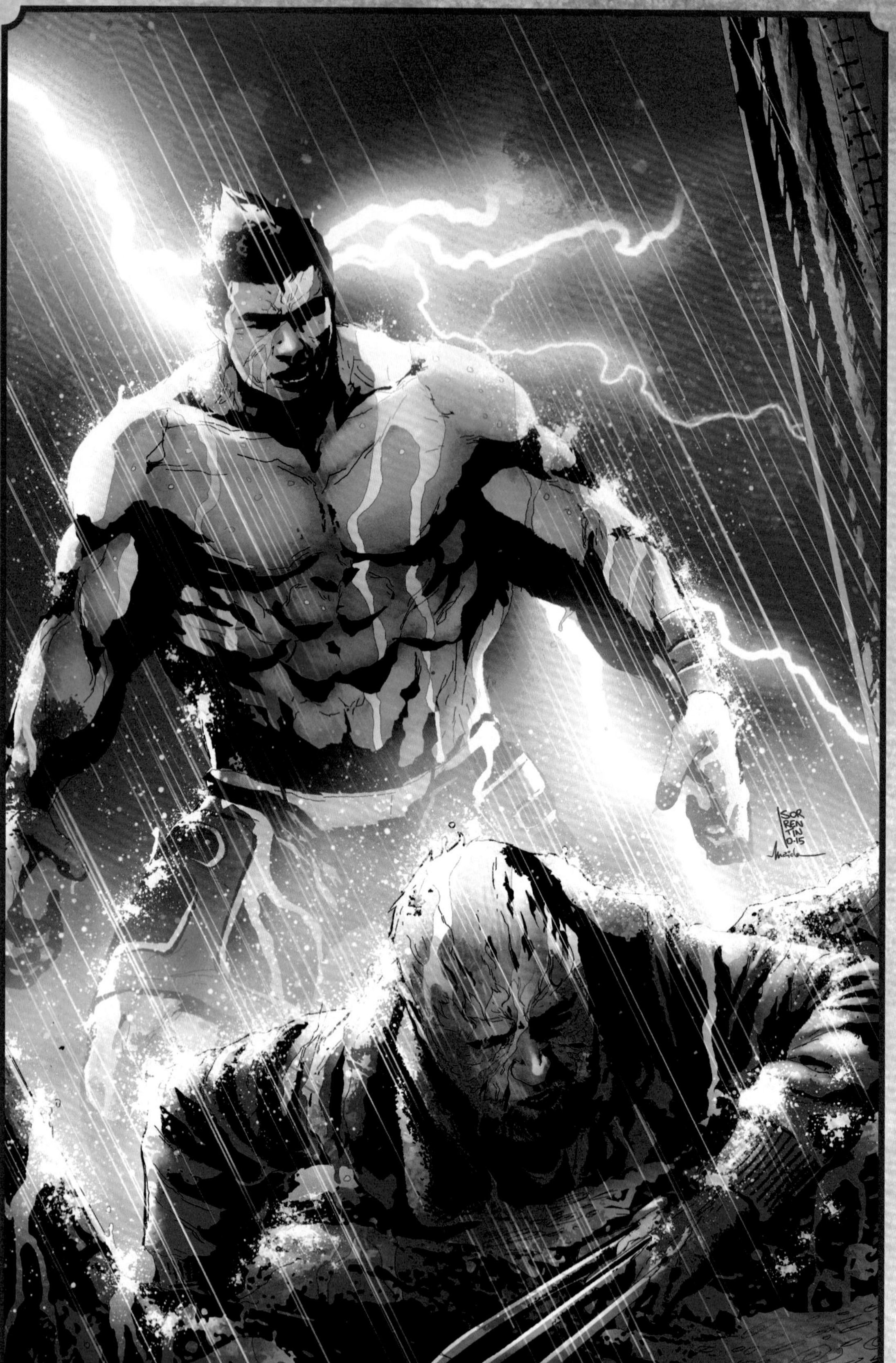

2

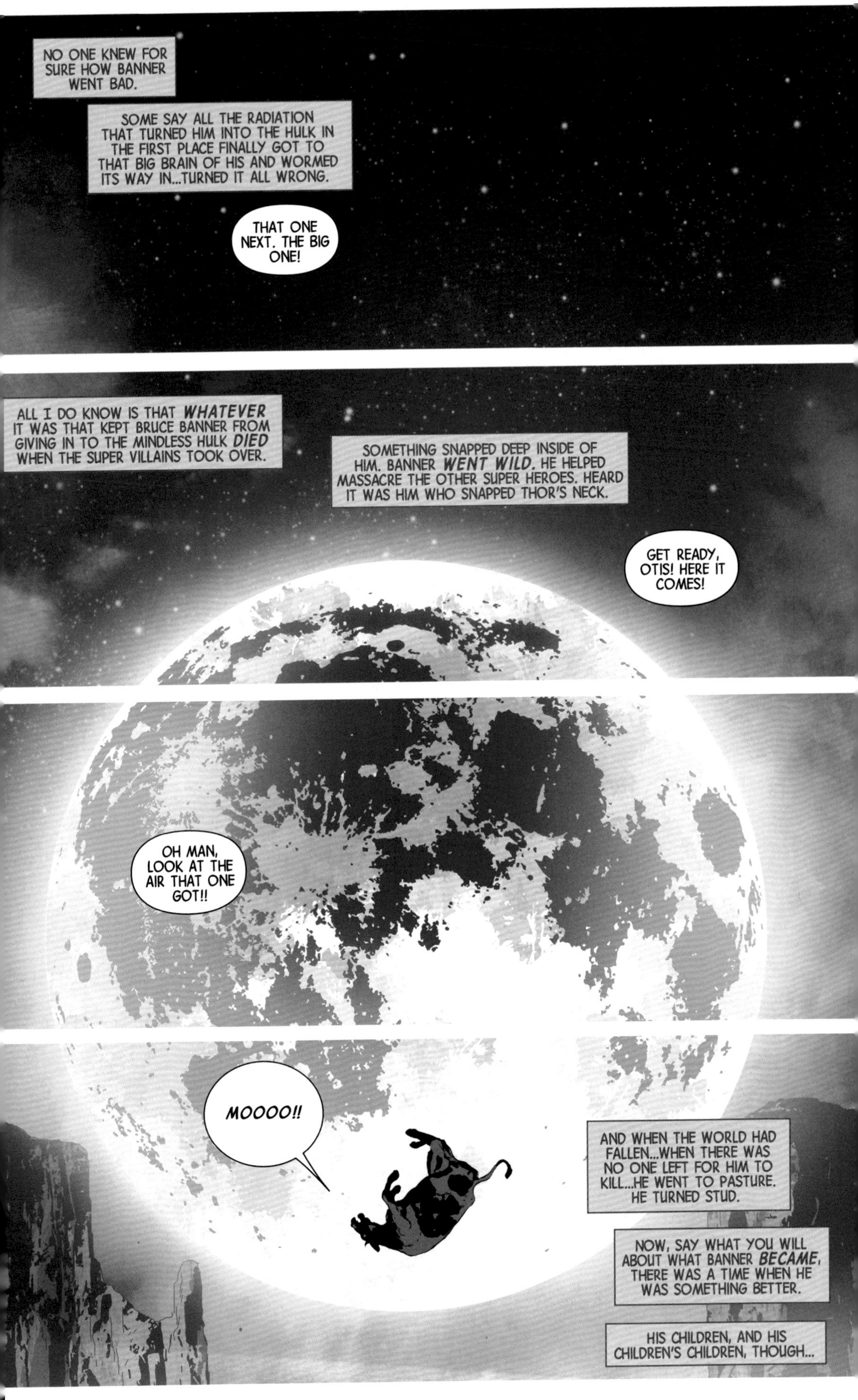
NO ONE KNEW FOR SURE HOW BANNER WENT BAD.
SOME SAY ALL THE RADIATION THAT TURNED HIM INTO THE HULK IN THE FIRST PLACE FINALLY GOT TO THAT BIG BRAIN OF HIS AND WORMED ITS WAY IN...TURNED IT ALL WRONG.
THAT ONE NEXT. THE BIG ONE!
ALL I DO KNOW IS THAT *WHATEVER* IT WAS THAT KEPT BRUCE BANNER FROM GIVING IN TO THE MINDLESS HULK *DIED* WHEN THE SUPER VILLAINS TOOK OVER.
SOMETHING SNAPPED DEEP INSIDE OF HIM. BANNER *WENT WILD.* HE HELPED MASSACRE THE OTHER SUPER HEROES. HEARD IT WAS HIM WHO SNAPPED THOR'S NECK.
GET READY, OTIS! HERE IT COMES!
OH MAN, LOOK AT THE AIR THAT ONE GOT!!
MOOOO!!
AND WHEN THE WORLD HAD FALLEN...WHEN THERE WAS NO ONE LEFT FOR HIM TO KILL...HE WENT TO PASTURE. HE TURNED STUD.
NOW, SAY WHAT YOU WILL ABOUT WHAT BANNER *BECAME*, THERE WAS A TIME WHEN HE WAS SOMETHING BETTER.
HIS CHILDREN, AND HIS CHILDREN'S CHILDREN, THOUGH...

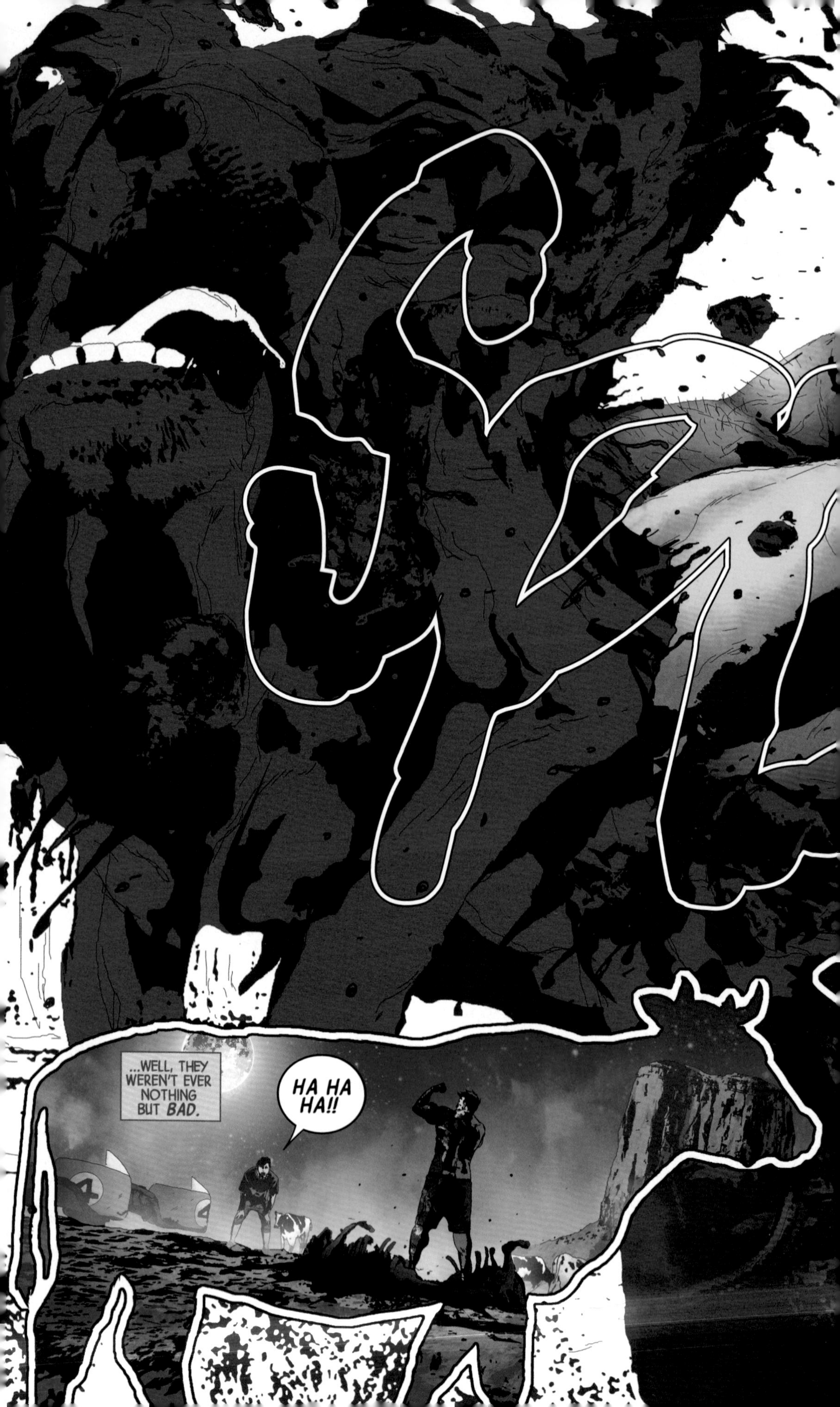
...WELL, THEY WEREN'T EVER NOTHING BUT *BAD*.
HA HA HA!!

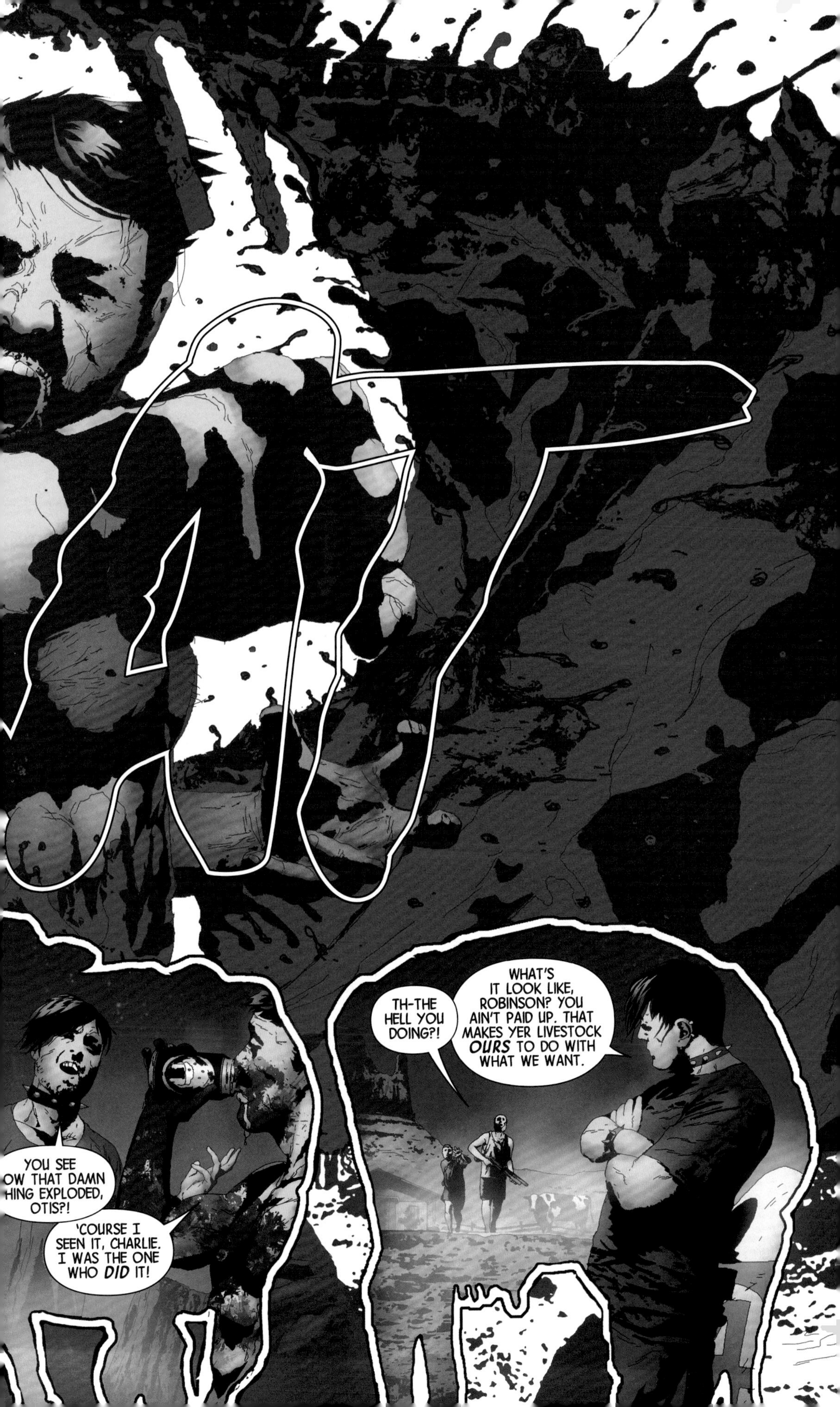

YOU SEE
OW THAT DAMN
HING EXPLODED,
OTIS?!
'COURSE I SEEN IT, CHARLIE. I WAS THE ONE WHO *DID* IT!
TH-THE HELL YOU DOING?!
WHAT'S IT LOOK LIKE, ROBINSON? YOU AIN'T PAID UP. THAT MAKES YER LIVESTOCK *OURS* TO DO WITH WHAT WE WANT.

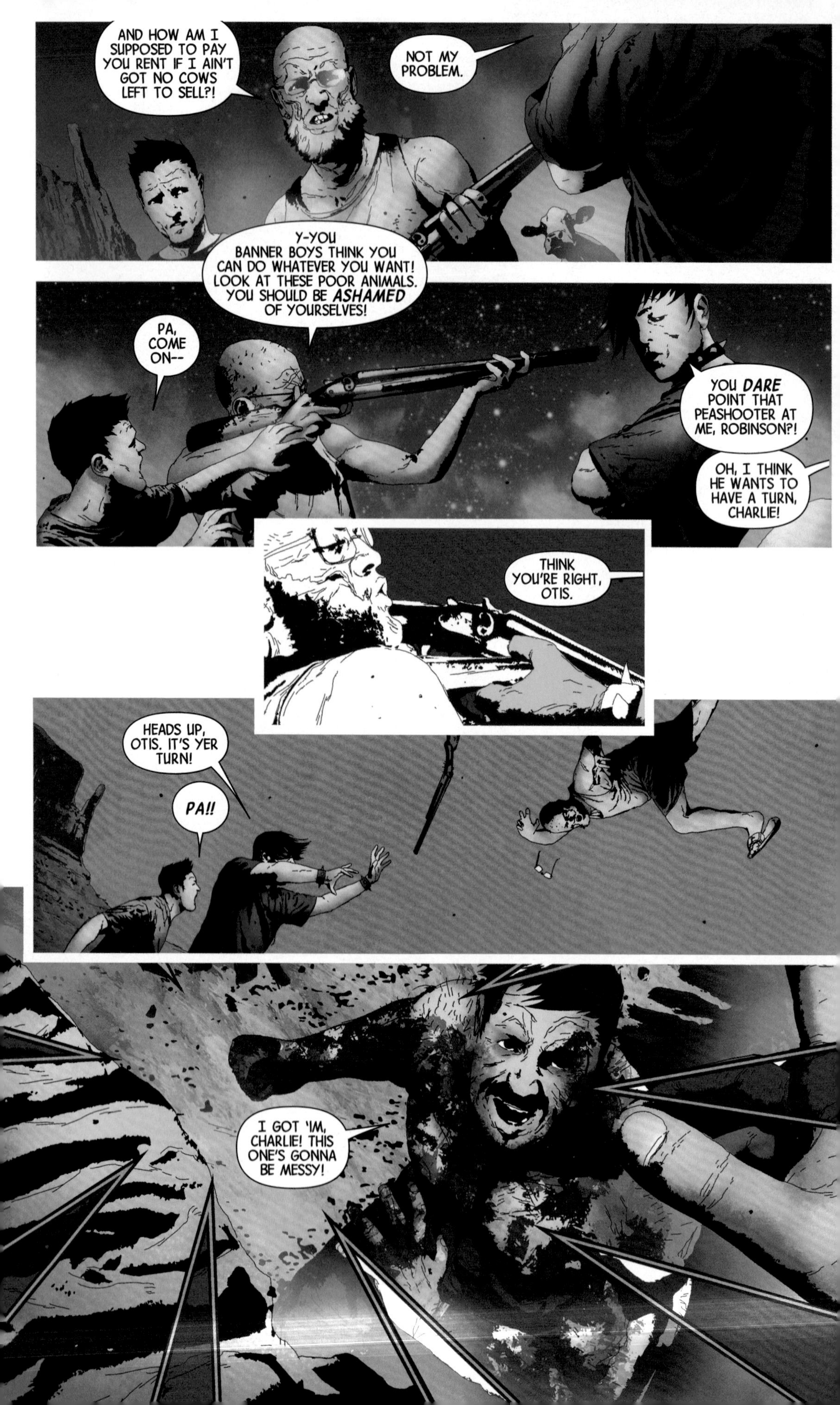
AND HOW AM I SUPPOSED TO PAY YOU RENT IF I AIN'T GOT NO COWS LEFT TO SELL?!
NOT MY PROBLEM.
Y-YOU BANNER BOYS THINK YOU CAN DO WHATEVER YOU WANT! LOOK AT THESE POOR ANIMALS. YOU SHOULD BE ASHAMED OF YOURSELVES!
PA, COME ON--
YOU DARE POINT THAT PEASHOOTER AT ME, ROBINSON?!
OH, I THINK HE WANTS TO HAVE A TURN, CHARLIE!
THINK YOU'RE RIGHT, OTIS.
HEADS UP, OTIS. IT'S YER TURN!
PA!!
I GOT 'IM, CHARLIE! THIS ONE'S GONNA BE MESSY!

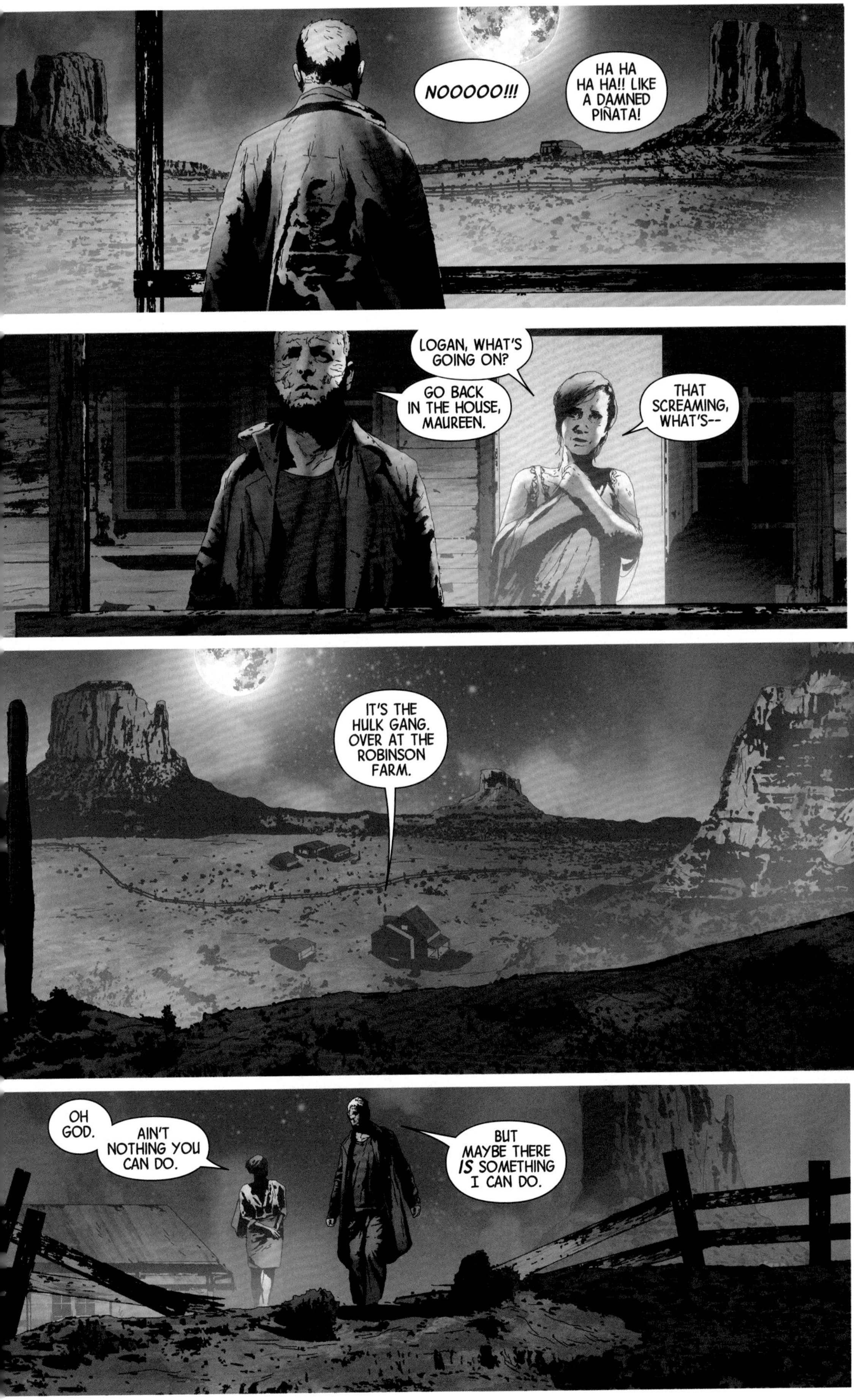
NOOOOO!!!
HA HA HA HA!! LIKE A DAMNED PIÑATA!
LOGAN, WHAT'S GOING ON?
GO BACK IN THE HOUSE, MAUREEN.
THAT SCREAMING, WHAT'S--
IT'S THE HULK GANG. OVER AT THE ROBINSON FARM.
OH GOD.
AIN'T NOTHING YOU CAN DO.
BUT MAYBE THERE *IS* SOMETHING I CAN DO.

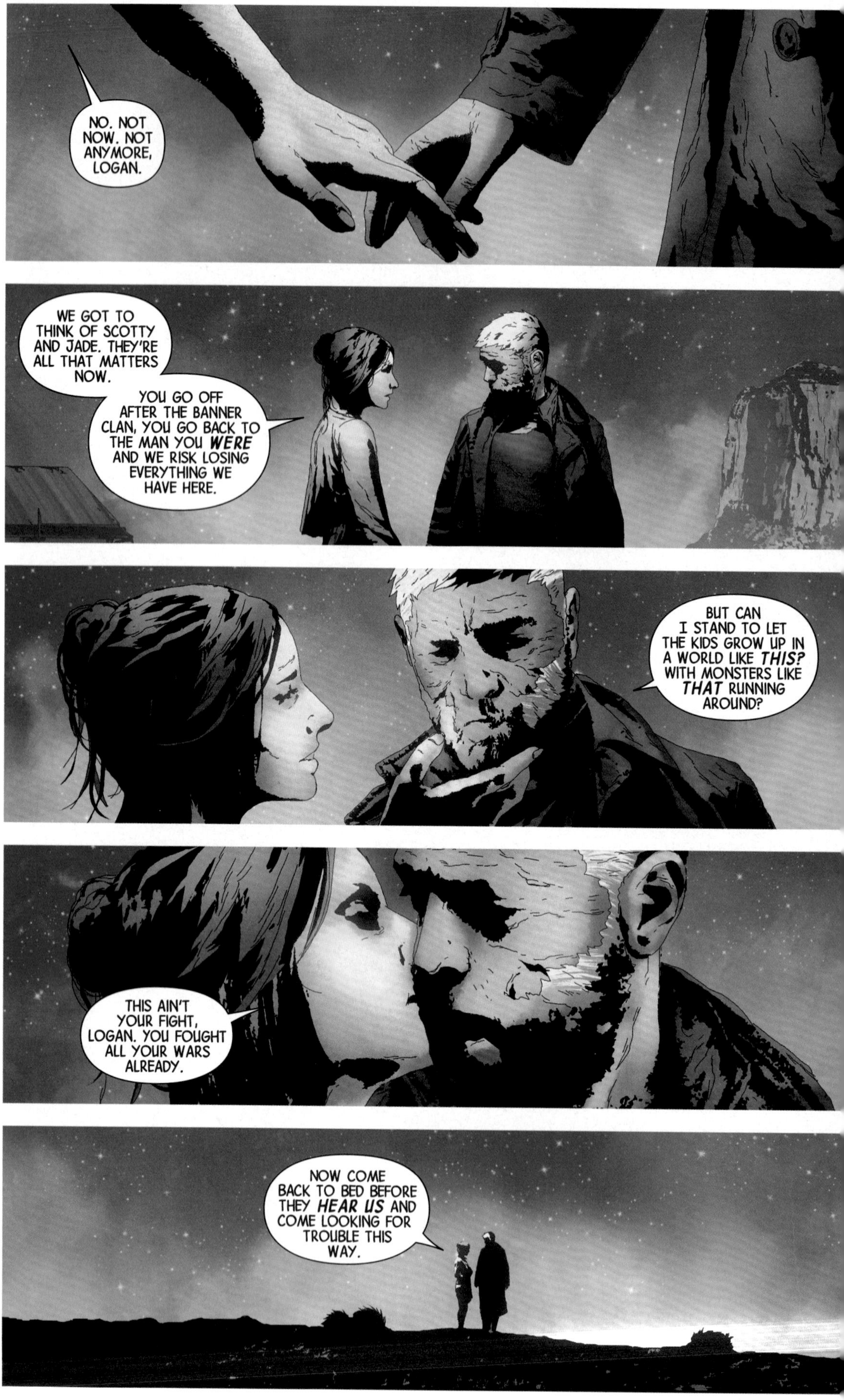
NO. NOT NOW. NOT ANYMORE, LOGAN.
WE GOT TO THINK OF SCOTTY AND JADE. THEY'RE ALL THAT MATTERS NOW.
YOU GO OFF AFTER THE BANNER CLAN, YOU GO BACK TO THE MAN YOU *WERE* AND WE RISK LOSING EVERYTHING WE HAVE HERE.
BUT CAN I STAND TO LET THE KIDS GROW UP IN A WORLD LIKE *THIS?* WITH MONSTERS LIKE *THAT* RUNNING AROUND?
THIS AIN'T YOUR FIGHT, LOGAN. YOU FOUGHT ALL YOUR WARS ALREADY.
NOW COME BACK TO BED BEFORE THEY *HEAR US* AND COME LOOKING FOR TROUBLE THIS WAY.

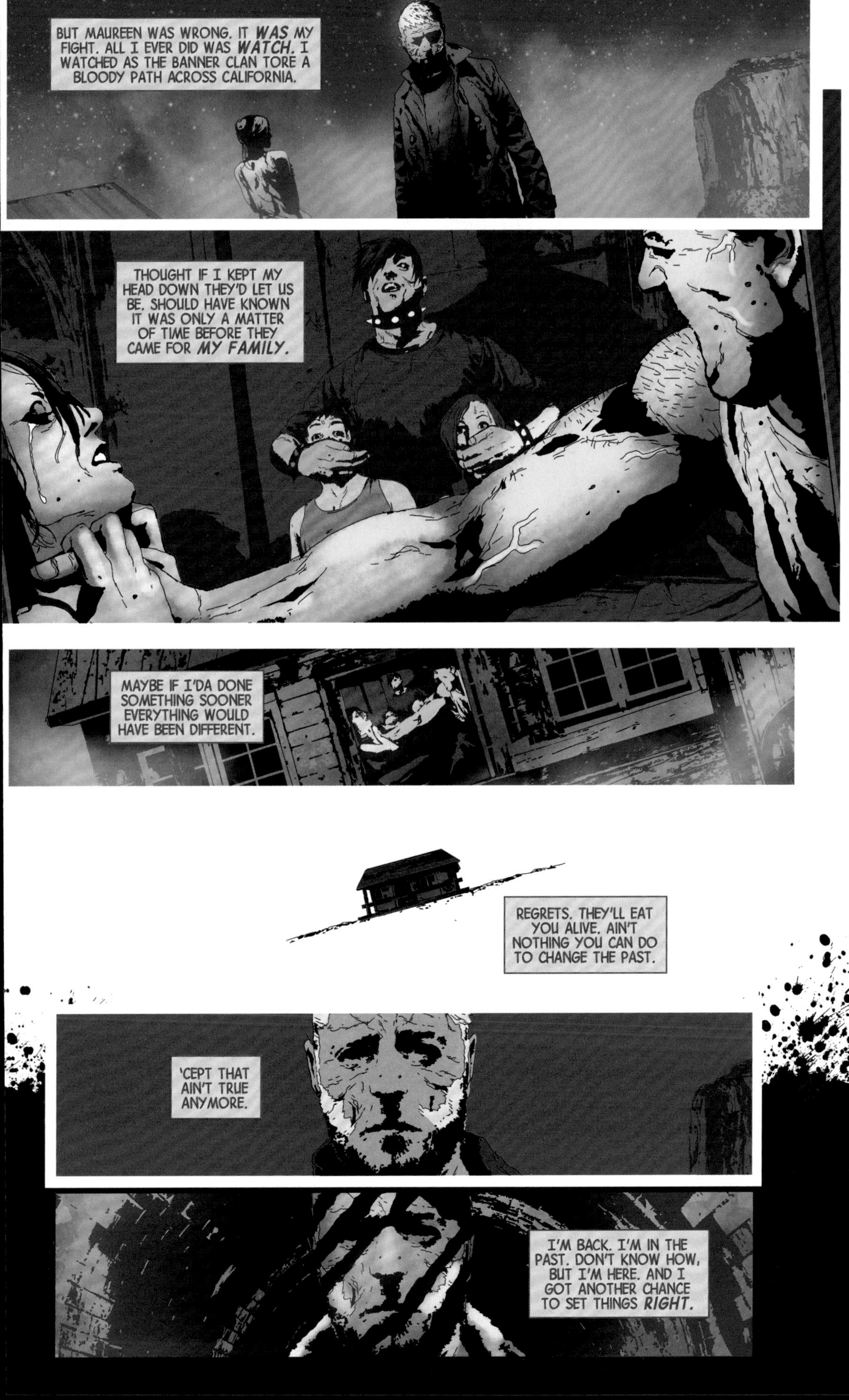

BUT MAUREEN WAS WRONG. IT *WAS* MY FIGHT. ALL I EVER DID WAS *WATCH.* I WATCHED AS THE BANNER CLAN TORE A BLOODY PATH ACROSS CALIFORNIA.
THOUGHT IF I KEPT MY HEAD DOWN THEY'D LET US BE. SHOULD HAVE KNOWN IT WAS ONLY A MATTER OF TIME BEFORE THEY CAME FOR *MY FAMILY.*
MAYBE IF I'DA DONE SOMETHING SOONER EVERYTHING WOULD HAVE BEEN DIFFERENT.
REGRETS. THEY'LL EAT YOU ALIVE. AIN'T NOTHING YOU CAN DO TO CHANGE THE PAST.
'CEPT THAT AIN'T TRUE ANYMORE.
I'M BACK. I'M IN THE PAST. DON'T KNOW HOW, BUT I'M HERE. AND I GOT ANOTHER CHANCE TO SET THINGS *RIGHT.*

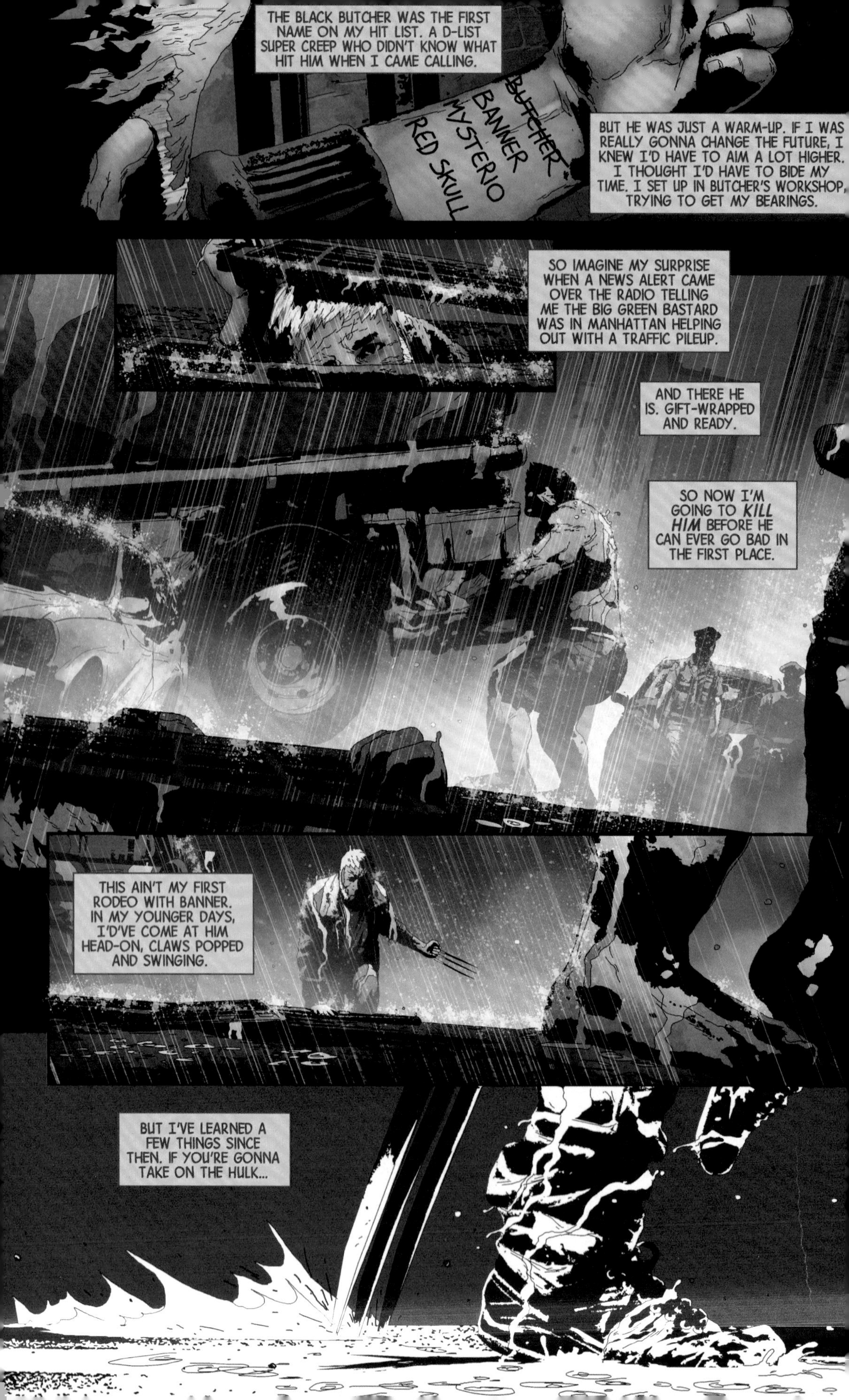
THE BLACK BUTCHER WAS THE FIRST NAME ON MY HIT LIST. A D-LIST SUPER CREEP WHO DIDN'T KNOW WHAT HIT HIM WHEN I CAME CALLING.
BUTCHER
BANNER
MYSTERIO
RED SKULL
BUT HE WAS JUST A WARM-UP. IF I WAS REALLY GONNA CHANGE THE FUTURE, I KNEW I'D HAVE TO AIM A LOT HIGHER. I THOUGHT I'D HAVE TO BIDE MY TIME. I SET UP IN BUTCHER'S WORKSHOP, TRYING TO GET MY BEARINGS.
SO IMAGINE MY SURPRISE WHEN A NEWS ALERT CAME OVER THE RADIO TELLING ME THE BIG GREEN BASTARD WAS IN MANHATTAN HELPING OUT WITH A TRAFFIC PILEUP.
AND THERE HE IS. GIFT-WRAPPED AND READY.
SO NOW I'M GOING TO *KILL HIM* BEFORE HE CAN EVER GO BAD IN THE FIRST PLACE.
THIS AIN'T MY FIRST RODEO WITH BANNER. IN MY YOUNGER DAYS, I'D'VE COME AT HIM HEAD-ON, CLAWS POPPED AND SWINGING.
BUT I'VE LEARNED A FEW THINGS SINCE THEN. IF YOU'RE GONNA TAKE ON THE HULK...

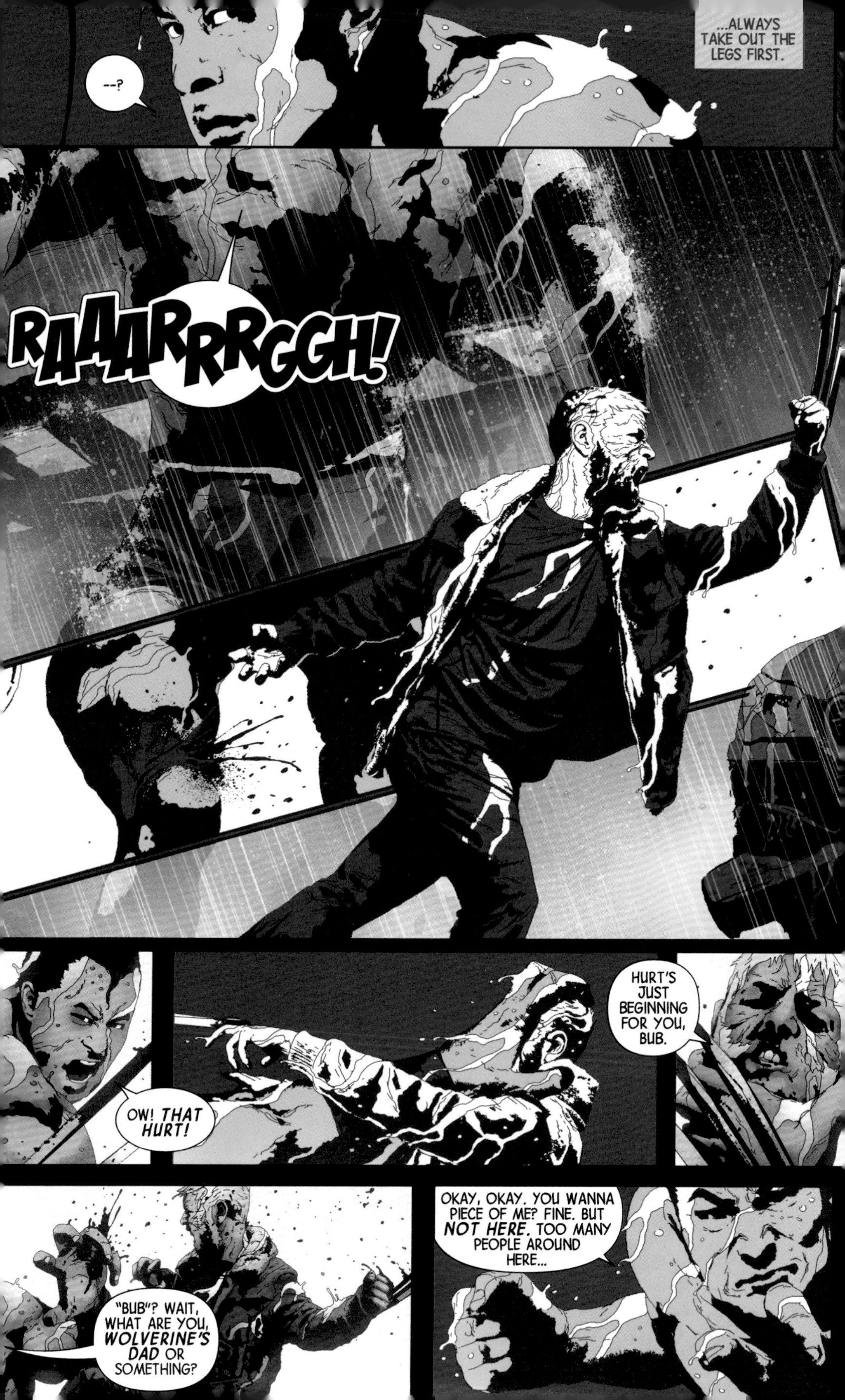
...ALWAYS TAKE OUT THE LEGS FIRST.
--?
RAAARRRGGH!
OW! THAT HURT!
HURT'S JUST BEGINNING FOR YOU, BUB.
"BUB"? WAIT, WHAT ARE YOU, WOLVERINE'S DAD OR SOMETHING?
OKAY, OKAY. YOU WANNA PIECE OF ME? FINE. BUT NOT HERE. TOO MANY PEOPLE AROUND HERE...

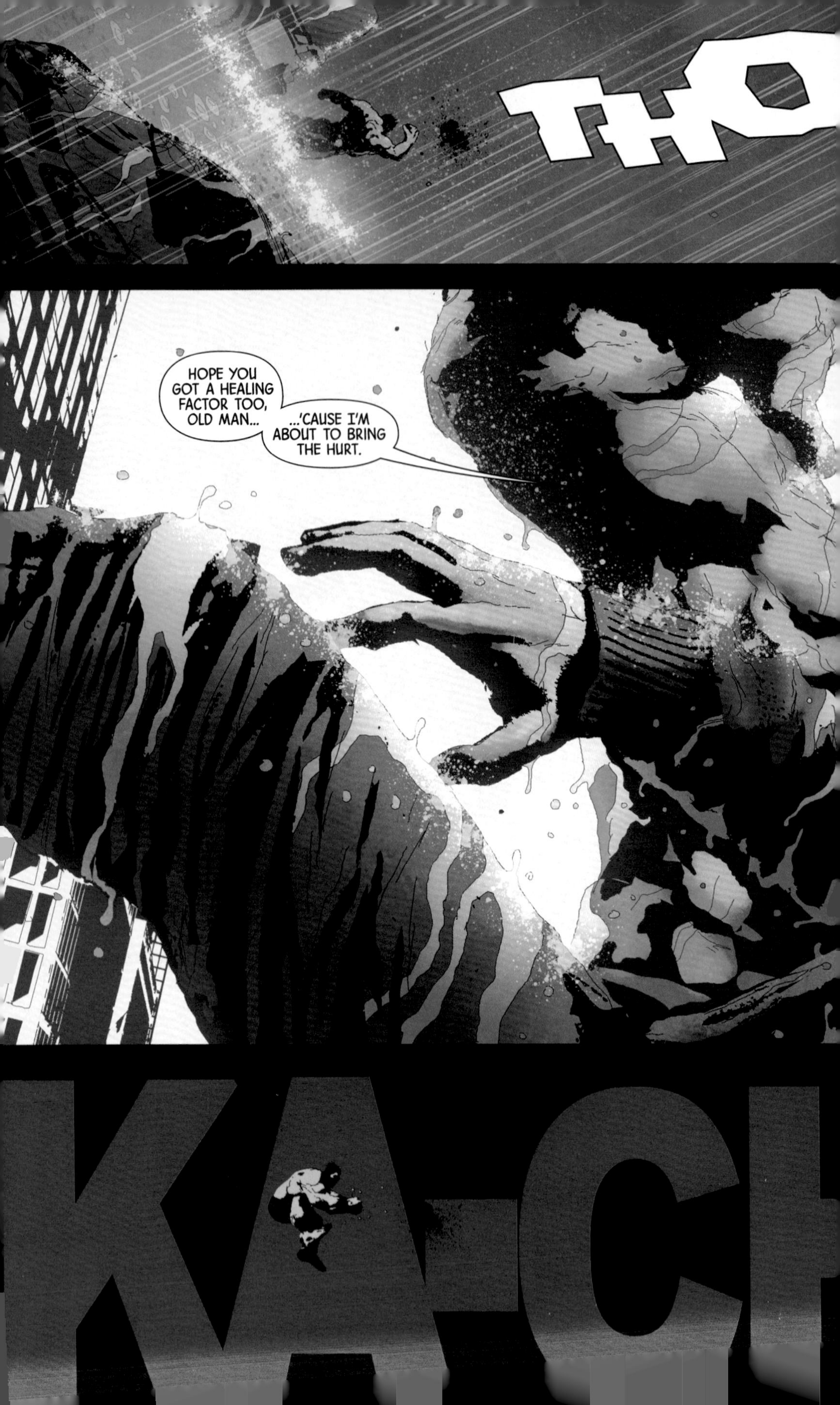
THO
HOPE YOU GOT A HEALING FACTOR TOO, OLD MAN...
...'CAUSE I'M ABOUT TO BRING THE HURT.
KA-CH

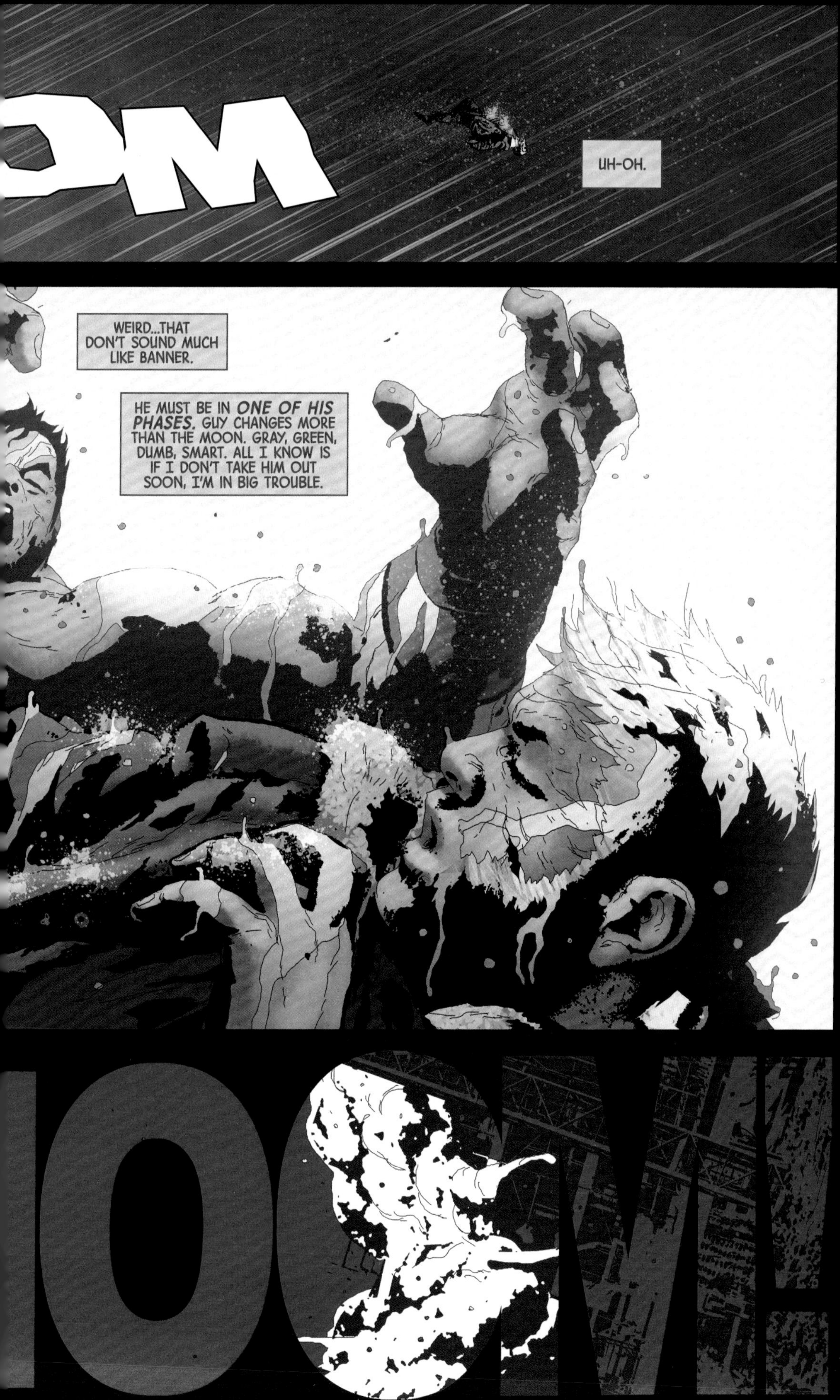
OM
UH-OH.
WEIRD...THAT DON'T SOUND MUCH LIKE BANNER.
HE MUST BE IN *ONE OF HIS PHASES*. GUY CHANGES MORE THAN THE MOON. GRAY, GREEN, DUMB, SMART. ALL I KNOW IS IF I DON'T TAKE HIM OUT SOON, I'M IN BIG TROUBLE.
OM!

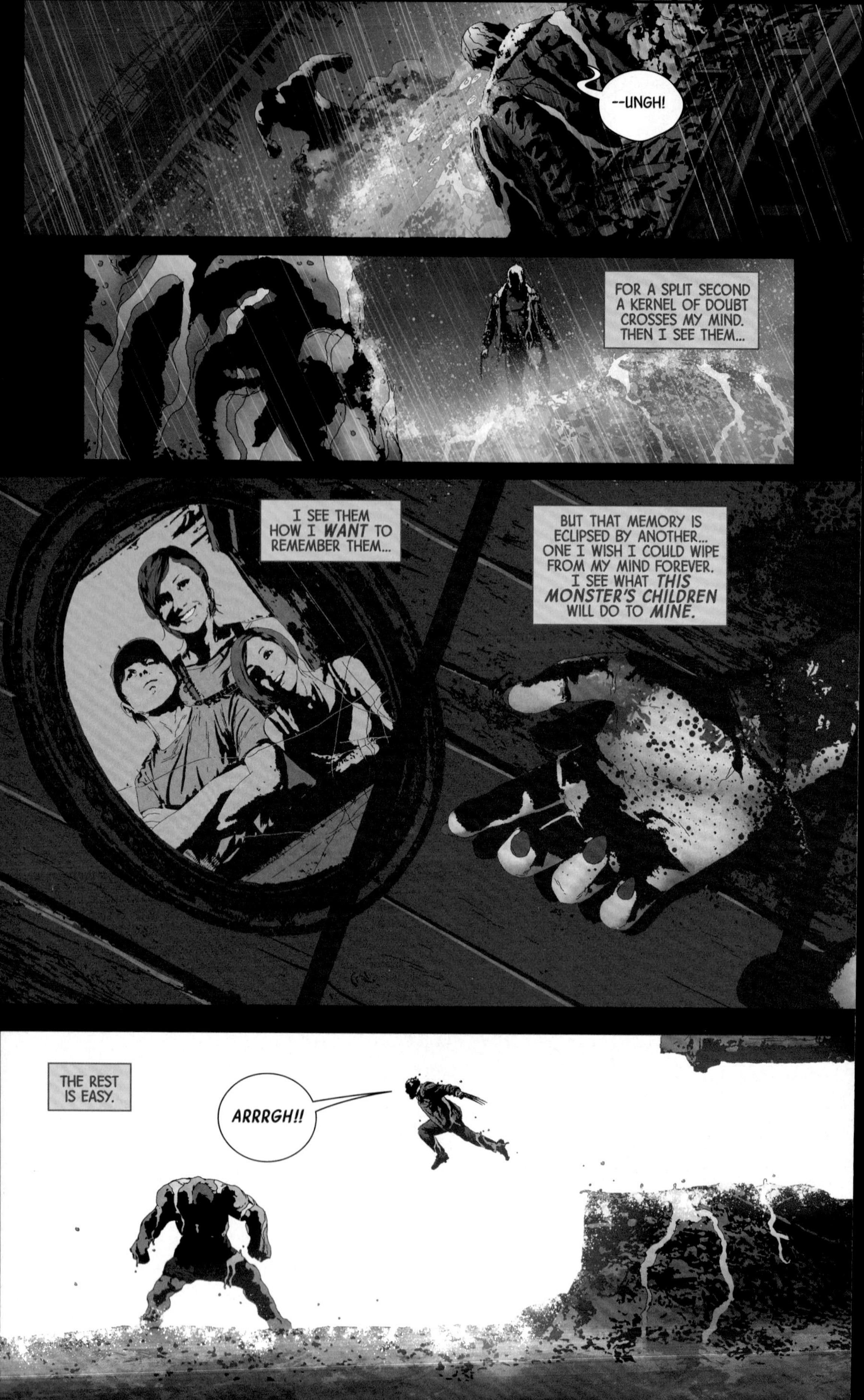
--UNGH!
FOR A SPLIT SECOND A KERNEL OF DOUBT CROSSES MY MIND. THEN I SEE THEM...
I SEE THEM HOW I WANT TO REMEMBER THEM...
BUT THAT MEMORY IS ECLIPSED BY ANOTHER... ONE I WISH I COULD WIPE FROM MY MIND FOREVER. I SEE WHAT THIS MONSTER'S CHILDREN WILL DO TO MINE.
THE REST IS EASY.
ARRRGH!!

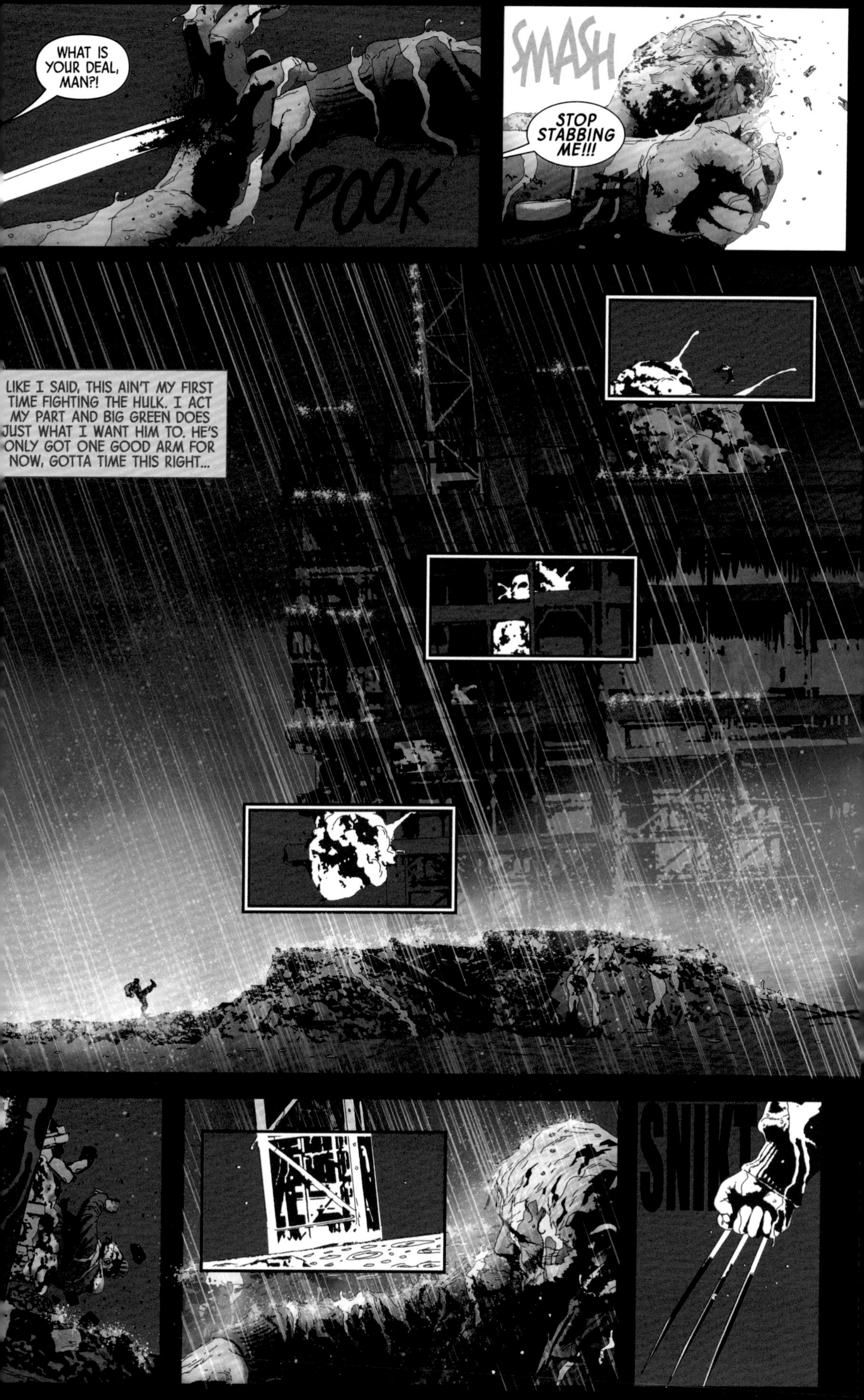

WHAT IS YOUR DEAL, MAN?!
POOK
SMASH
STOP STABBING ME!!!
LIKE I SAID, THIS AIN'T MY FIRST TIME FIGHTING THE HULK. I ACT MY PART AND BIG GREEN DOES JUST WHAT I WANT HIM TO. HE'S ONLY GOT ONE GOOD ARM FOR NOW, GOTTA TIME THIS RIGHT...
SNIKT

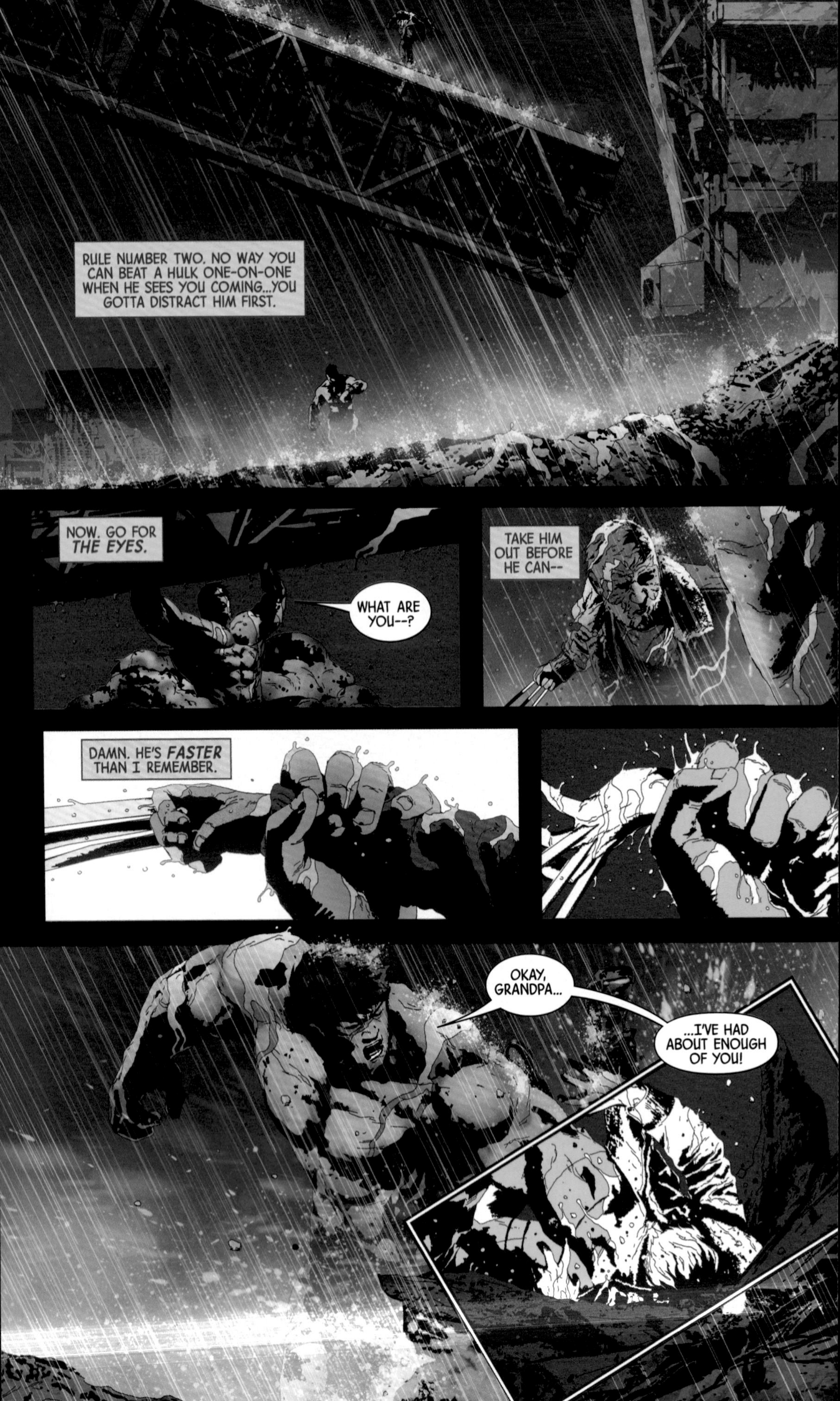
RULE NUMBER TWO. NO WAY YOU CAN BEAT A HULK ONE-ON-ONE WHEN HE SEES YOU COMING...YOU GOTTA DISTRACT HIM FIRST.
NOW. GO FOR *THE EYES.*
WHAT ARE YOU--?
TAKE HIM OUT BEFORE HE CAN--
DAMN. HE'S *FASTER* THAN I REMEMBER.
OKAY, GRANDPA...
...I'VE HAD ABOUT ENOUGH OF YOU!

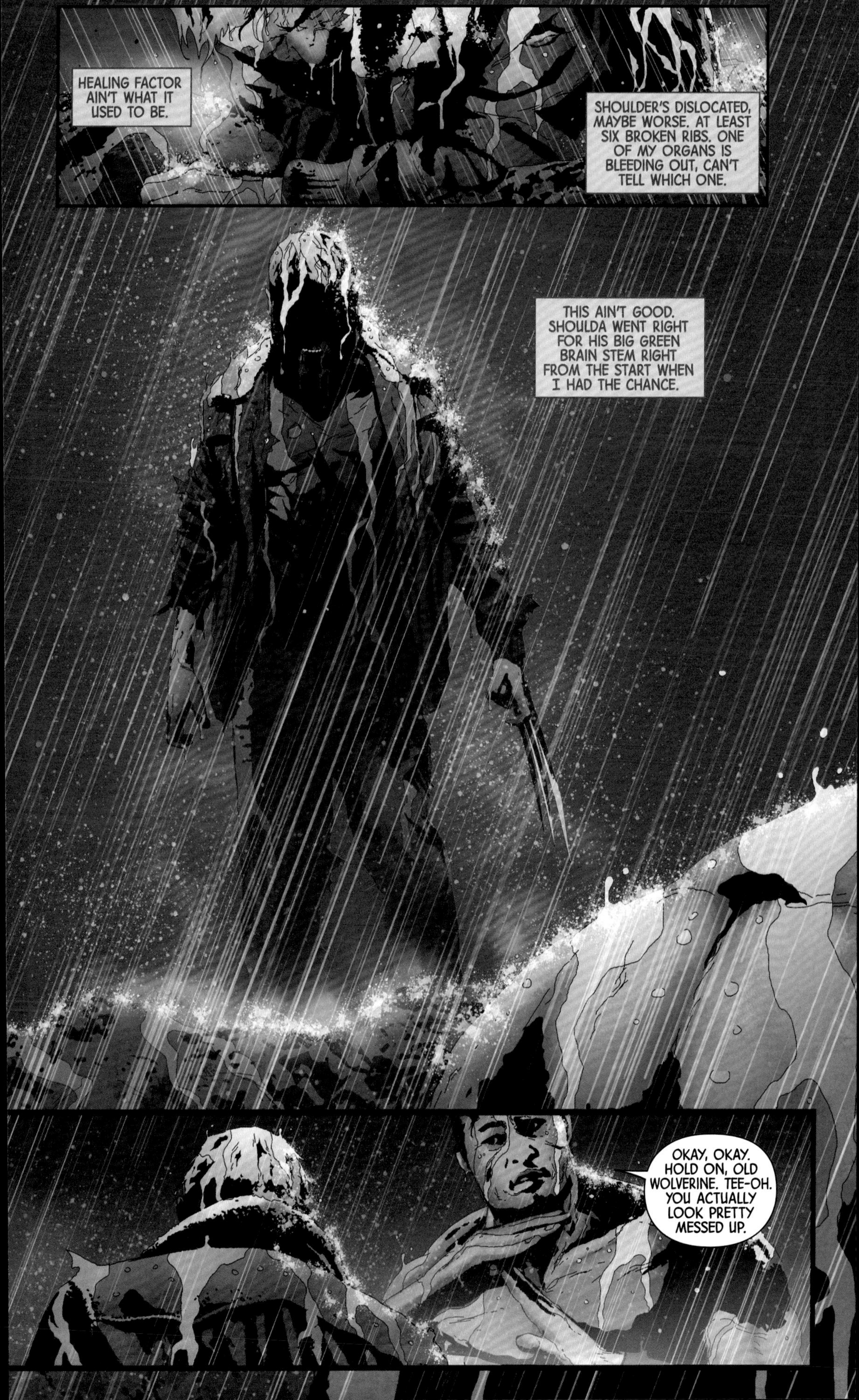
HEALING FACTOR AIN'T WHAT IT USED TO BE.
SHOULDER'S DISLOCATED, MAYBE WORSE. AT LEAST SIX BROKEN RIBS. ONE OF MY ORGANS IS BLEEDING OUT, CAN'T TELL WHICH ONE.
THIS AIN'T GOOD. SHOULDA WENT RIGHT FOR HIS BIG GREEN BRAIN STEM RIGHT FROM THE START WHEN I HAD THE CHANCE.
OKAY, OKAY. HOLD ON, OLD WOLVERINE. TEE-OH. YOU ACTUALLY LOOK PRETTY MESSED UP.

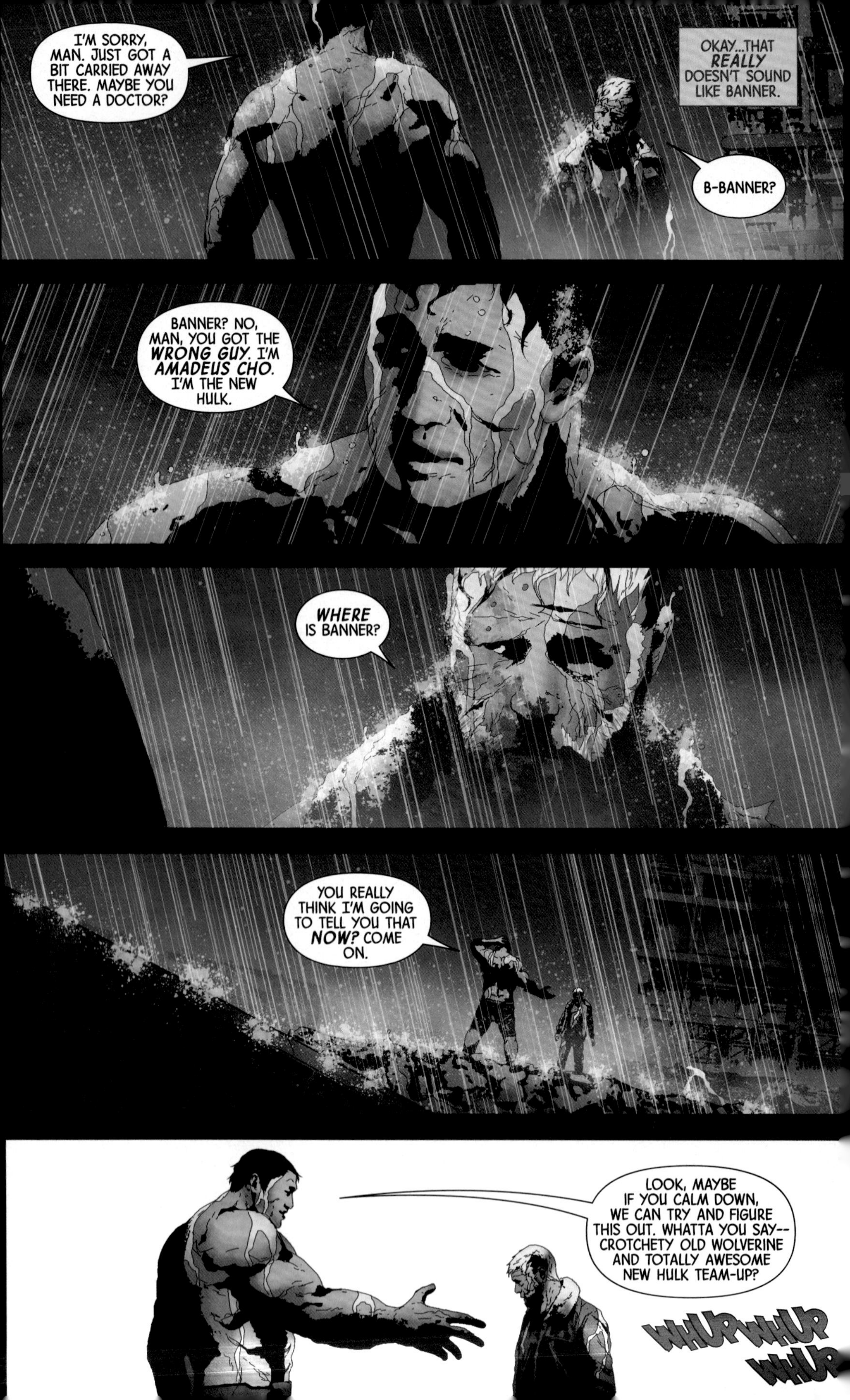
I'M SORRY, MAN. JUST GOT A BIT CARRIED AWAY THERE. MAYBE YOU NEED A DOCTOR?
OKAY...THAT REALLY DOESN'T SOUND LIKE BANNER.
B-BANNER?
BANNER? NO, MAN, YOU GOT THE WRONG GUY. I'M AMADEUS CHO. I'M THE NEW HULK.
WHERE IS BANNER?
YOU REALLY THINK I'M GOING TO TELL YOU THAT NOW? COME ON.
LOOK, MAYBE IF YOU CALM DOWN, WE CAN TRY AND FIGURE THIS OUT. WHATTA YOU SAY-- CROTCHETY OLD WOLVERINE AND TOTALLY AWESOME NEW HULK TEAM-UP?
WHUP WHUP WHUP

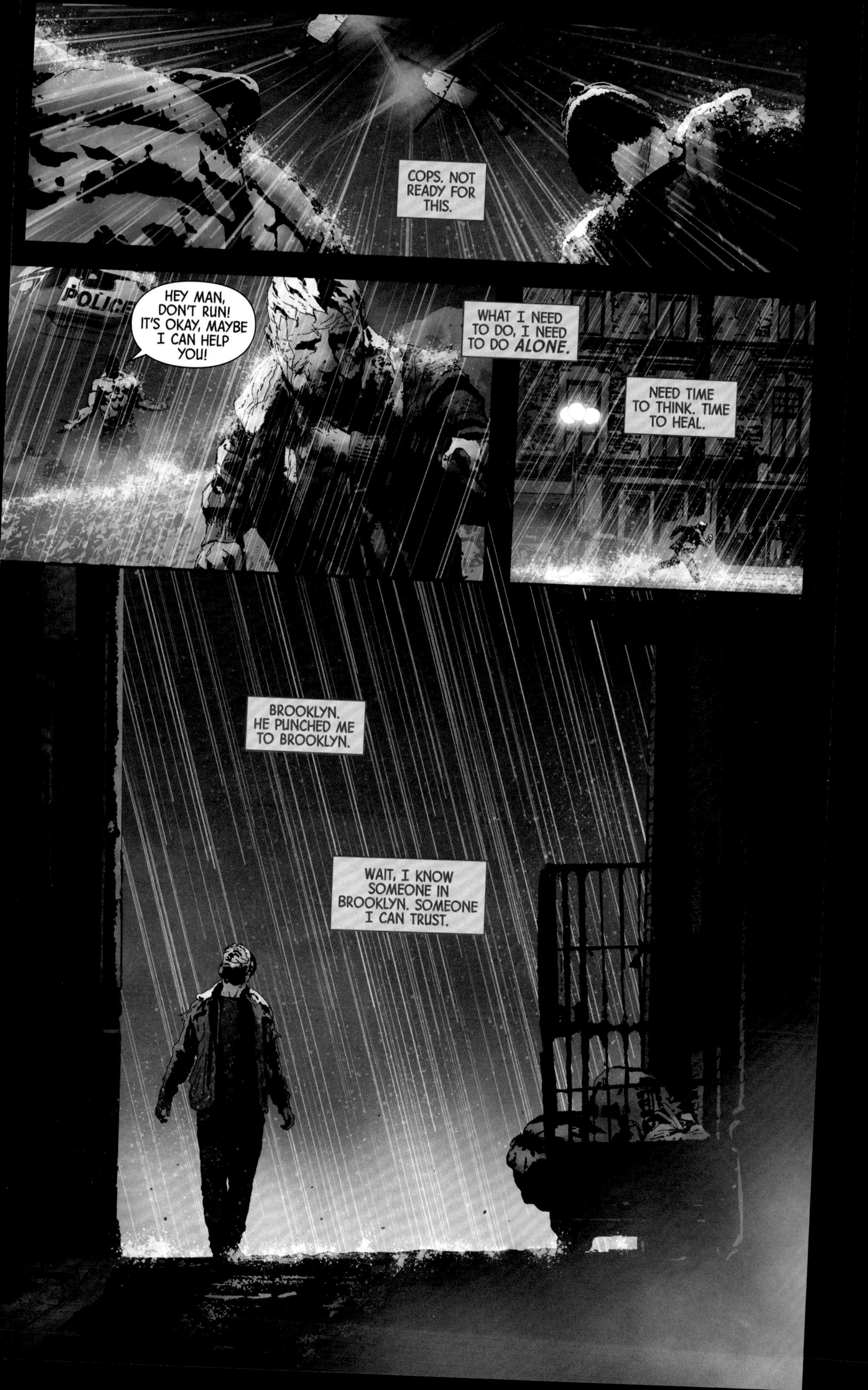
COPS. NOT READY FOR THIS.
POLICE
HEY MAN, DON'T RUN! IT'S OKAY, MAYBE I CAN HELP YOU!
WHAT I NEED TO DO, I NEED TO DO ALONE.
NEED TIME TO THINK. TIME TO HEAL.
BROOKLYN. HE PUNCHED ME TO BROOKLYN.
WAIT, I KNOW SOMEONE IN BROOKLYN. SOMEONE I CAN TRUST.

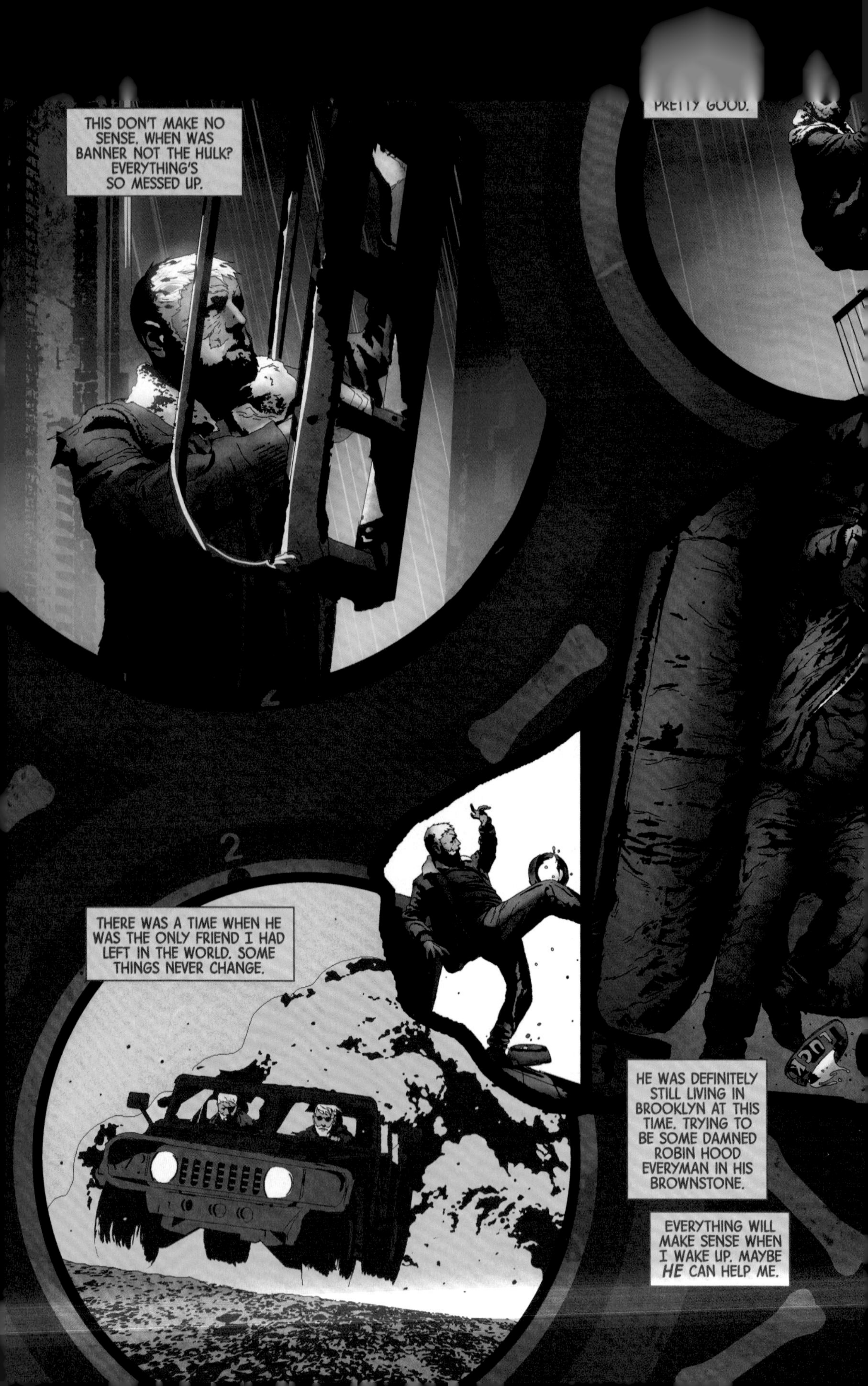
THIS DON'T MAKE NO SENSE. WHEN WAS BANNER NOT THE HULK? EVERYTHING'S SO MESSED UP.
PRETTY GOOD.
THERE WAS A TIME WHEN HE WAS THE ONLY FRIEND I HAD LEFT IN THE WORLD. SOME THINGS NEVER CHANGE.
HE WAS DEFINITELY STILL LIVING IN BROOKLYN AT THIS TIME. TRYING TO BE SOME DAMNED ROBIN HOOD EVERYMAN IN HIS BROWNSTONE.
EVERYTHING WILL MAKE SENSE WHEN I WAKE UP. MAYBE HE CAN HELP ME.

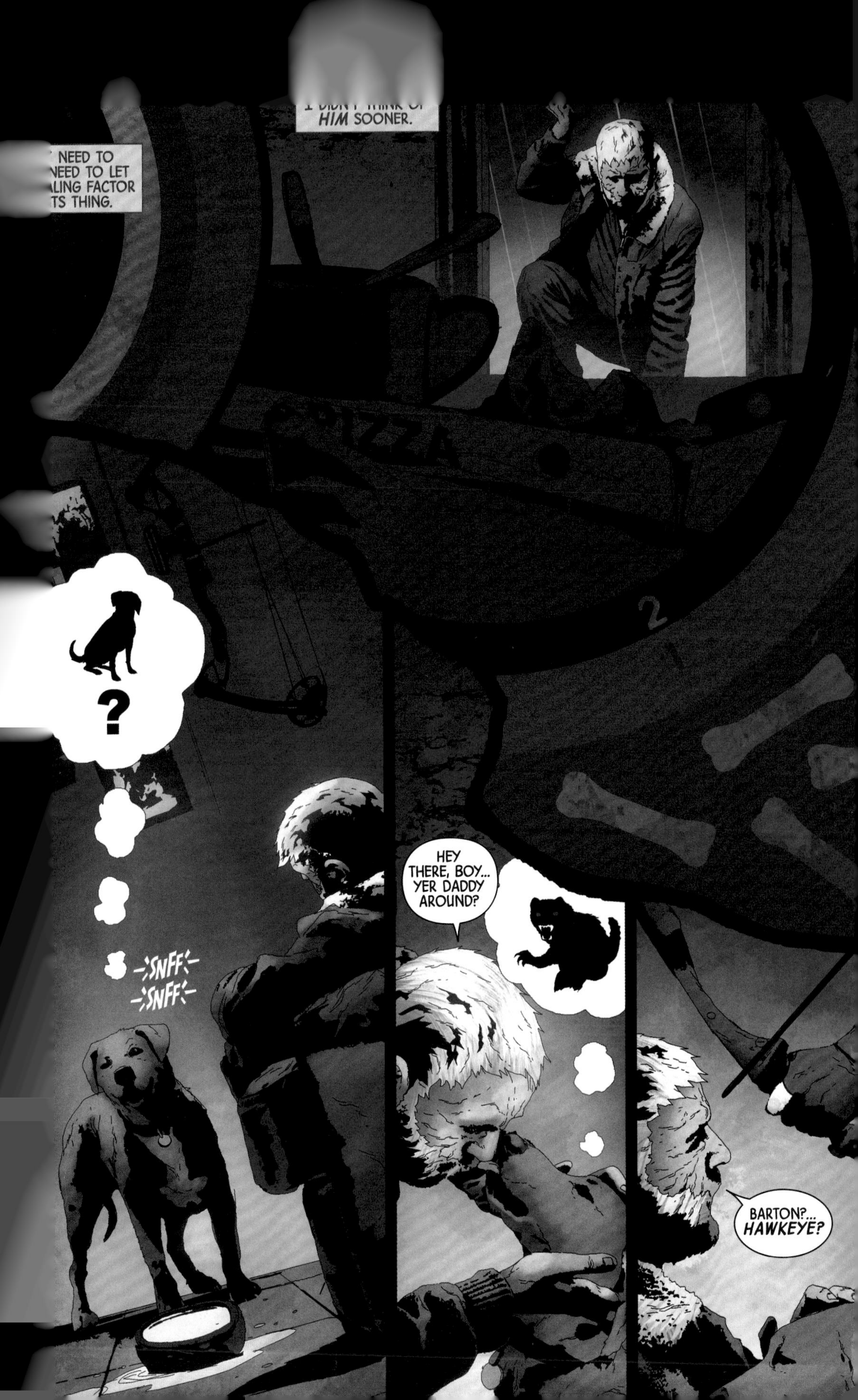

HIM SOONER.
NEED TO NEED TO LET FACTOR THING.
PIZZA
?
SNFF SNFF
HEY THERE, BOY... YER DADDY AROUND?
BARTON?... HAWKEYE?

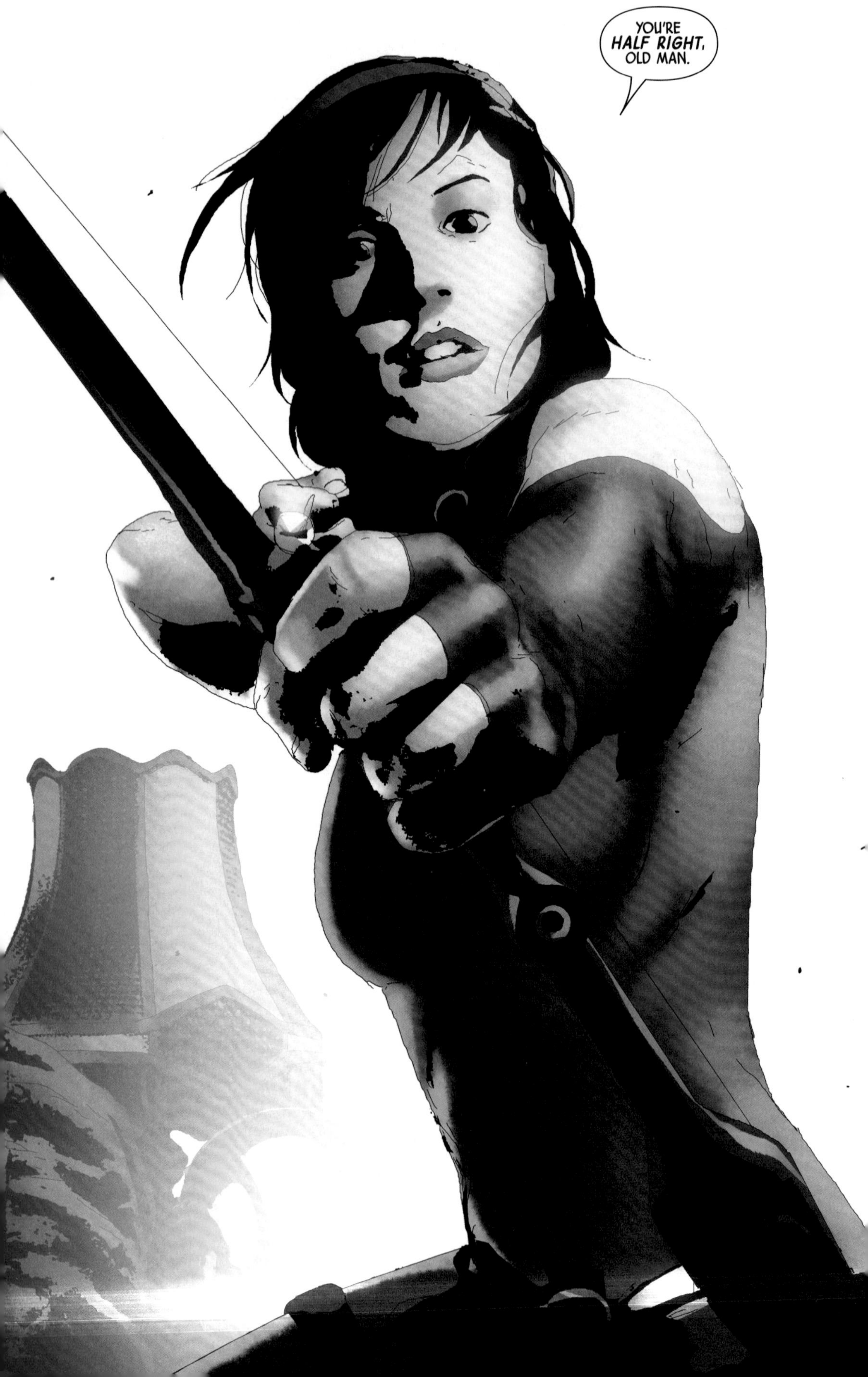
YOU'RE *HALF RIGHT*, OLD MAN.

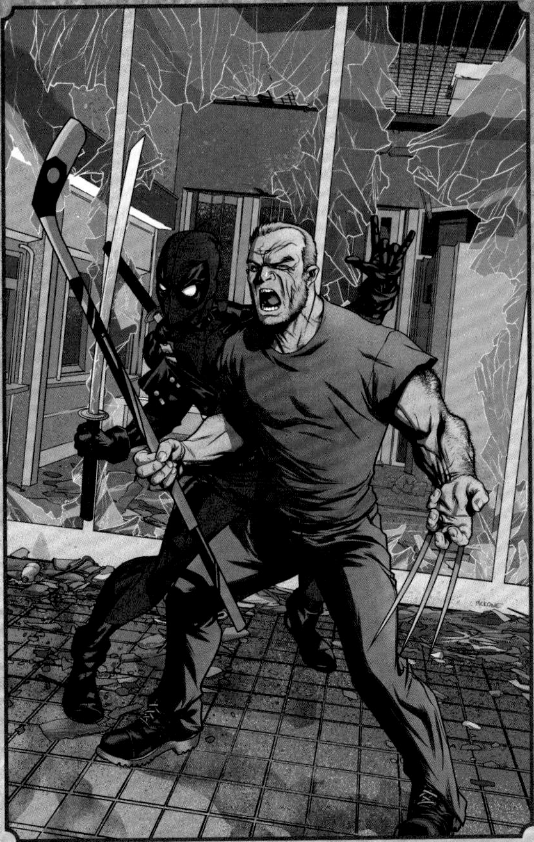

#1 DEADPOOL VARIANT BY MIKE McKONE

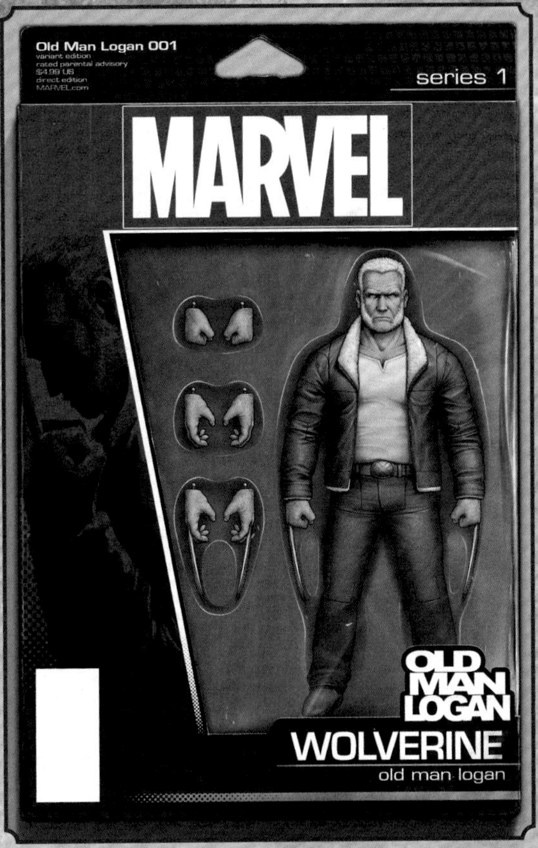
Old Man Logan 001
variant edition
rated parental advisory
$4.99 US
direct edition
MARVEL.com
series 1
MARVEL
OLD MAN LOGAN
WOLVERINE
old man logan

#1 ACTION FIGURE VARIANT BY JOHN TYLER CHRISTOPHER

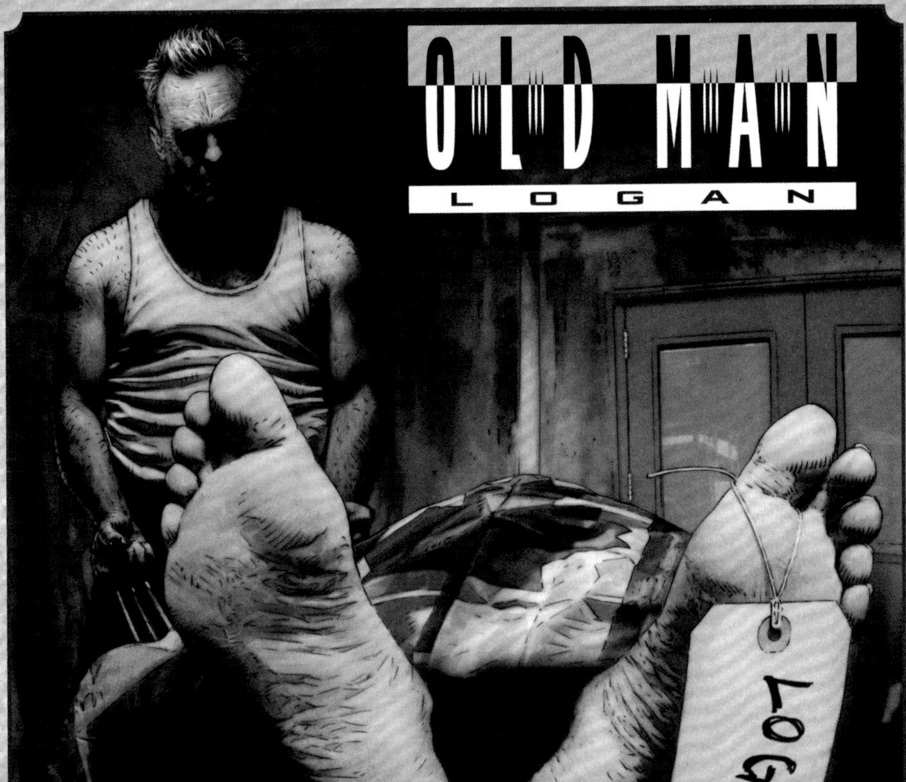
OLD MAN
LOGAN
LOGAN

#1 HIP-HOP VARIANT BY TIM BRADSTREET

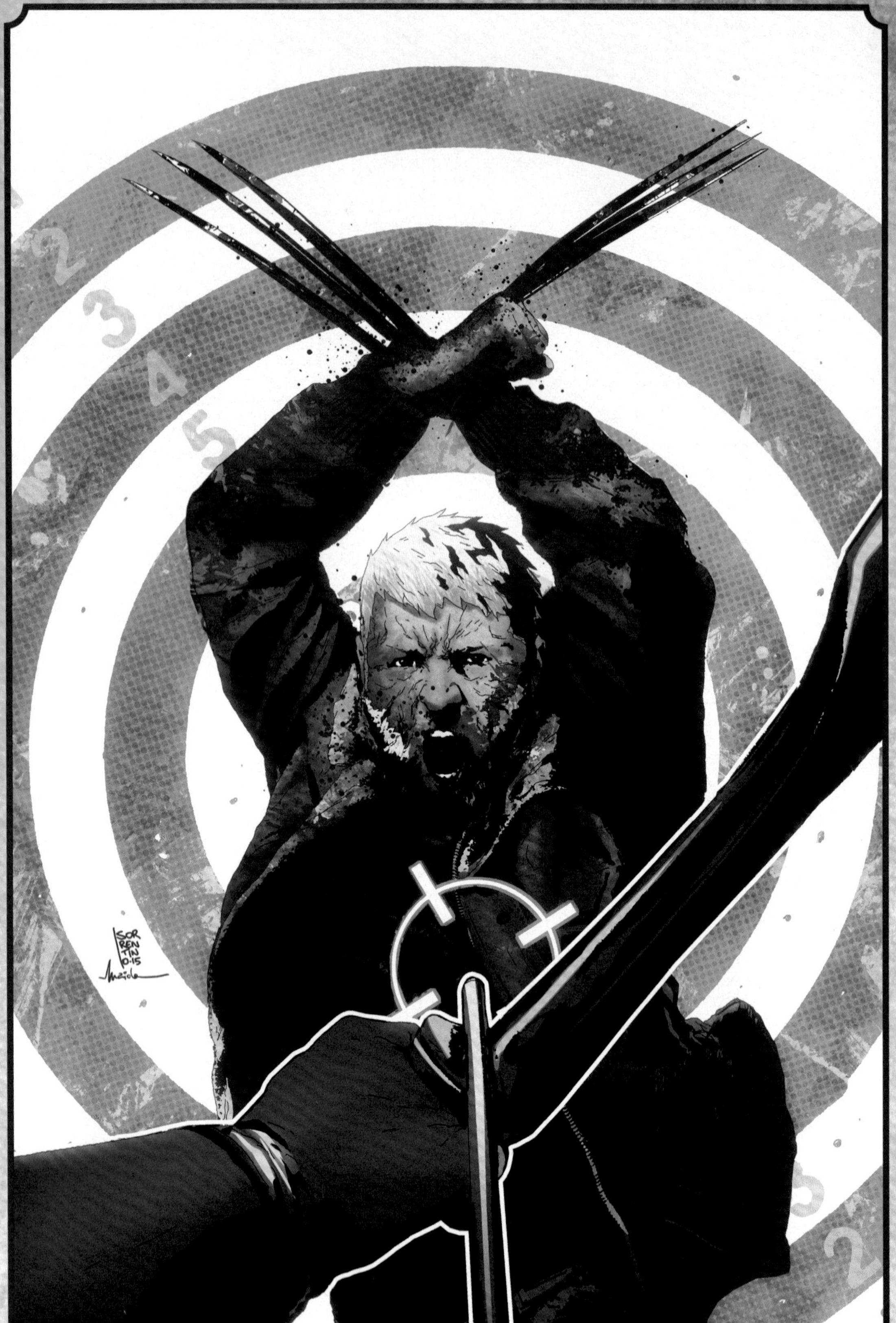

3

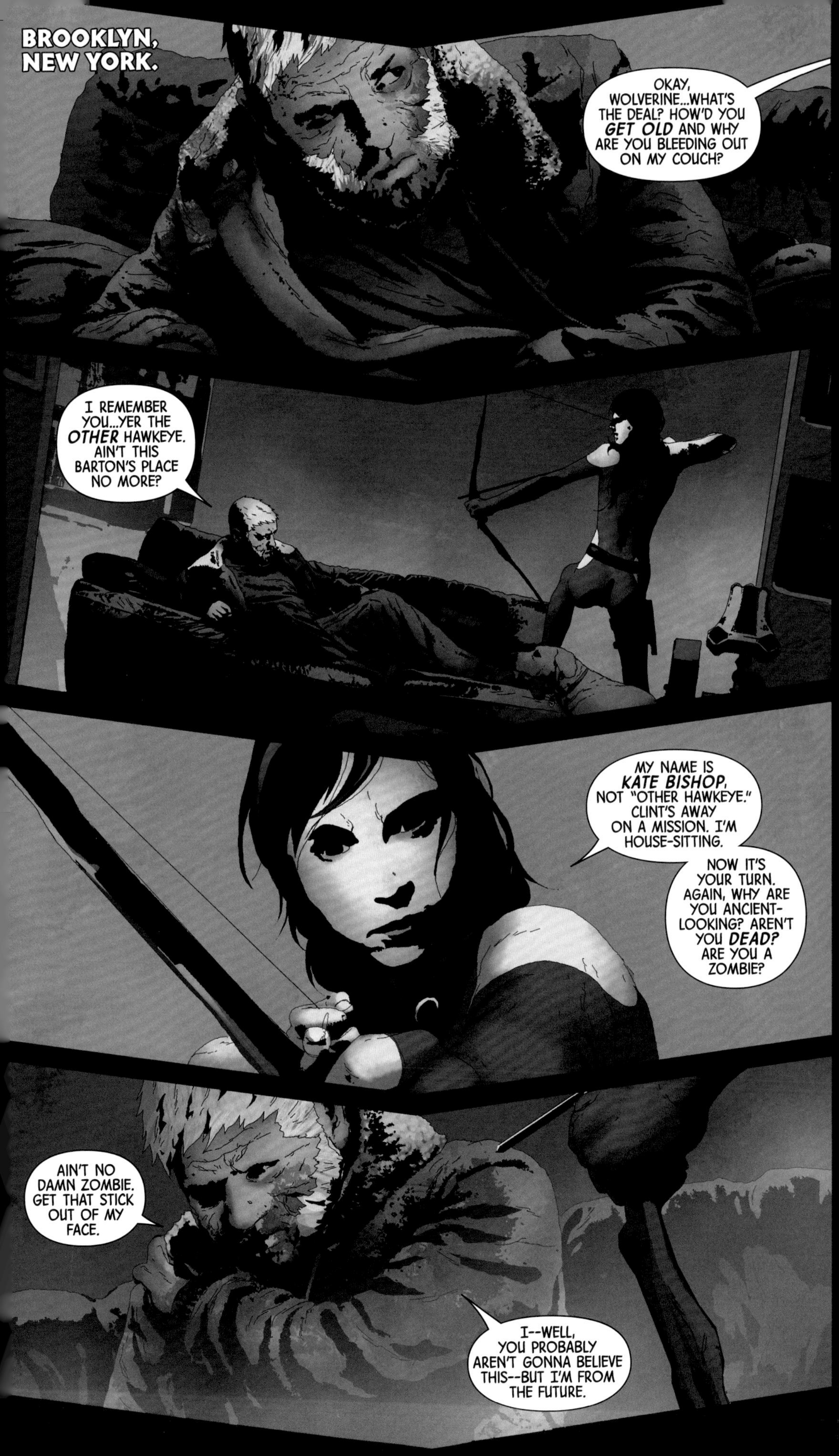
BROOKLYN, NEW YORK.
OKAY, WOLVERINE...WHAT'S THE DEAL? HOW'D YOU GET OLD AND WHY ARE YOU BLEEDING OUT ON MY COUCH?
I REMEMBER YOU...YER THE OTHER HAWKEYE. AIN'T THIS BARTON'S PLACE NO MORE?
MY NAME IS KATE BISHOP, NOT "OTHER HAWKEYE." CLINT'S AWAY ON A MISSION. I'M HOUSE-SITTING.
NOW IT'S YOUR TURN. AGAIN, WHY ARE YOU ANCIENT-LOOKING? AREN'T YOU DEAD? ARE YOU A ZOMBIE?
AIN'T NO DAMN ZOMBIE. GET THAT STICK OUT OF MY FACE.
I--WELL, YOU PROBABLY AREN'T GONNA BELIEVE THIS--BUT I'M FROM THE FUTURE.

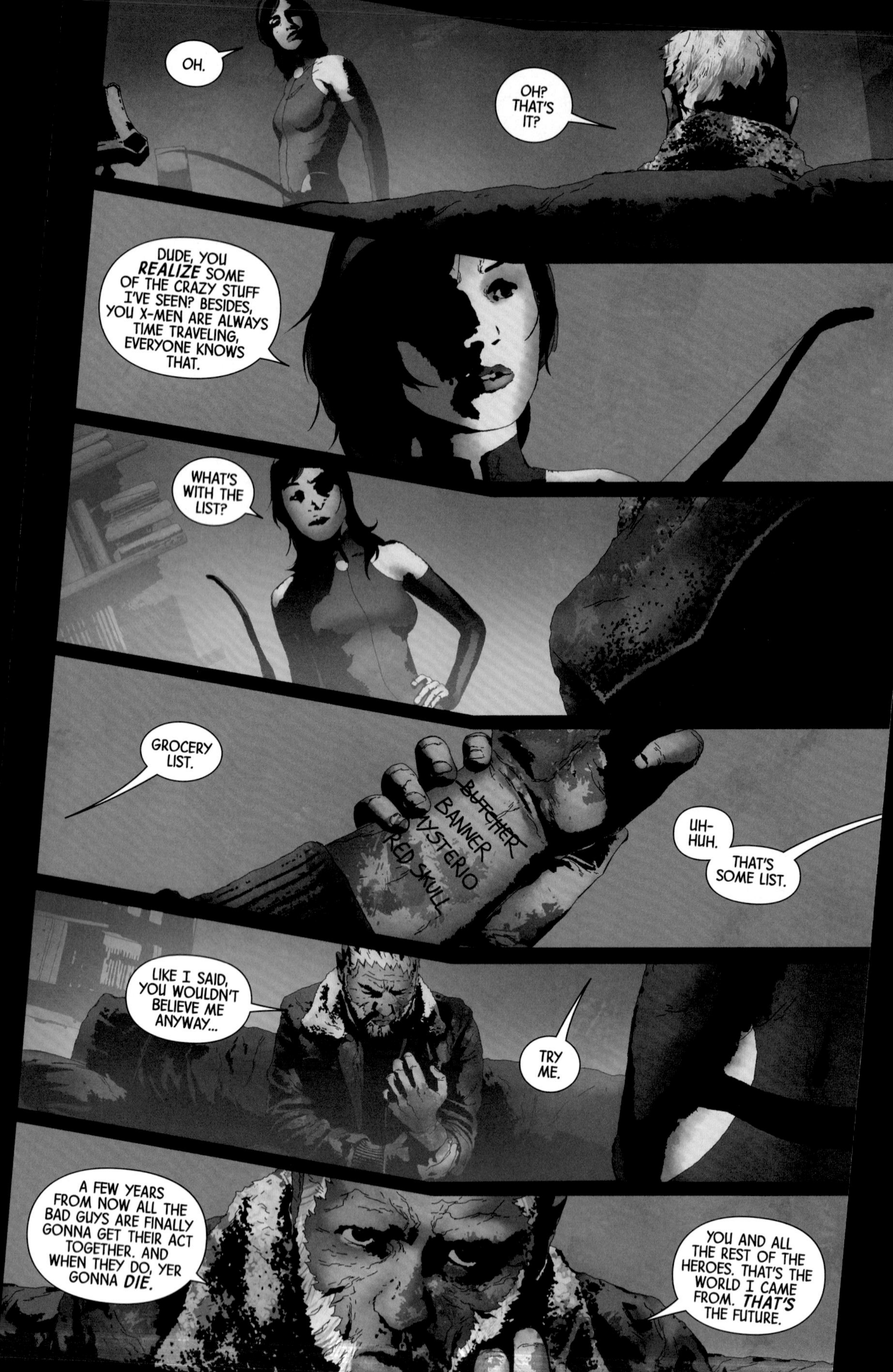

OH.
OH? THAT'S IT?
DUDE, YOU *REALIZE* SOME OF THE CRAZY STUFF I'VE SEEN? BESIDES, YOU X-MEN ARE ALWAYS TIME TRAVELING, EVERYONE KNOWS THAT.
WHAT'S WITH THE LIST?
GROCERY LIST.
~~BUTCHER~~
BANNER
MYSTERIO
RED SKULL
UH-HUH.
THAT'S SOME LIST.
LIKE I SAID, YOU WOULDN'T BELIEVE ME ANYWAY...
TRY ME.
A FEW YEARS FROM NOW ALL THE BAD GUYS ARE FINALLY GONNA GET THEIR ACT TOGETHER. AND WHEN THEY DO, YER GONNA *DIE*.
YOU AND ALL THE REST OF THE HEROES. THAT'S THE WORLD I CAME FROM. *THAT'S* THE FUTURE.

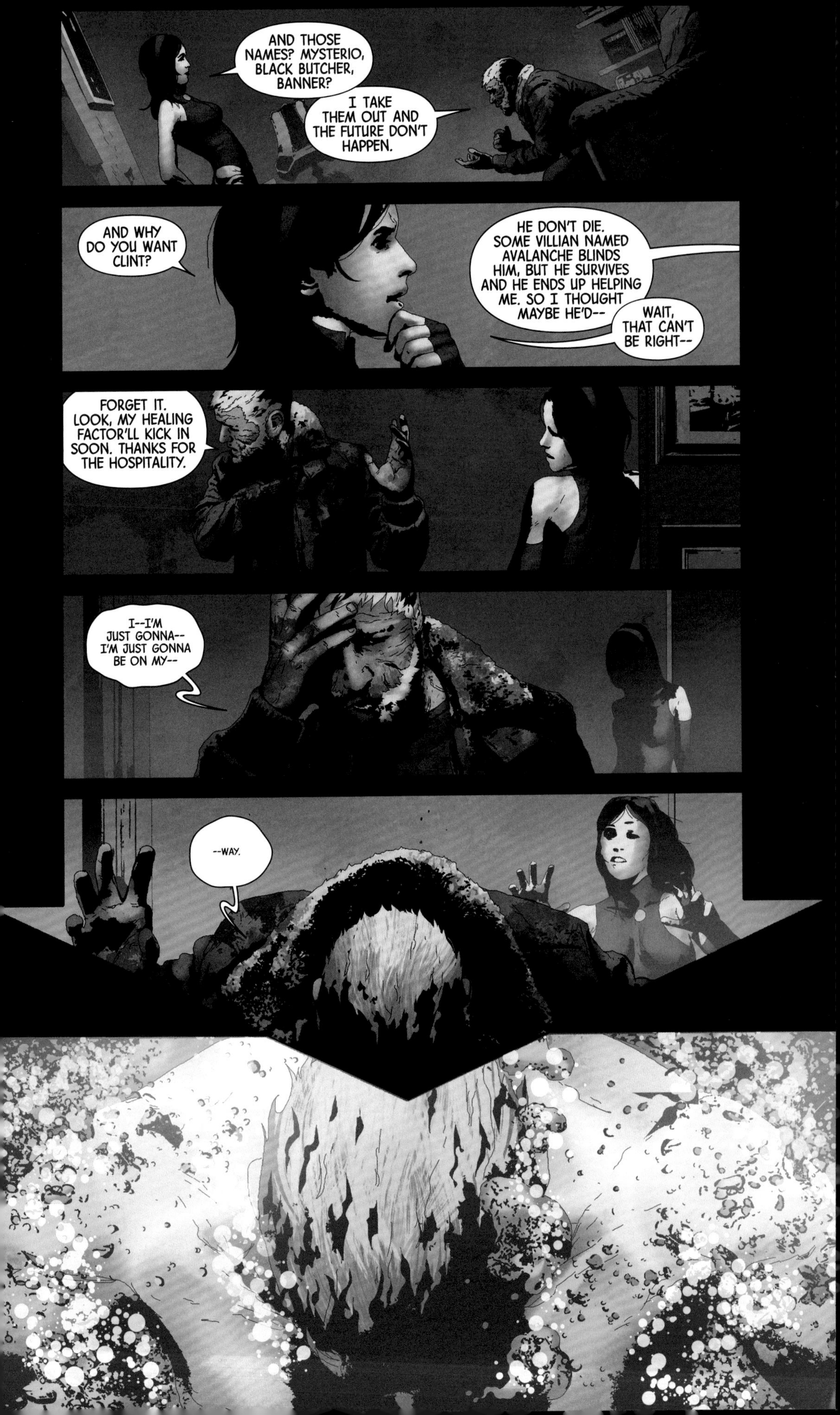
AND THOSE NAMES? MYSTERIO, BLACK BUTCHER, BANNER?
I TAKE THEM OUT AND THE FUTURE DON'T HAPPEN.
AND WHY DO YOU WANT CLINT?
HE DON'T DIE. SOME VILLIAN NAMED AVALANCHE BLINDS HIM, BUT HE SURVIVES AND HE ENDS UP HELPING ME. SO I THOUGHT MAYBE HE'D--
WAIT, THAT CAN'T BE RIGHT--
FORGET IT. LOOK, MY HEALING FACTOR'LL KICK IN SOON. THANKS FOR THE HOSPITALITY.
I--I'M JUST GONNA-- I'M JUST GONNA BE ON MY--
--WAY.

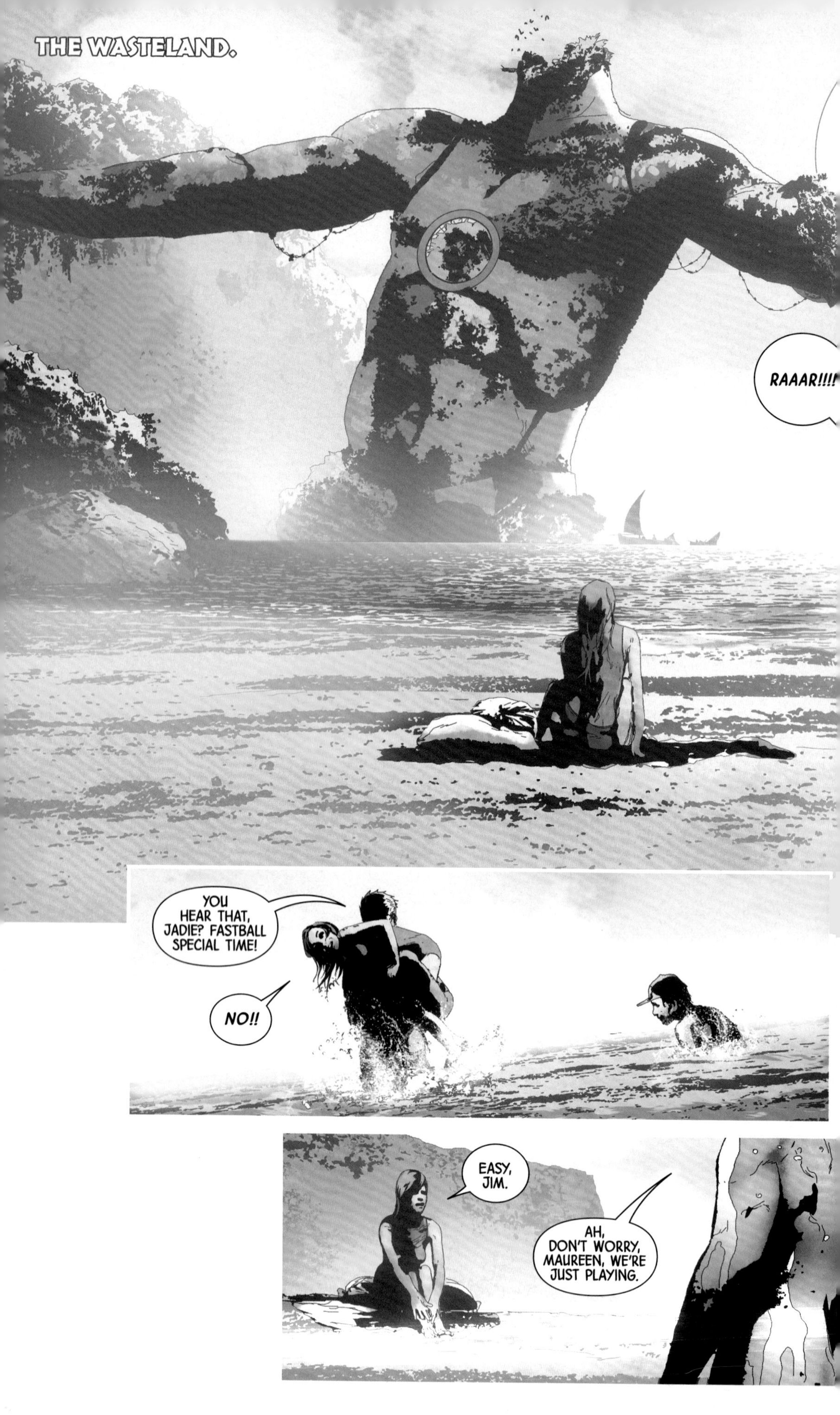
THE WASTELAND.
RAAAR!!!!
YOU HEAR THAT, JADIE? FASTBALL SPECIAL TIME!
NO!!
EASY, JIM.
AH, DON'T WORRY, MAUREEN, WE'RE JUST PLAYING.

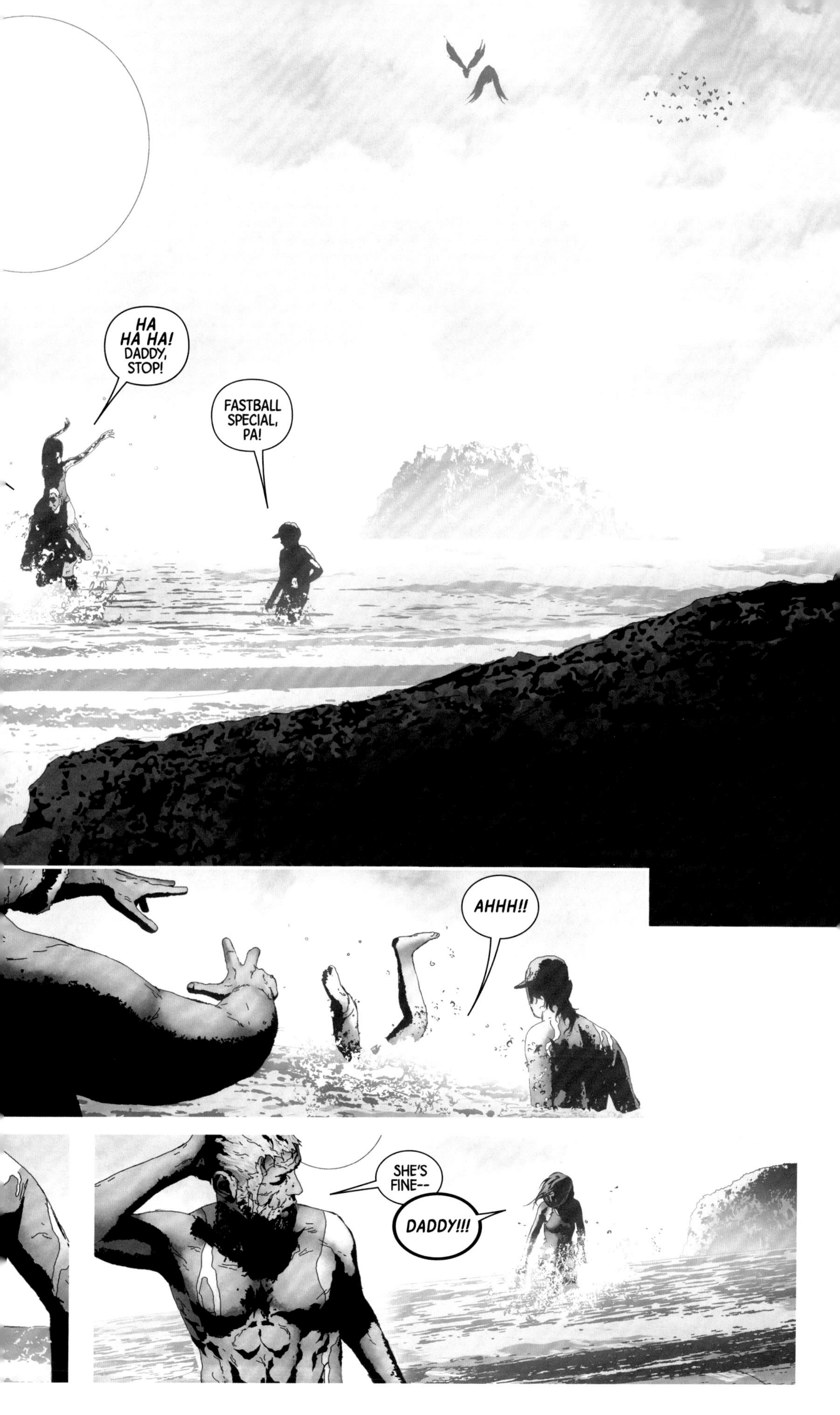
HA HA HA! DADDY, STOP!
FASTBALL SPECIAL, PA!
AHHH!!
SHE'S FINE--
DADDY!!!

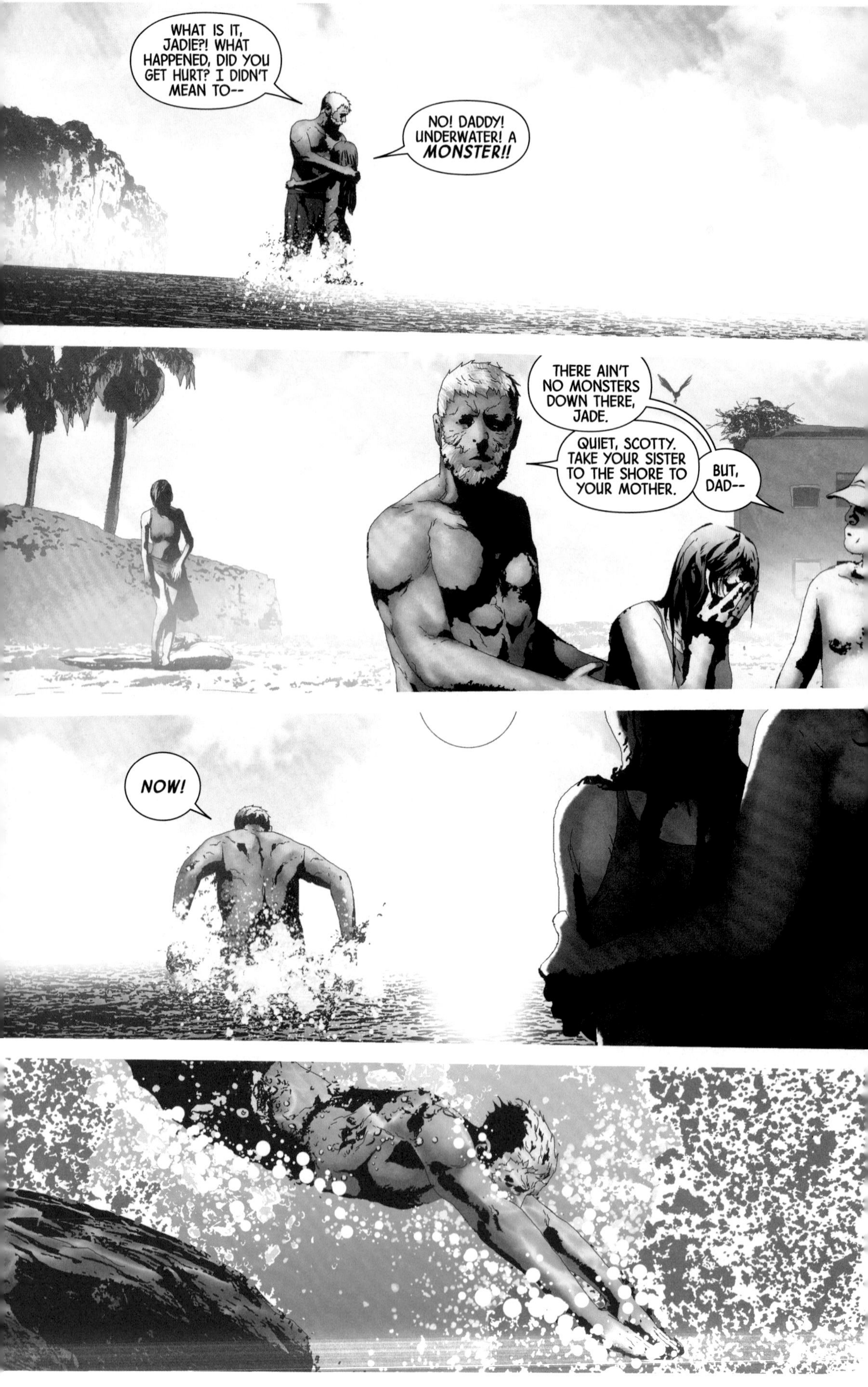
WHAT IS IT, JADIE?! WHAT HAPPENED, DID YOU GET HURT? I DIDN'T MEAN TO--
NO! DADDY! UNDERWATER! A MONSTER!!
THERE AIN'T NO MONSTERS DOWN THERE, JADE.
QUIET, SCOTTY. TAKE YOUR SISTER TO THE SHORE TO YOUR MOTHER.
BUT, DAD--
NOW!

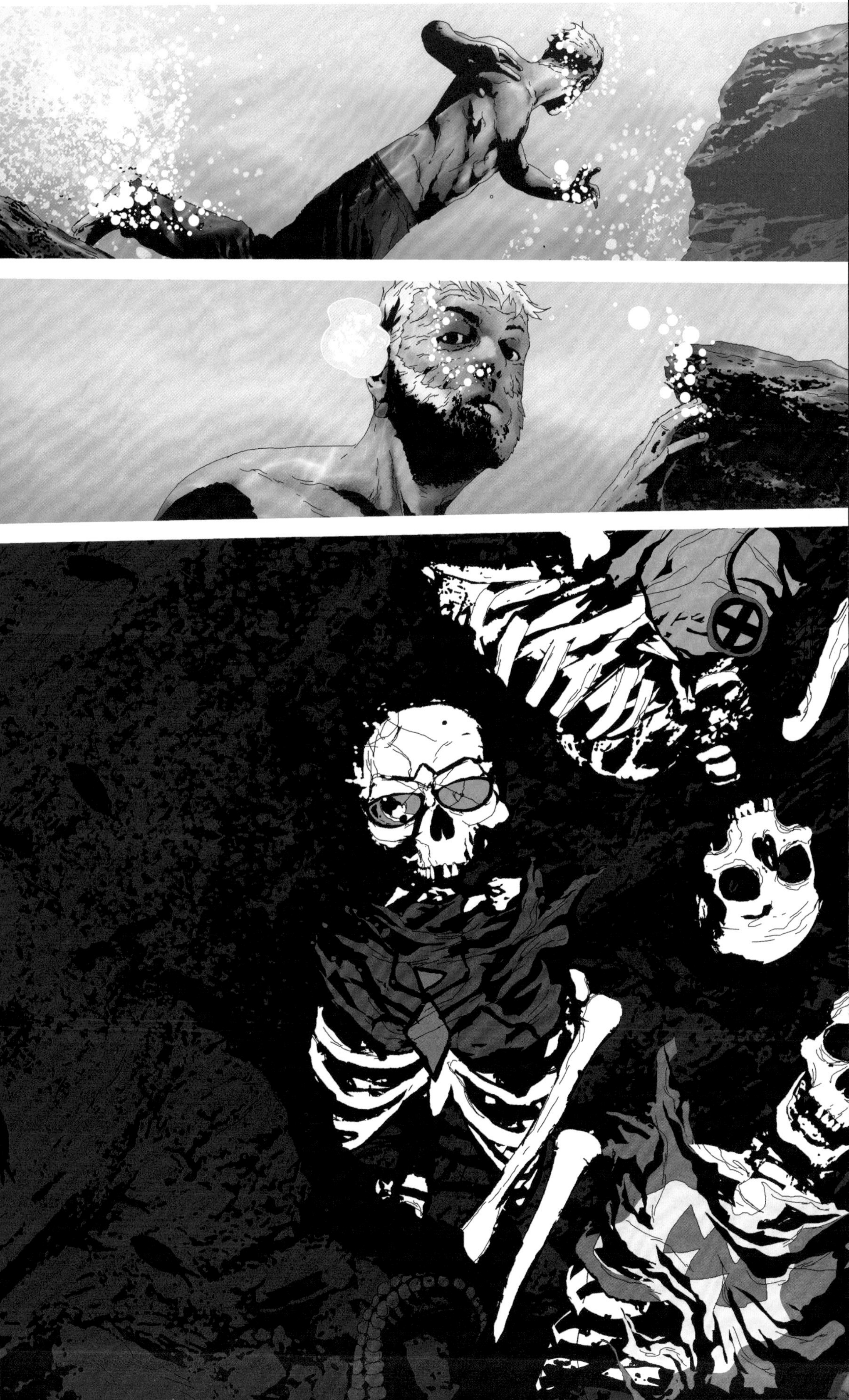

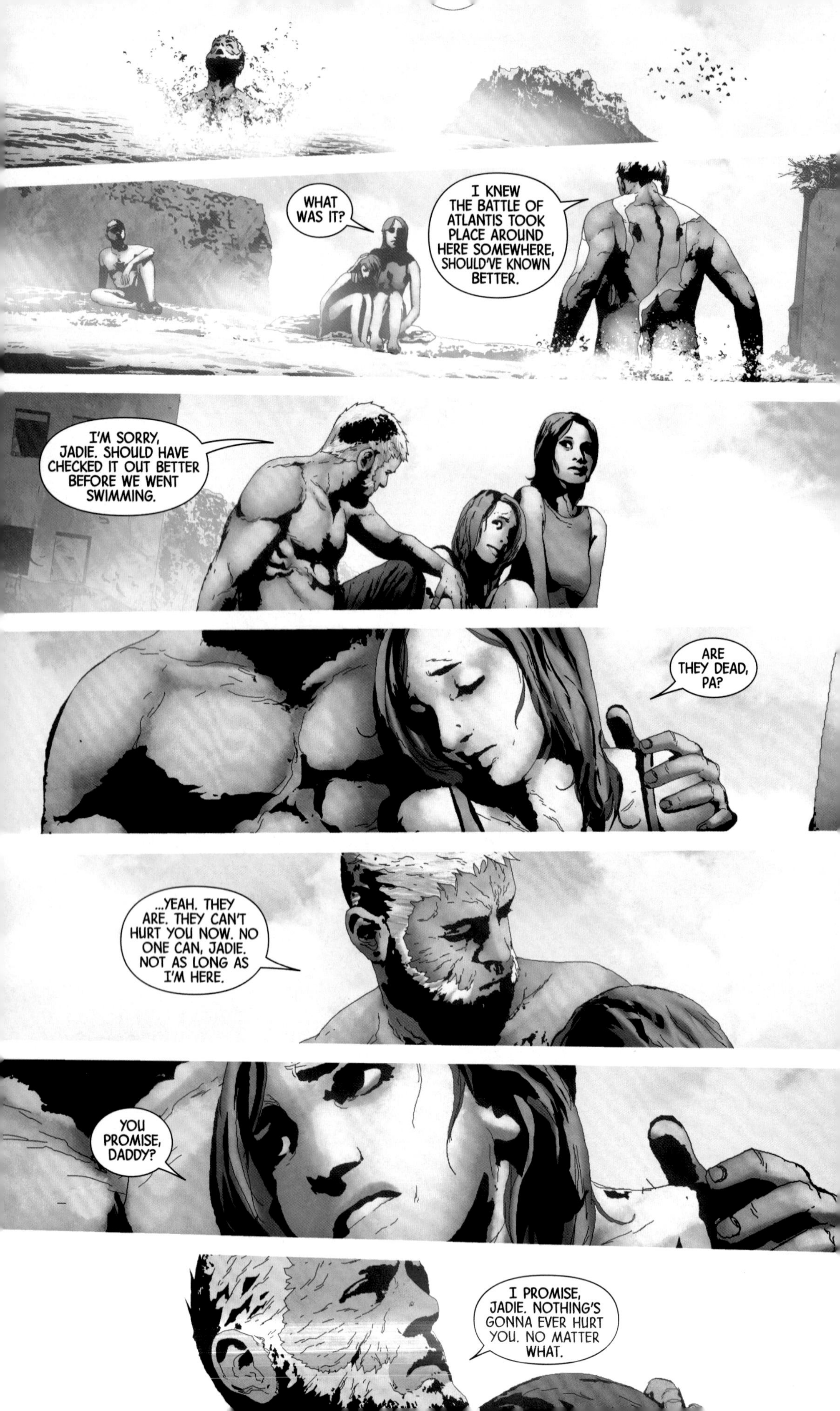
WHAT WAS IT?
I KNEW THE BATTLE OF ATLANTIS TOOK PLACE AROUND HERE SOMEWHERE, SHOULD'VE KNOWN BETTER.
I'M SORRY, JADIE. SHOULD HAVE CHECKED IT OUT BETTER BEFORE WE WENT SWIMMING.
ARE THEY DEAD, PA?
...YEAH. THEY ARE. THEY CAN'T HURT YOU NOW. NO ONE CAN, JADIE. NOT AS LONG AS I'M HERE.
YOU PROMISE, DADDY?
I PROMISE, JADIE. NOTHING'S GONNA EVER HURT YOU. NO MATTER WHAT.

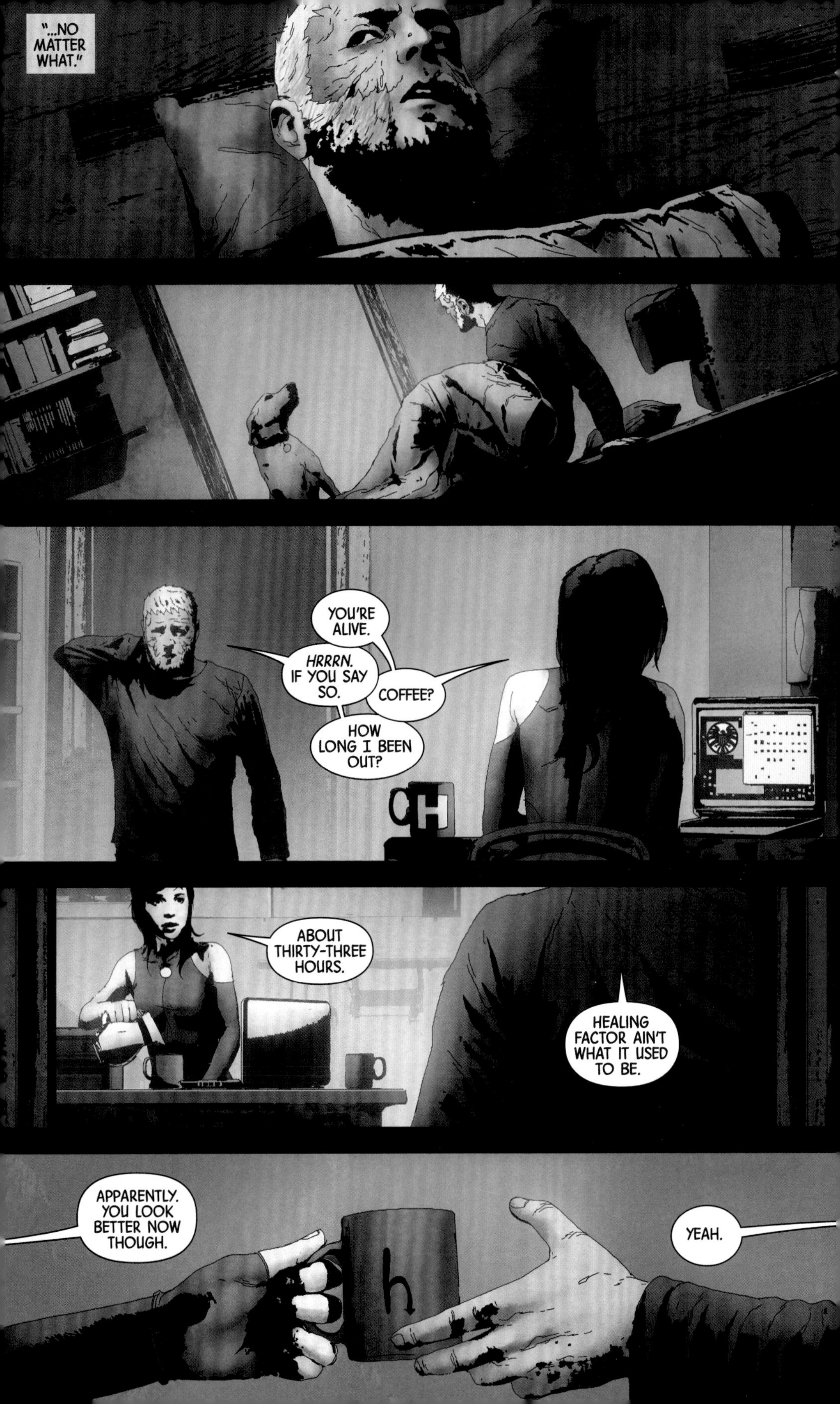
"...NO MATTER WHAT."
YOU'RE ALIVE.
HRRRN. IF YOU SAY SO.
COFFEE?
HOW LONG I BEEN OUT?
ABOUT THIRTY-THREE HOURS.
HEALING FACTOR AIN'T WHAT IT USED TO BE.
APPARENTLY. YOU LOOK BETTER NOW THOUGH.
YEAH.

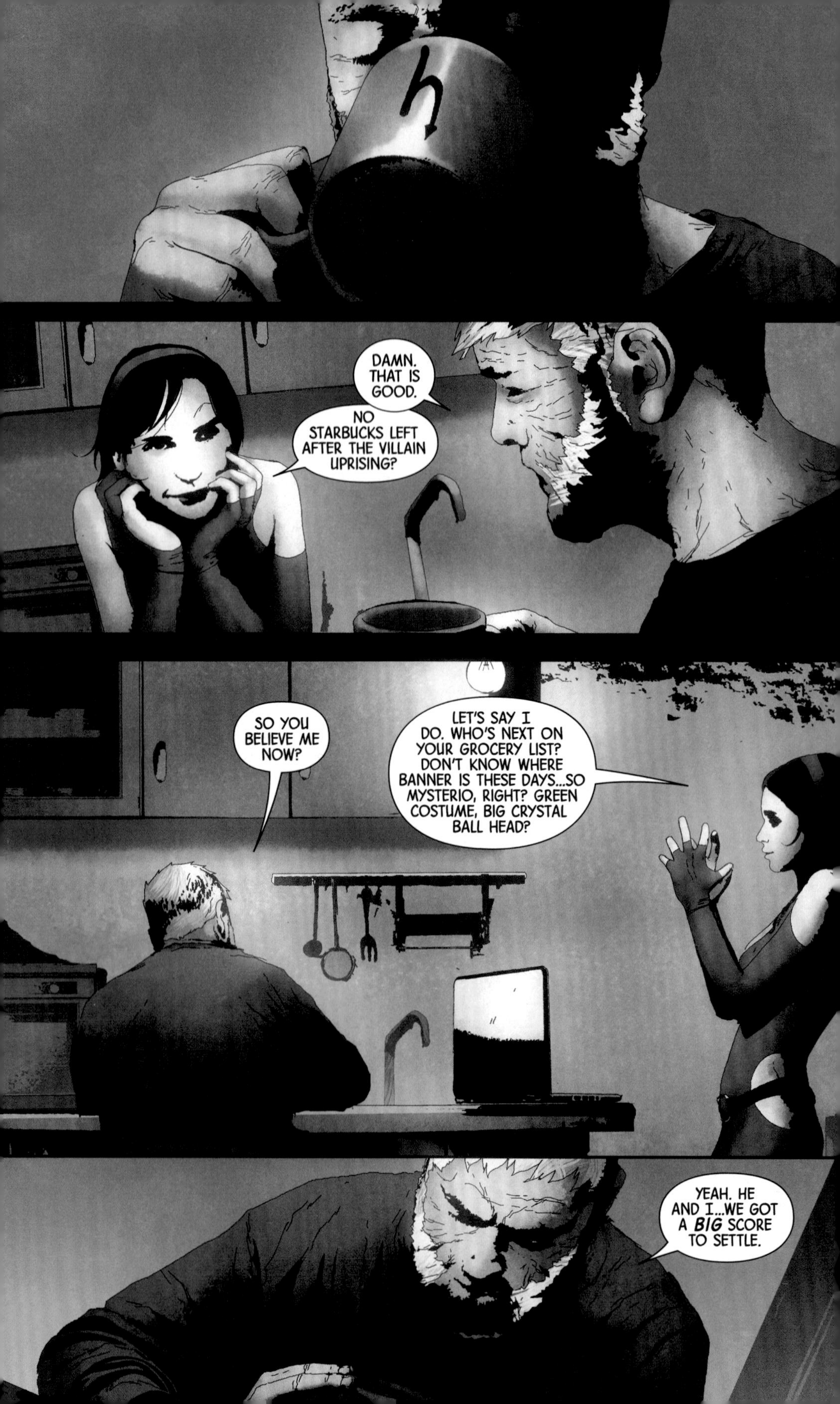
DAMN. THAT IS GOOD.
NO STARBUCKS LEFT AFTER THE VILLAIN UPRISING?
SO YOU BELIEVE ME NOW?
LET'S SAY I DO. WHO'S NEXT ON YOUR GROCERY LIST? DON'T KNOW WHERE BANNER IS THESE DAYS...SO MYSTERIO, RIGHT? GREEN COSTUME, BIG CRYSTAL BALL HEAD?
YEAH. HE AND I...WE GOT A ***BIG*** SCORE TO SETTLE.

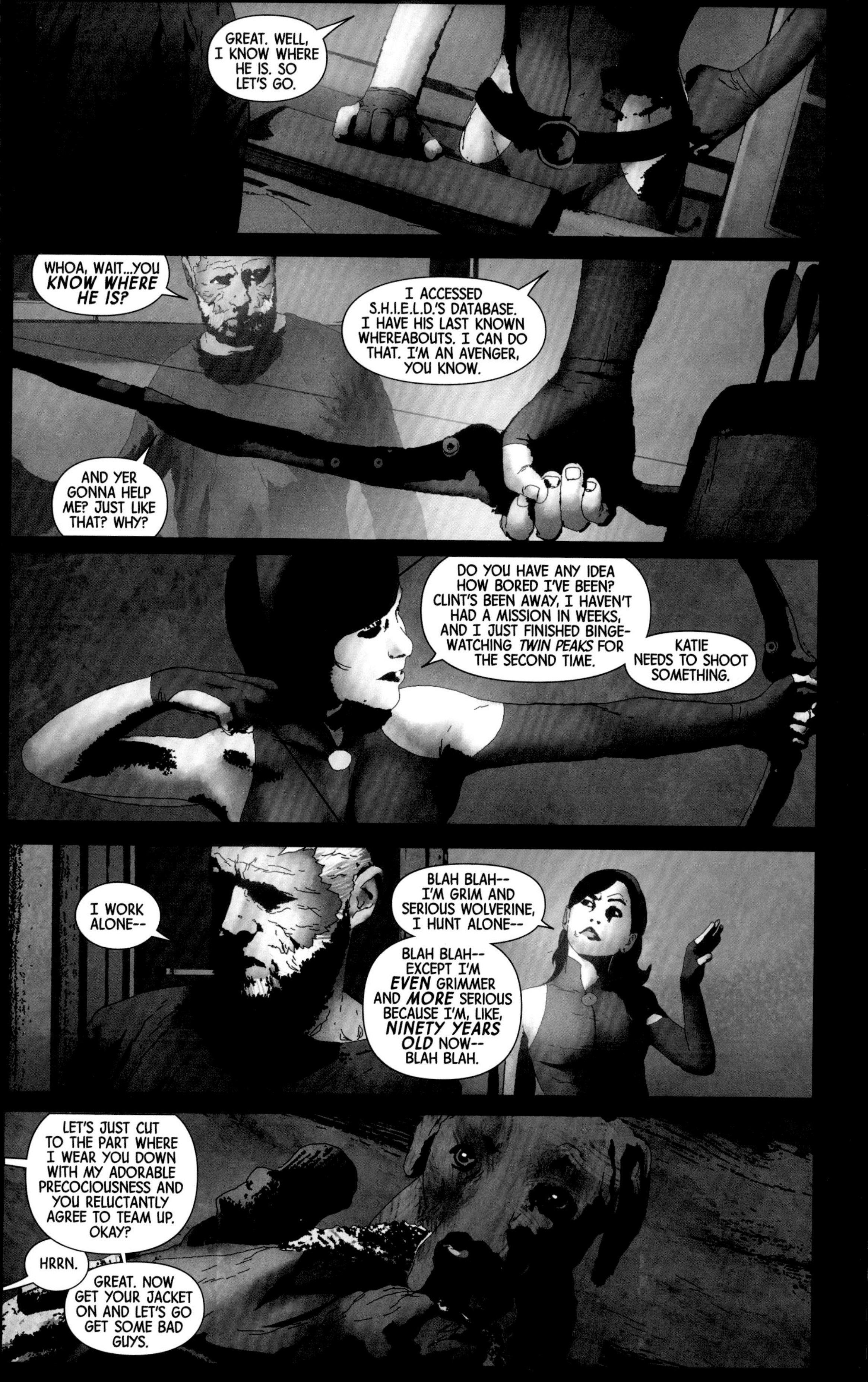
GREAT. WELL, I KNOW WHERE HE IS. SO LET'S GO.
WHOA, WAIT...YOU *KNOW WHERE HE IS?*
I ACCESSED S.H.I.E.L.D.'S DATABASE. I HAVE HIS LAST KNOWN WHEREABOUTS. I CAN DO THAT. I'M AN AVENGER, YOU KNOW.
AND YER GONNA HELP ME? JUST LIKE THAT? WHY?
DO YOU HAVE ANY IDEA HOW BORED I'VE BEEN? CLINT'S BEEN AWAY, I HAVEN'T HAD A MISSION IN WEEKS, AND I JUST FINISHED BINGE-WATCHING *TWIN PEAKS* FOR THE SECOND TIME.
KATIE NEEDS TO SHOOT SOMETHING.
I WORK ALONE--
BLAH BLAH-- I'M GRIM AND SERIOUS WOLVERINE, I HUNT ALONE--
BLAH BLAH-- EXCEPT I'M *EVEN* GRIMMER AND *MORE* SERIOUS BECAUSE I'M, LIKE, *NINETY YEARS OLD* NOW-- BLAH BLAH.
LET'S JUST CUT TO THE PART WHERE I WEAR YOU DOWN WITH MY ADORABLE PRECOCIOUSNESS AND YOU RELUCTANTLY AGREE TO TEAM UP. OKAY?
HRRN.
GREAT. NOW GET YOUR JACKET ON AND LET'S GO GET SOME BAD GUYS.

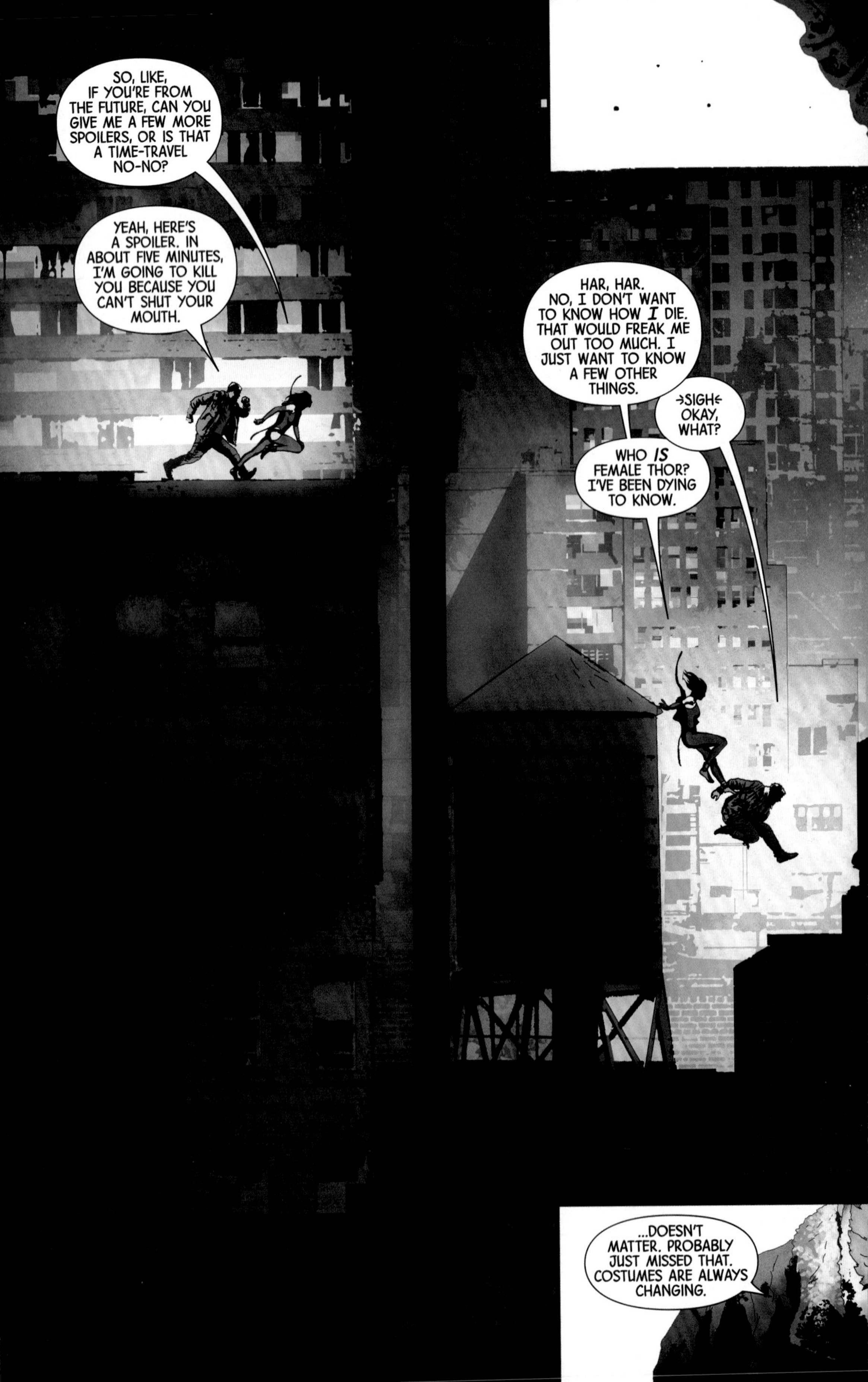
SO, LIKE, IF YOU'RE FROM THE FUTURE, CAN YOU GIVE ME A FEW MORE SPOILERS, OR IS THAT A TIME-TRAVEL NO-NO?
YEAH, HERE'S A SPOILER. IN ABOUT FIVE MINUTES, I'M GOING TO KILL YOU BECAUSE YOU CAN'T SHUT YOUR MOUTH.
HAR, HAR. NO, I DON'T WANT TO KNOW HOW *I* DIE. THAT WOULD FREAK ME OUT TOO MUCH. I JUST WANT TO KNOW A FEW OTHER THINGS.
→SIGH← OKAY, WHAT?
WHO *IS* FEMALE THOR? I'VE BEEN DYING TO KNOW.
...DOESN'T MATTER. PROBABLY JUST MISSED THAT. COSTUMES ARE ALWAYS CHANGING.

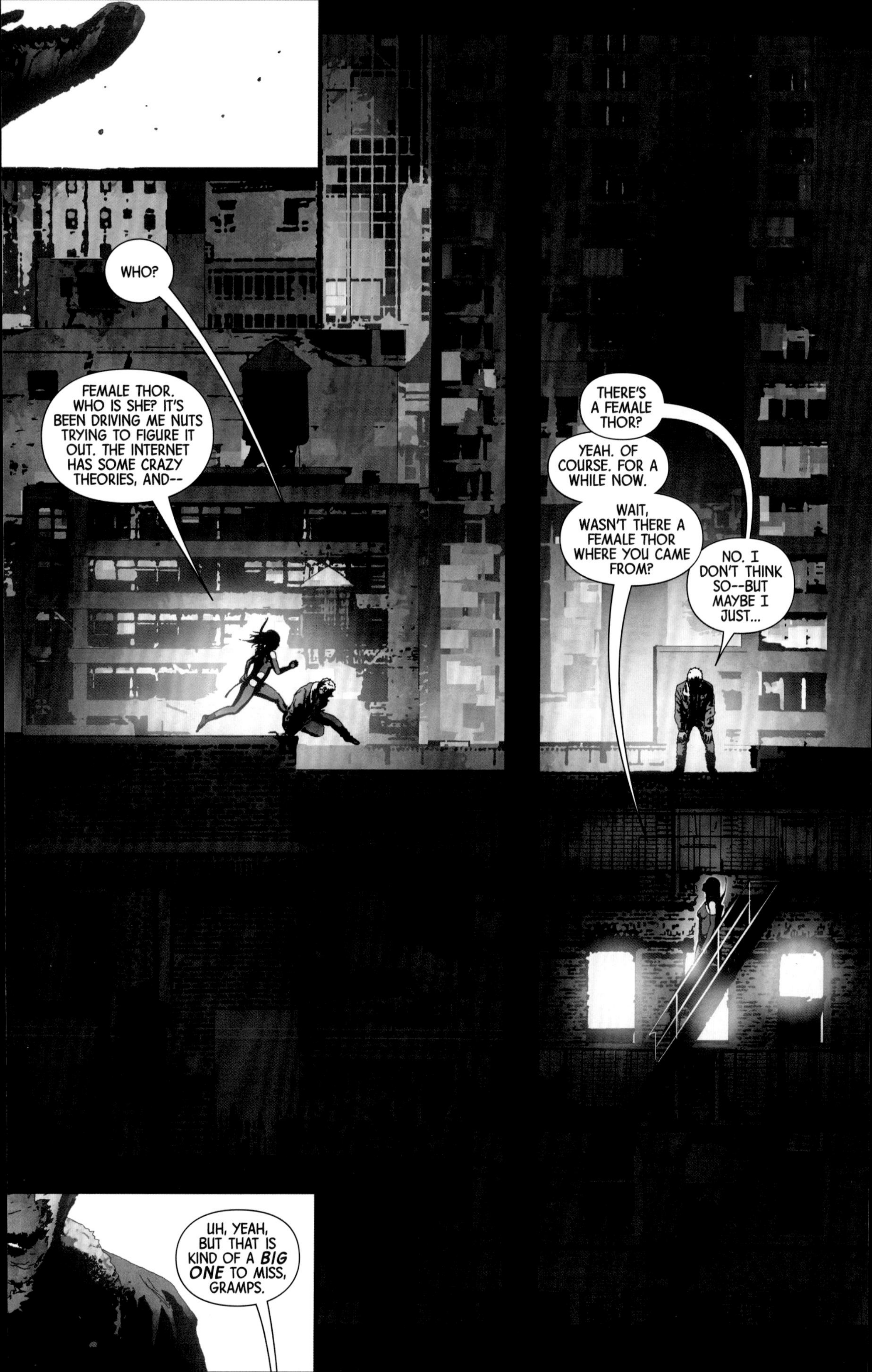
WHO?
FEMALE THOR. WHO IS SHE? IT'S BEEN DRIVING ME NUTS TRYING TO FIGURE IT OUT. THE INTERNET HAS SOME CRAZY THEORIES, AND--
THERE'S A FEMALE THOR?
YEAH. OF COURSE. FOR A WHILE NOW.
WAIT, WASN'T THERE A FEMALE THOR WHERE YOU CAME FROM?
NO. I DON'T THINK SO--BUT MAYBE I JUST...
UH, YEAH, BUT THAT IS KIND OF A BIG ONE TO MISS, GRAMPS.

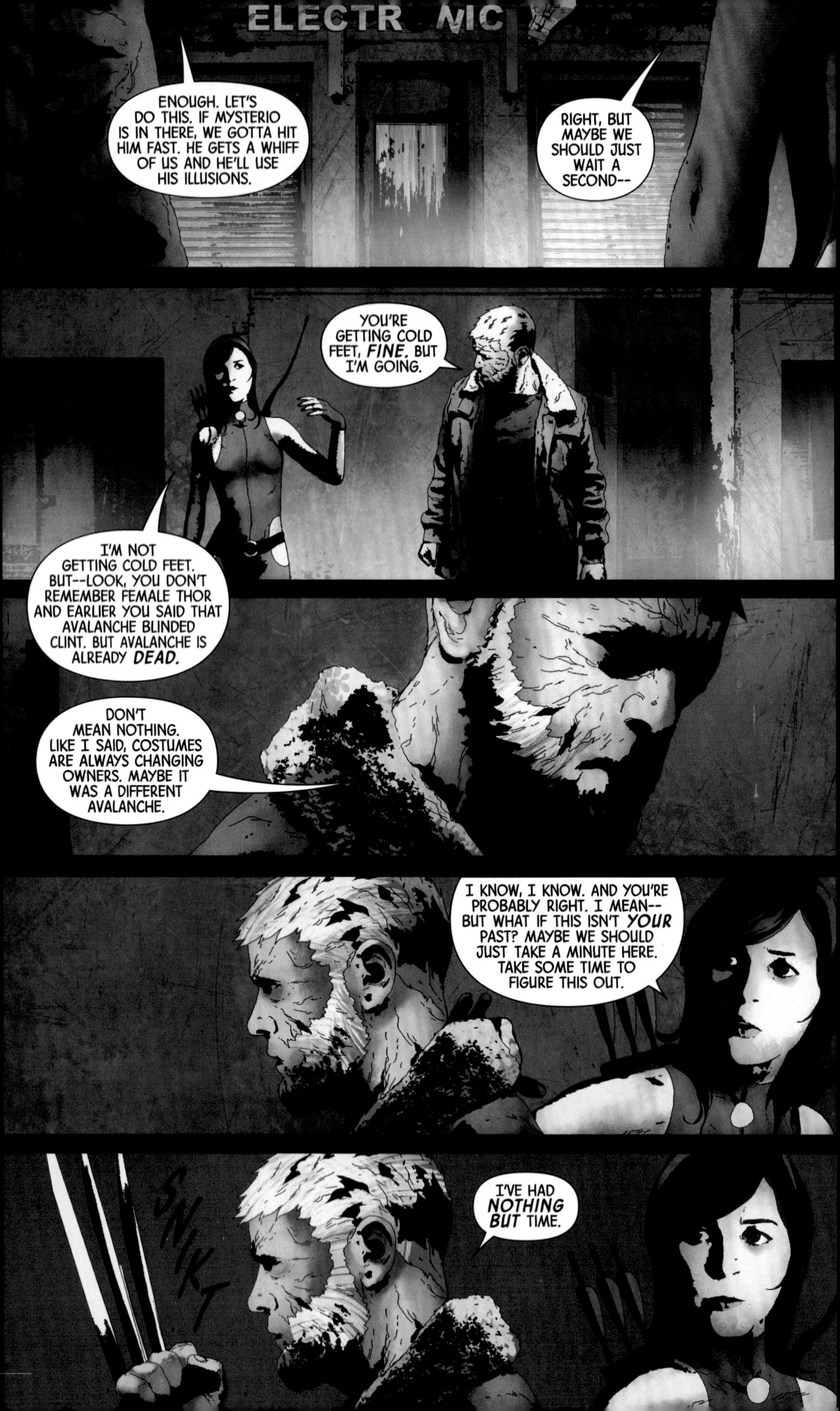
ELECTR NIC
ENOUGH. LET'S DO THIS. IF MYSTERIO IS IN THERE, WE GOTTA HIT HIM FAST. HE GETS A WHIFF OF US AND HE'LL USE HIS ILLUSIONS.
RIGHT, BUT MAYBE WE SHOULD JUST WAIT A SECOND--
YOU'RE GETTING COLD FEET, FINE. BUT I'M GOING.
I'M NOT GETTING COLD FEET. BUT--LOOK, YOU DON'T REMEMBER FEMALE THOR AND EARLIER YOU SAID THAT AVALANCHE BLINDED CLINT. BUT AVALANCHE IS ALREADY DEAD.
DON'T MEAN NOTHING. LIKE I SAID, COSTUMES ARE ALWAYS CHANGING OWNERS. MAYBE IT WAS A DIFFERENT AVALANCHE.
I KNOW, I KNOW. AND YOU'RE PROBABLY RIGHT. I MEAN-- BUT WHAT IF THIS ISN'T YOUR PAST? MAYBE WE SHOULD JUST TAKE A MINUTE HERE. TAKE SOME TIME TO FIGURE THIS OUT.
SNIKT
I'VE HAD NOTHING BUT TIME.

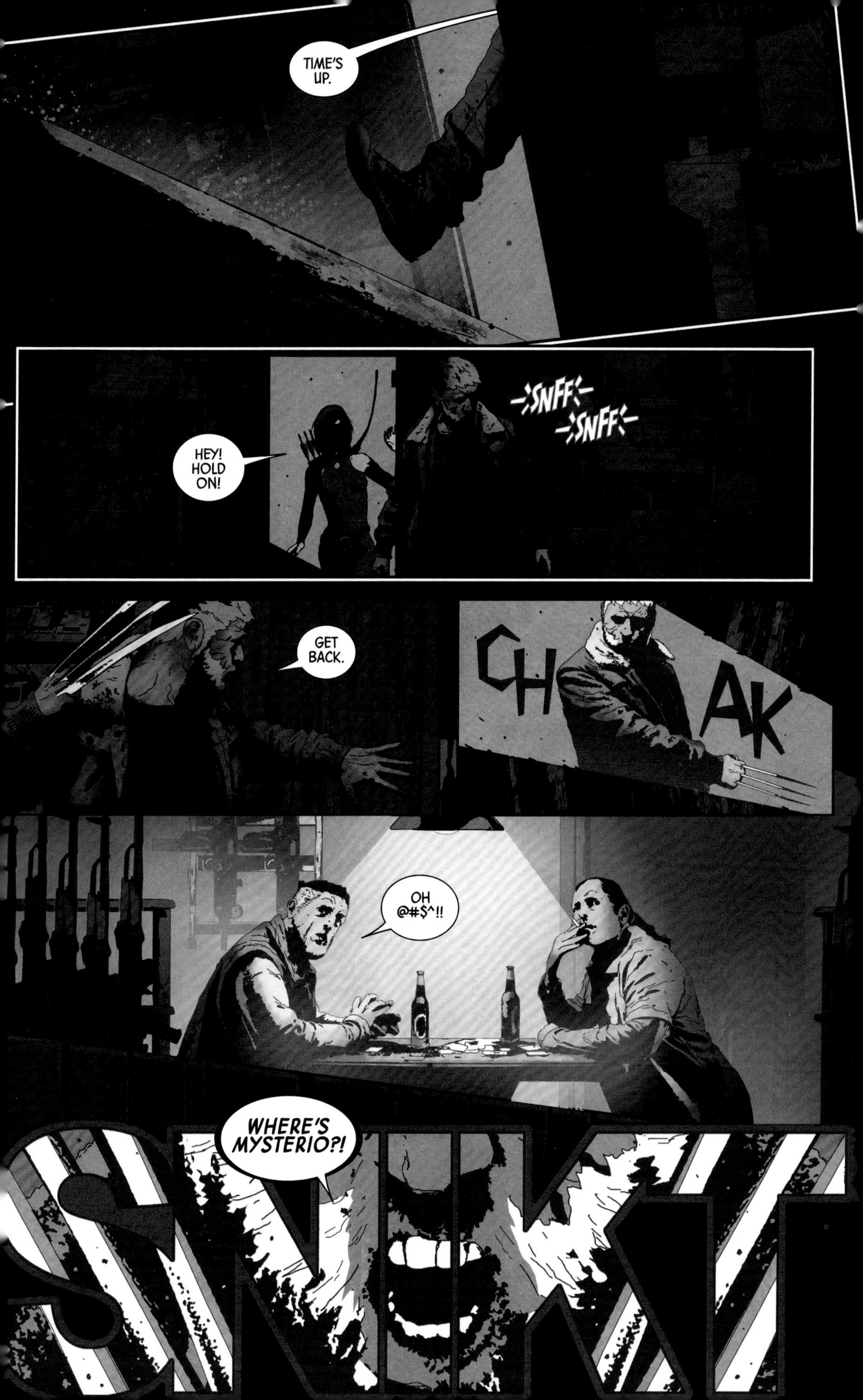
TIME'S UP.
HEY! HOLD ON!
SNFF
SNFF
GET BACK.
CHAK
OH @#$^!!
WHERE'S MYSTERIO?!
SNIKT

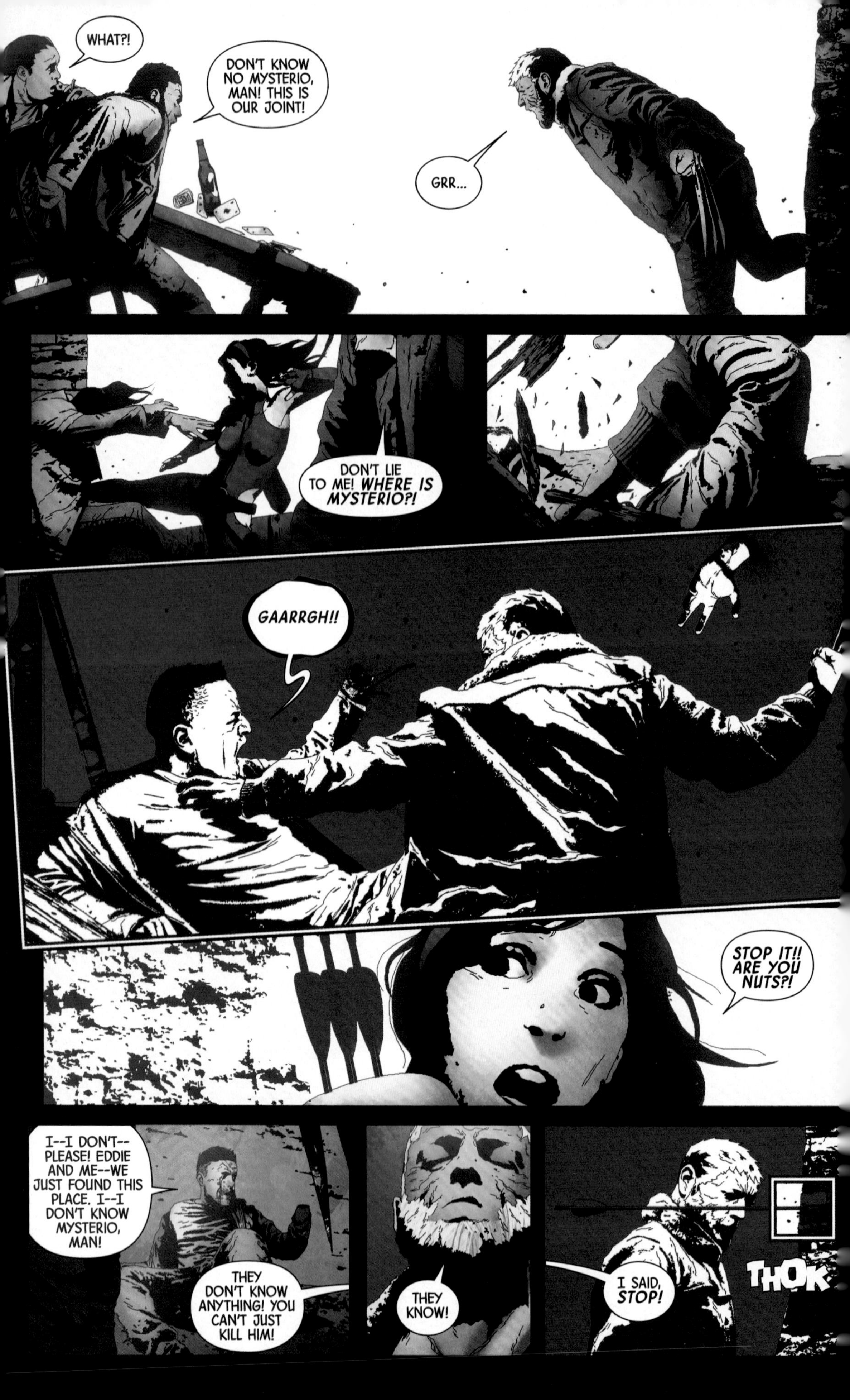
WHAT?!
DON'T KNOW NO MYSTERIO, MAN! THIS IS OUR JOINT!
GRR...
DON'T LIE TO ME! WHERE IS MYSTERIO?!
GAARRGH!!
STOP IT!! ARE YOU NUTS?!
I--I DON'T-- PLEASE! EDDIE AND ME--WE JUST FOUND THIS PLACE. I--I DON'T KNOW MYSTERIO, MAN!
THEY DON'T KNOW ANYTHING! YOU CAN'T JUST KILL HIM!
THEY KNOW!
I SAID, STOP!
THOK

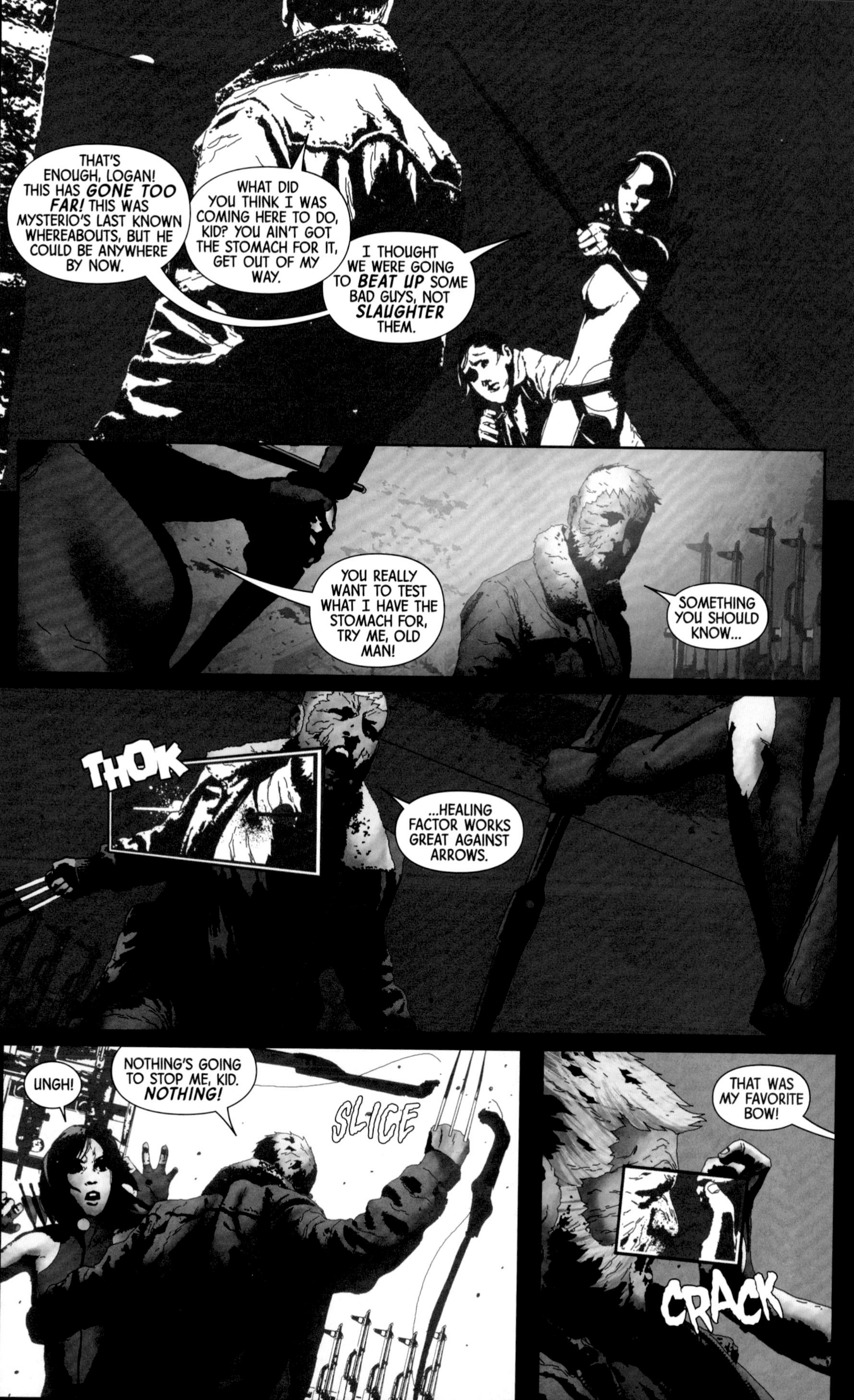
THAT'S ENOUGH, LOGAN! THIS HAS GONE TOO FAR! THIS WAS MYSTERIO'S LAST KNOWN WHEREABOUTS, BUT HE COULD BE ANYWHERE BY NOW.
WHAT DID YOU THINK I WAS COMING HERE TO DO, KID? YOU AIN'T GOT THE STOMACH FOR IT, GET OUT OF MY WAY.
I THOUGHT WE WERE GOING TO BEAT UP SOME BAD GUYS, NOT SLAUGHTER THEM.
YOU REALLY WANT TO TEST WHAT I HAVE THE STOMACH FOR, TRY ME, OLD MAN!
SOMETHING YOU SHOULD KNOW...
THOK
...HEALING FACTOR WORKS GREAT AGAINST ARROWS.
UNGH!
NOTHING'S GOING TO STOP ME, KID. NOTHING!
SLICE
THAT WAS MY FAVORITE BOW!
CRACK

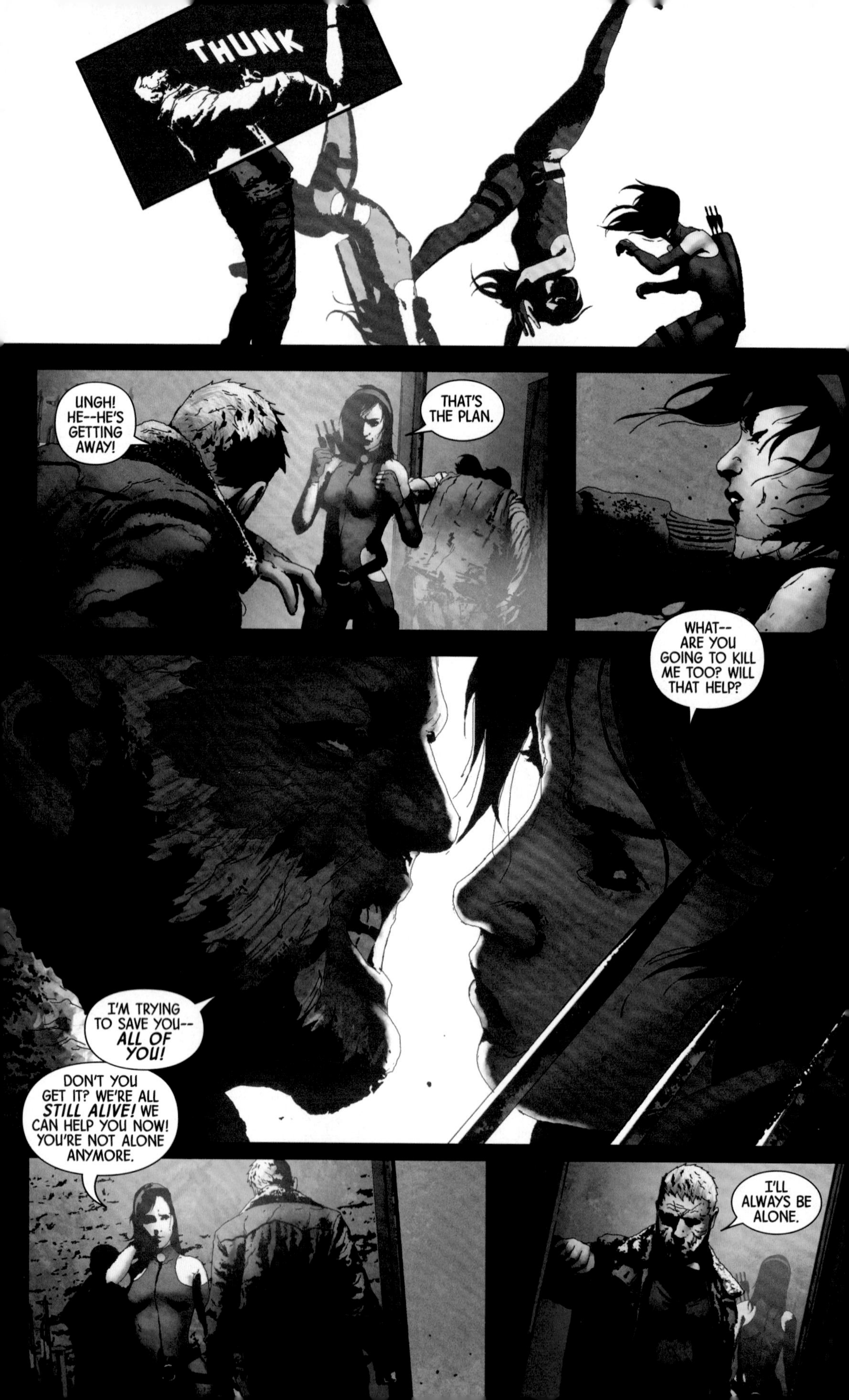
THUNK
UNGH! HE--HE'S GETTING AWAY!
THAT'S THE PLAN.
WHAT-- ARE YOU GOING TO KILL ME TOO? WILL THAT HELP?
I'M TRYING TO SAVE YOU-- ALL OF YOU!
DON'T YOU GET IT? WE'RE ALL STILL ALIVE! WE CAN HELP YOU NOW! YOU'RE NOT ALONE ANYMORE.
I'LL ALWAYS BE ALONE.

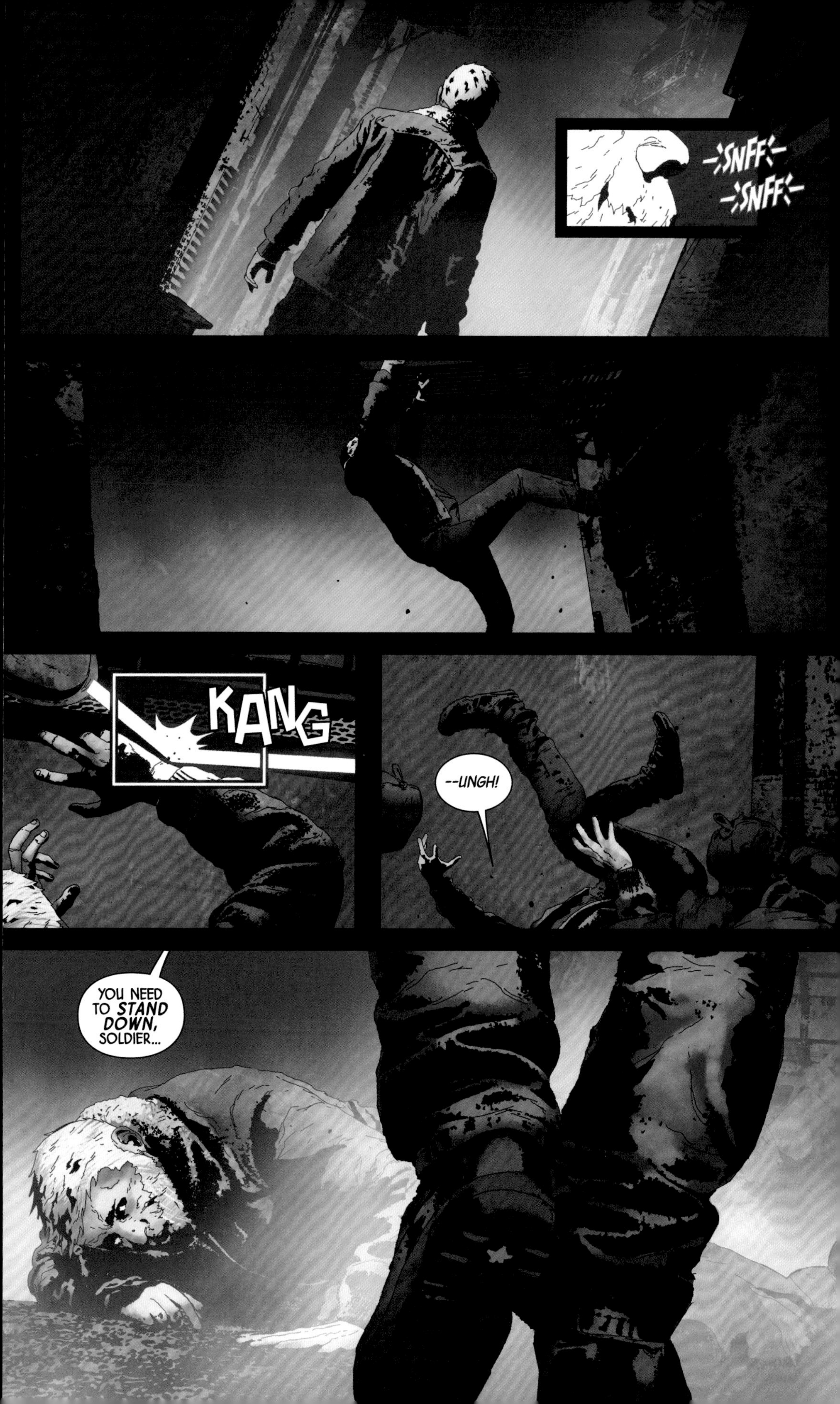
-SNFF-
-SNFF-
KANG
--UNGH!
YOU NEED TO STAND DOWN, SOLDIER...

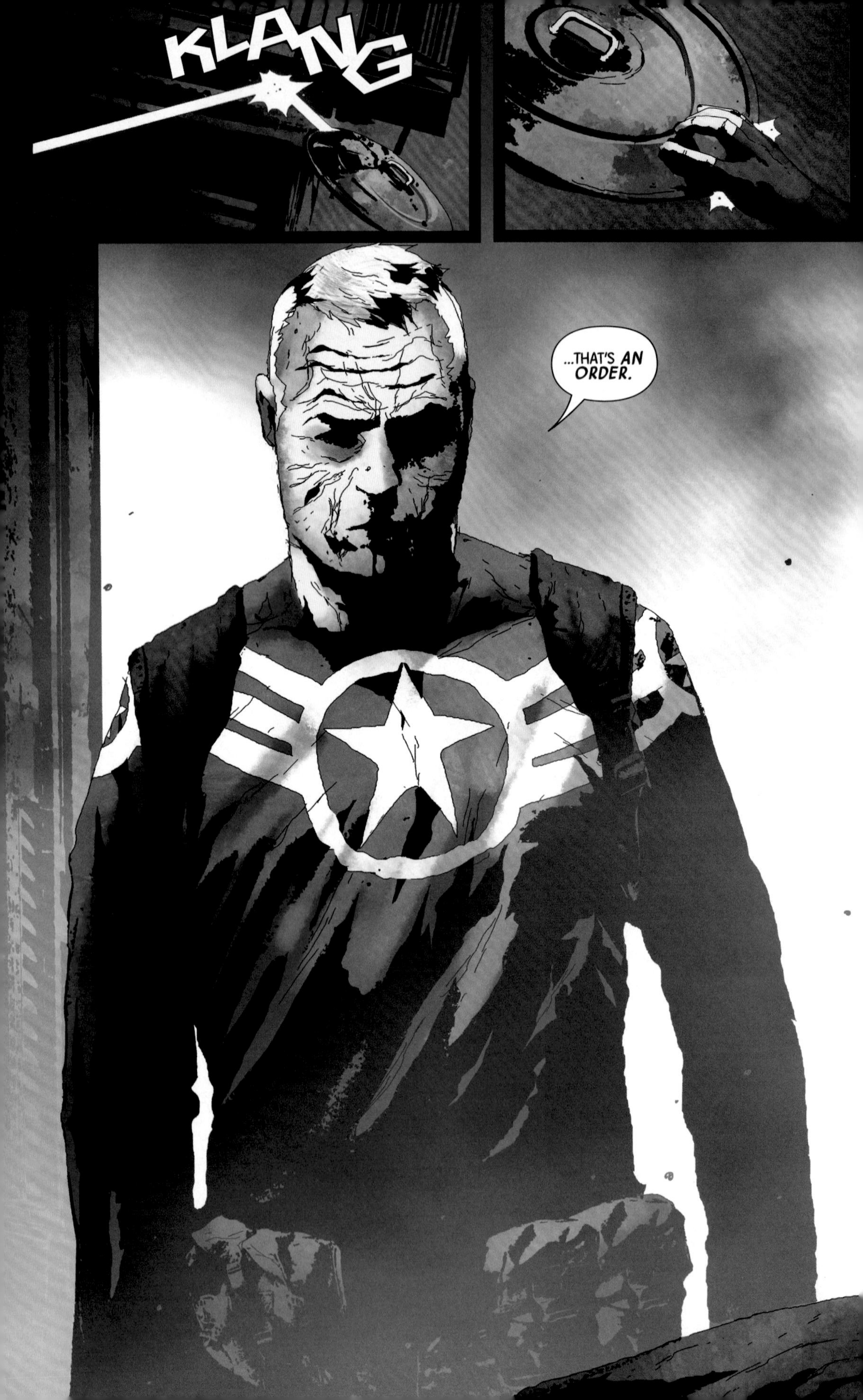
KLANG
...THAT'S AN ORDER.

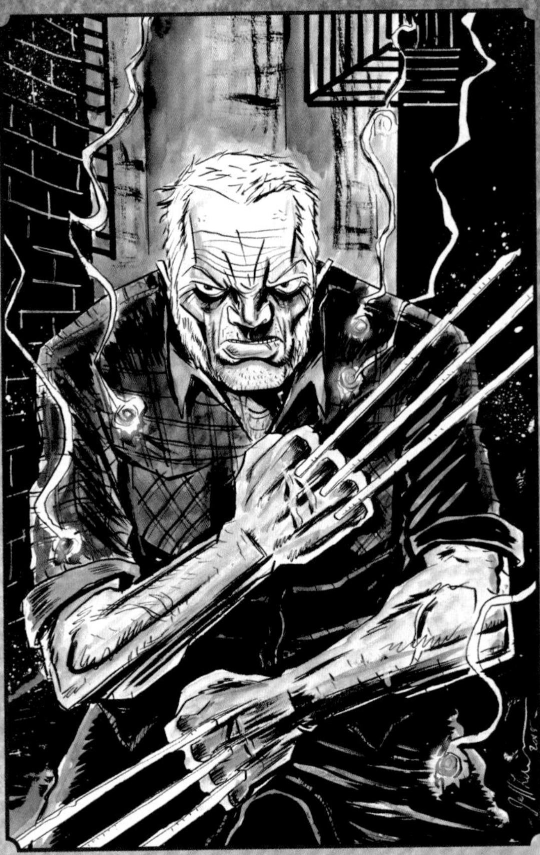

#1 VARIANT BY
JEFF LEMIRE

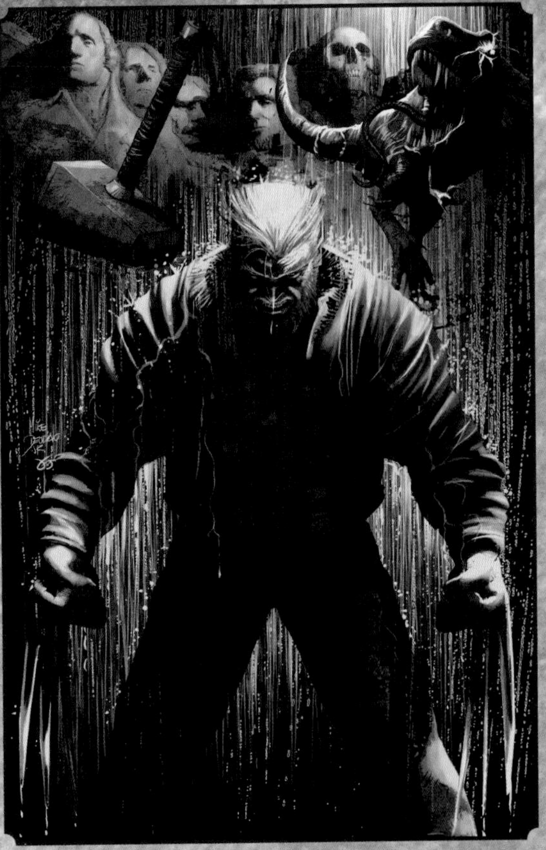

#1 VARIANT BY MIKE DEODATO
& FRANK MARTIN JR.

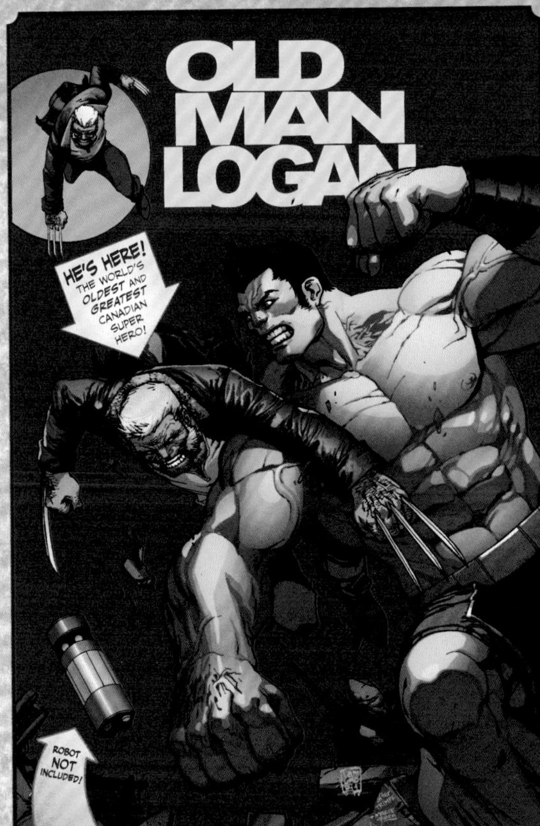
OLD MAN LOGAN
HE'S HERE! THE WORLD'S OLDEST AND GREATEST CANADIAN SUPER HERO!
ROBOT NOT INCLUDED!

#2 VARIANT BY
GIUSEPPE CAMUNCOLI
& MARTE GRACIA

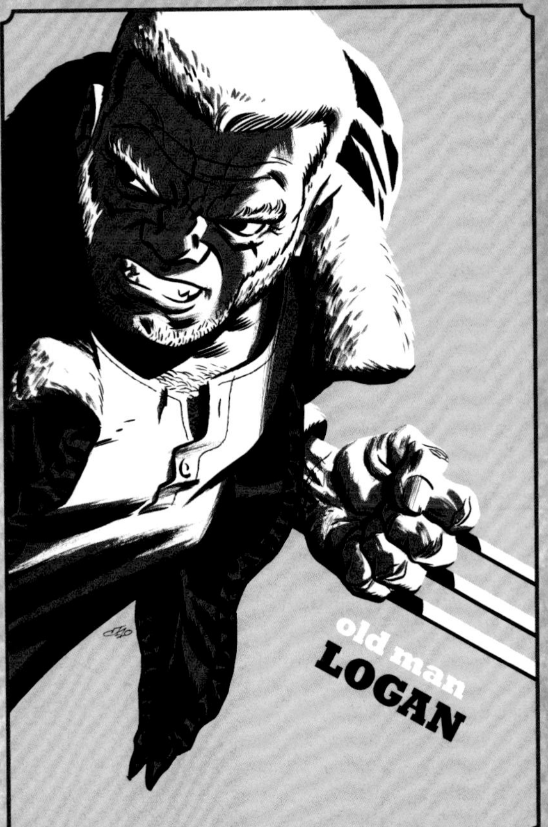
old man
LOGAN

#2 VARIANT BY
MICHAEL CHO

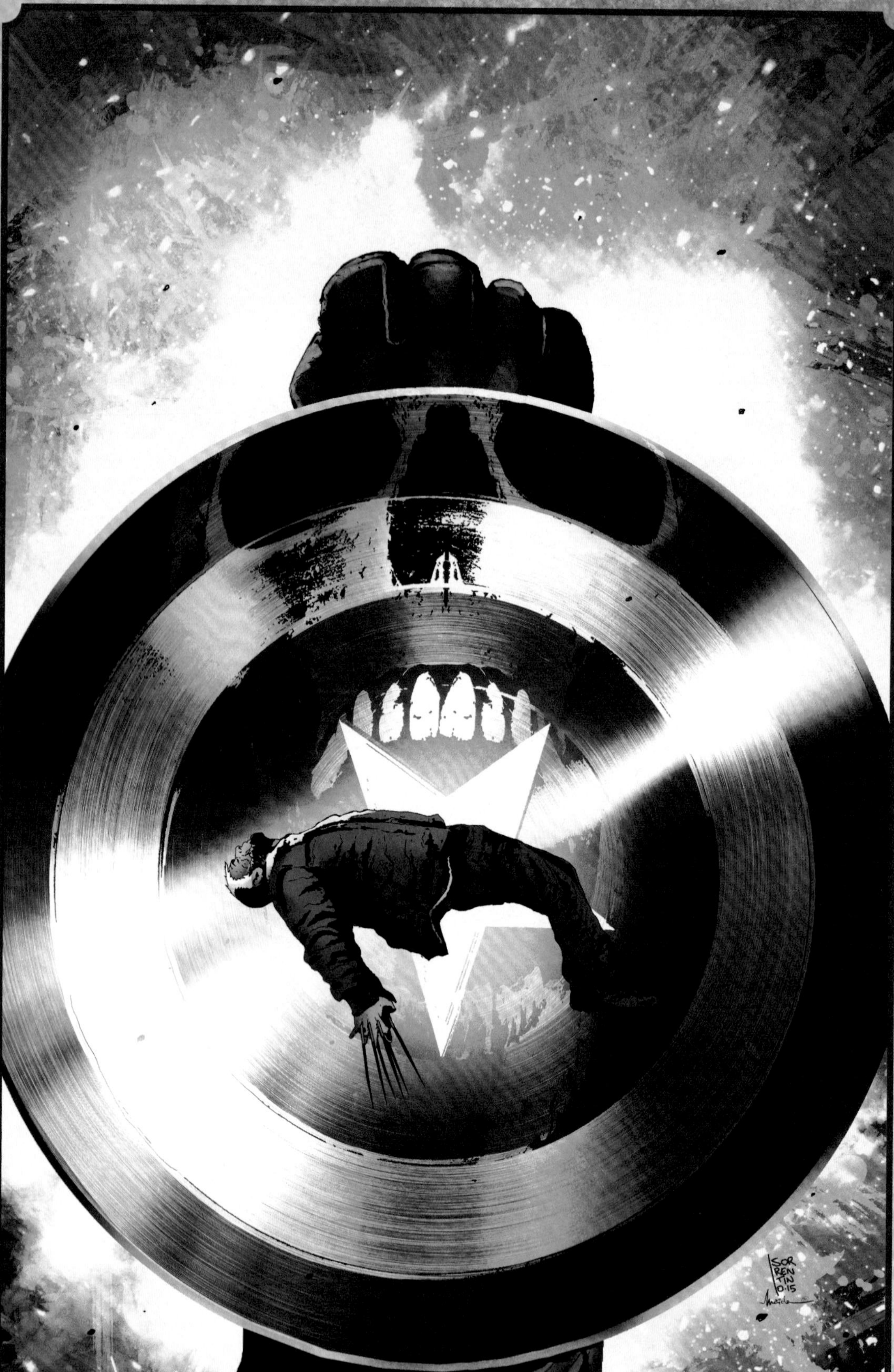
SOR
REN
TIN
O.15

4

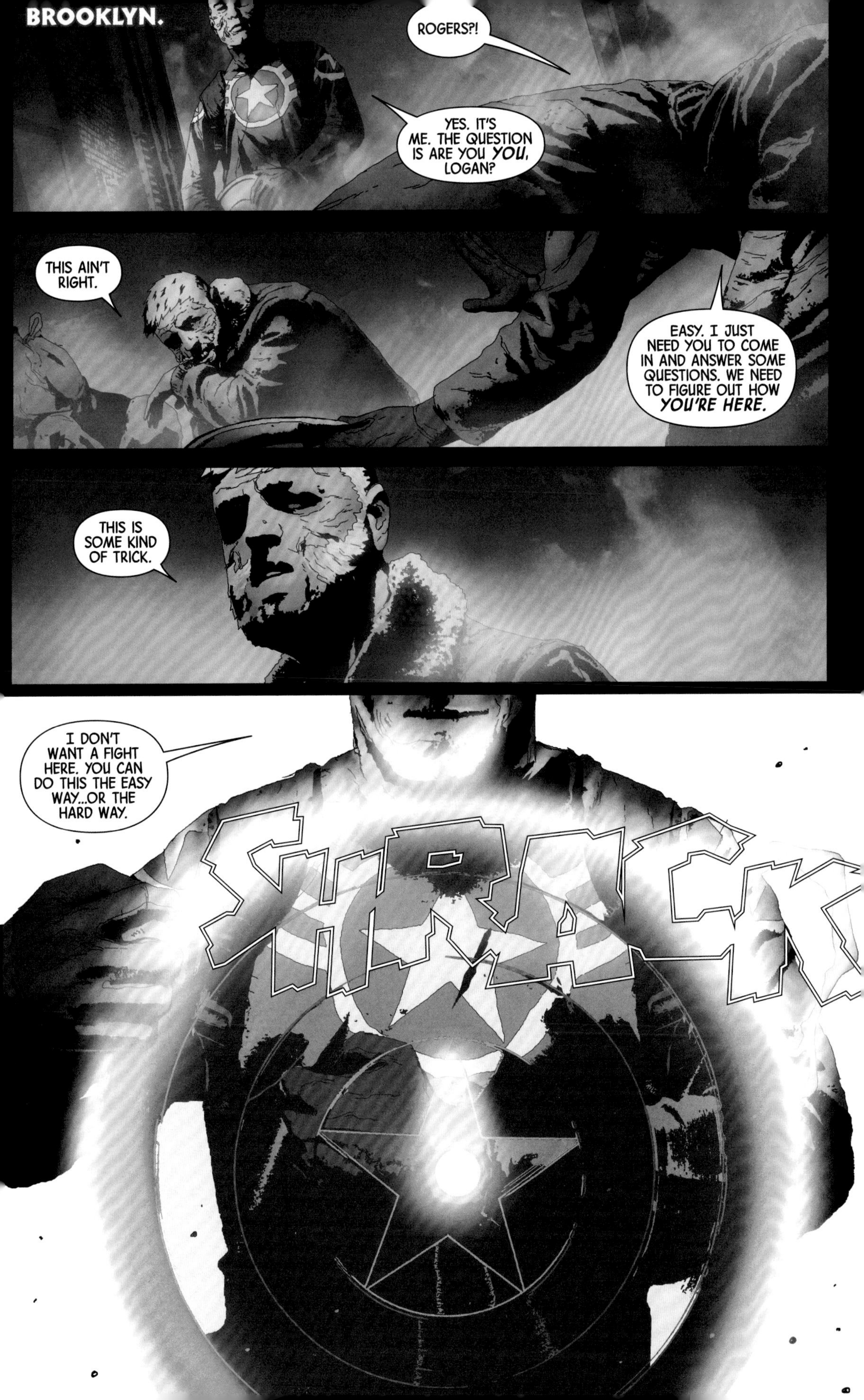
BROOKLYN.
ROGERS?!
YES, IT'S ME. THE QUESTION IS ARE YOU *YOU*, LOGAN?
THIS AIN'T RIGHT.
EASY. I JUST NEED YOU TO COME IN AND ANSWER SOME QUESTIONS. WE NEED TO FIGURE OUT HOW *YOU'RE HERE.*
THIS IS SOME KIND OF TRICK.
I DON'T WANT A FIGHT HERE. YOU CAN DO THIS THE EASY WAY...OR THE HARD WAY.
SHRACK

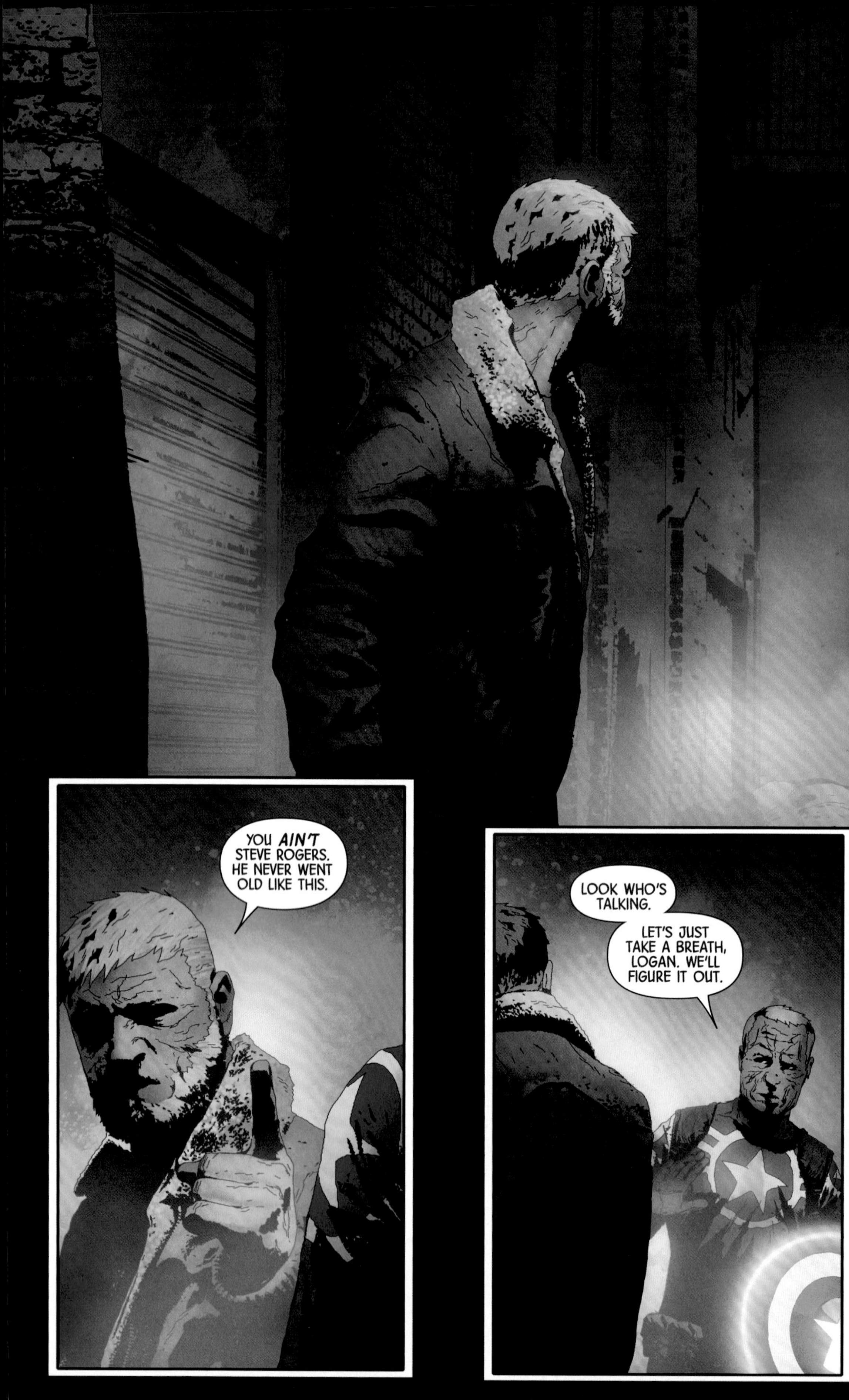
YOU *AIN'T* STEVE ROGERS. HE NEVER WENT OLD LIKE THIS.
LOOK WHO'S TALKING.
LET'S JUST TAKE A BREATH, LOGAN. WE'LL FIGURE IT OUT.

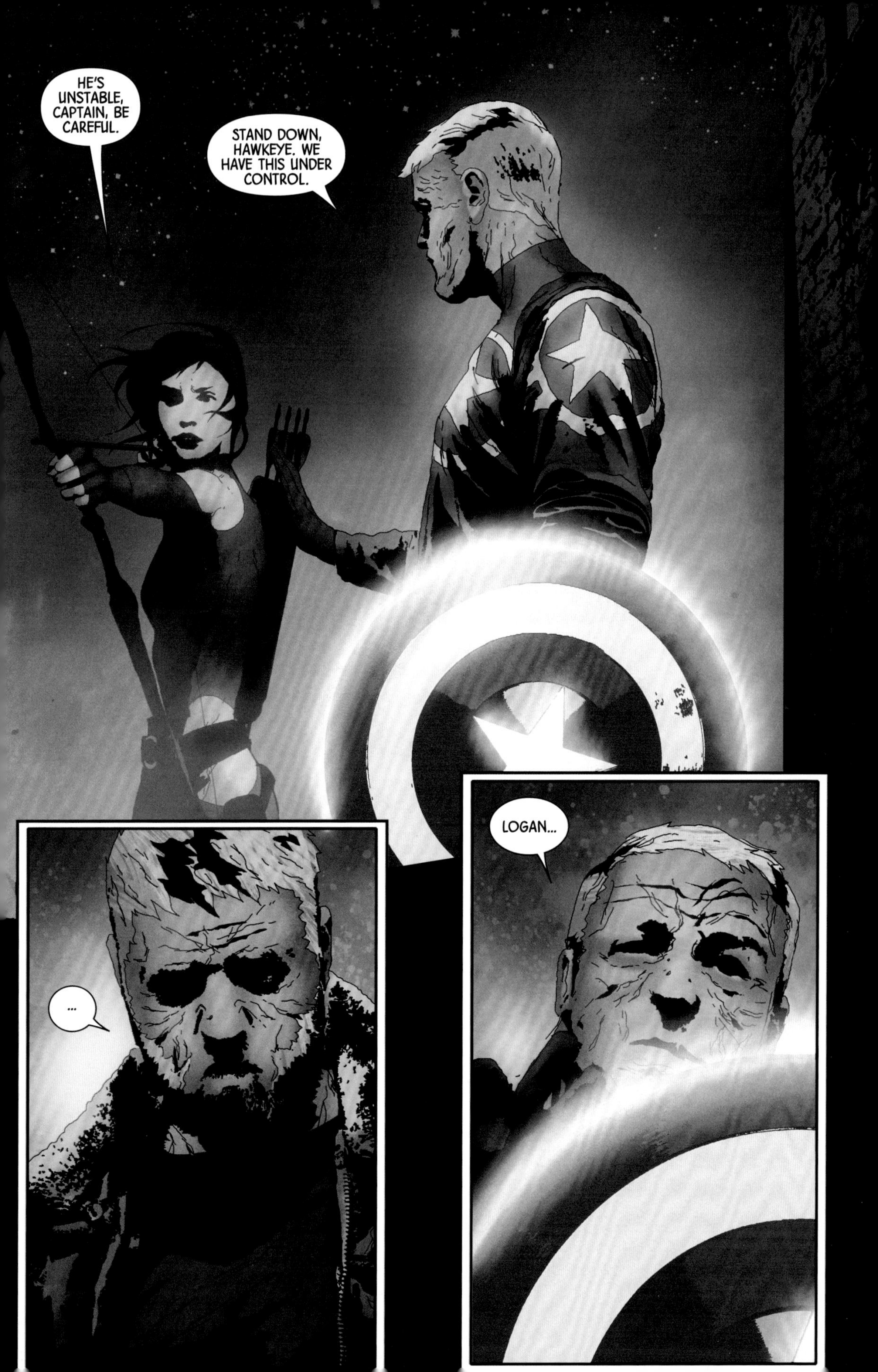
HE'S UNSTABLE, CAPTAIN, BE CAREFUL.
STAND DOWN, HAWKEYE. WE HAVE THIS UNDER CONTROL.
...
LOGAN...

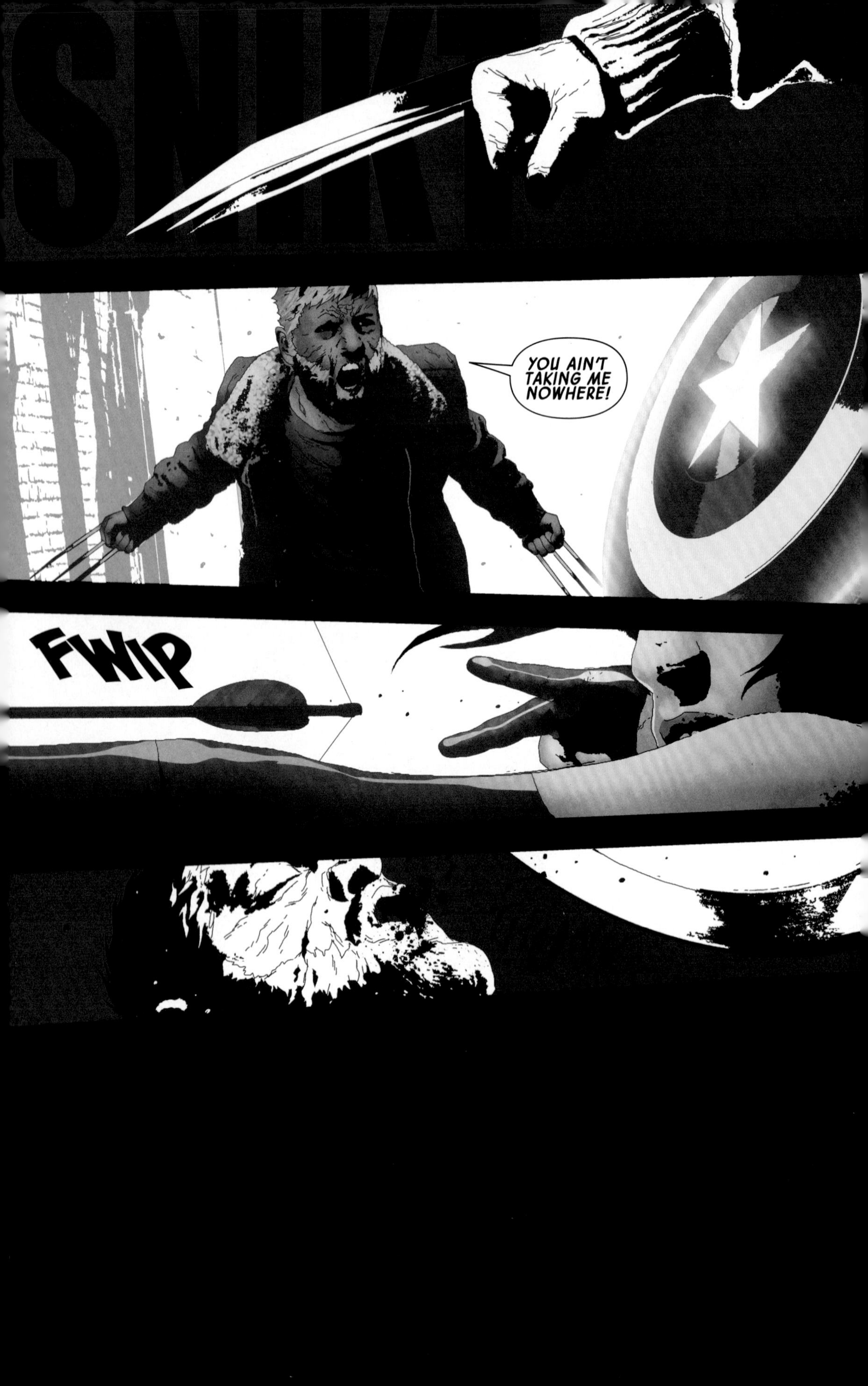
SNIKT
YOU AIN'T TAKING ME NOWHERE!
FWIP

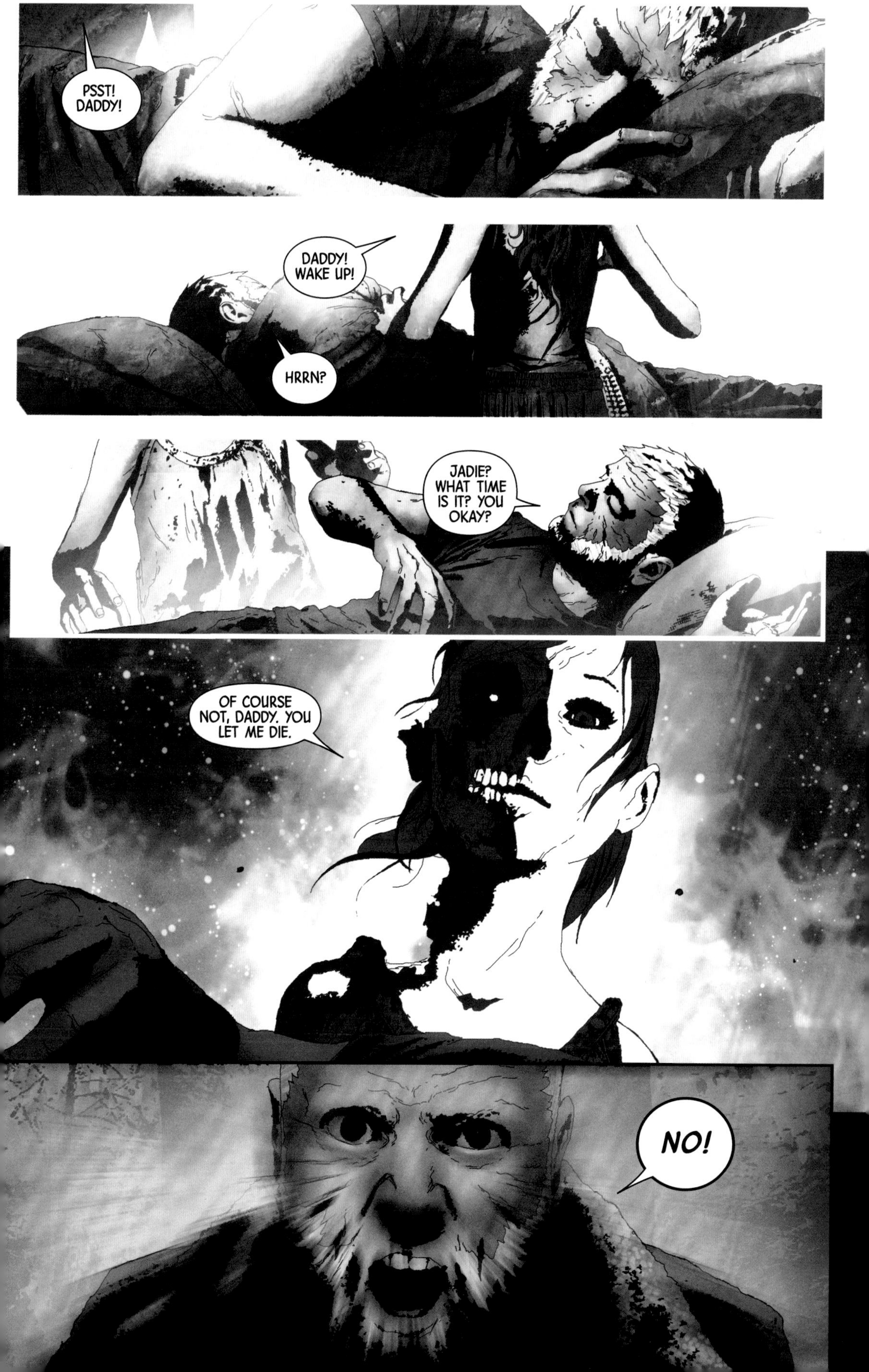
PSST! DADDY!
DADDY! WAKE UP!
HRRN?
JADIE? WHAT TIME IS IT? YOU OKAY?
OF COURSE NOT, DADDY. YOU LET ME DIE.
NO!

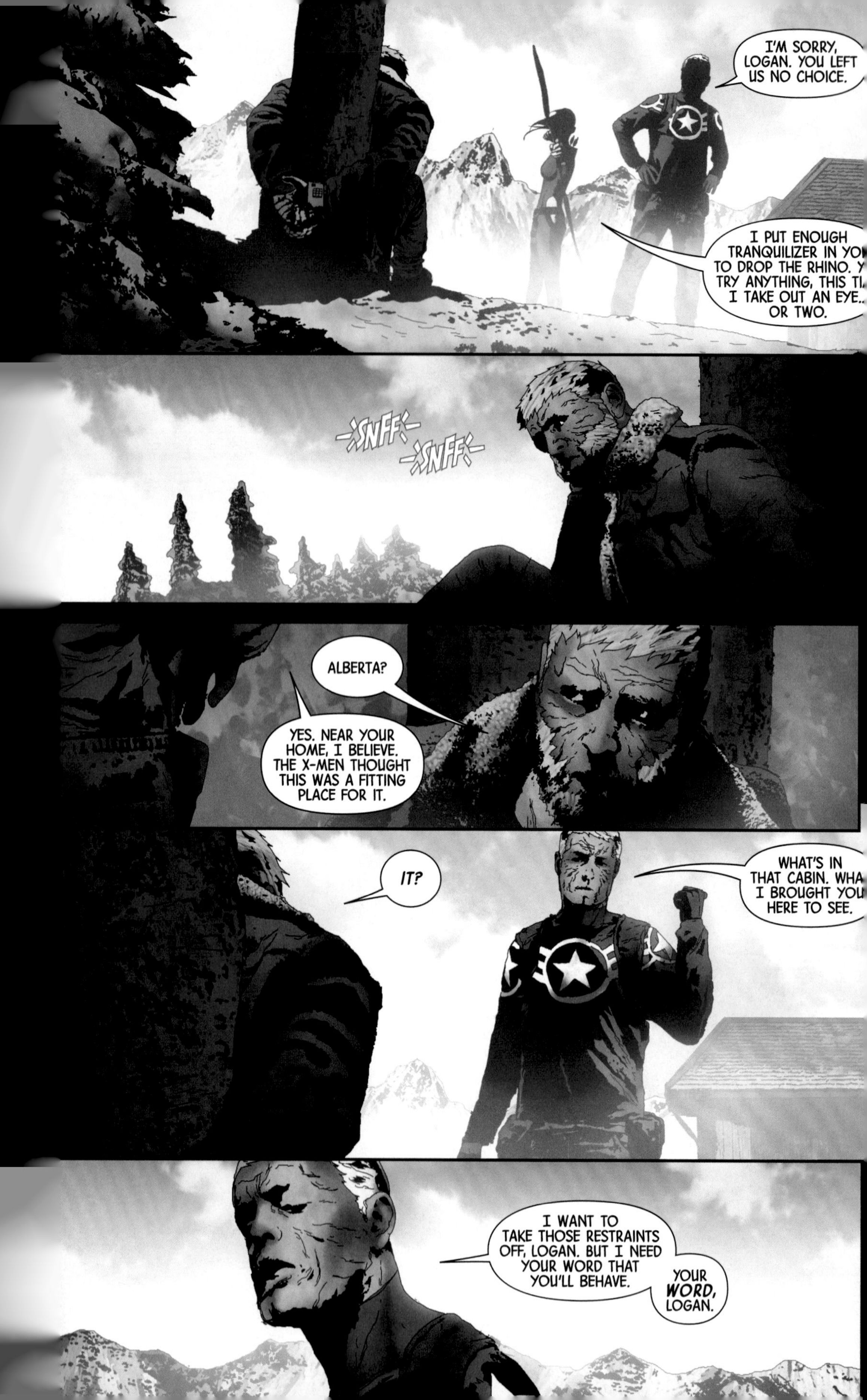
I'M SORRY, LOGAN. YOU LEFT US NO CHOICE.
I PUT ENOUGH TRANQUILIZER IN YO TO DROP THE RHINO. Y TRY ANYTHING, THIS TI I TAKE OUT AN EYE.. OR TWO.
SNFF SNFF
ALBERTA?
YES. NEAR YOUR HOME, I BELIEVE. THE X-MEN THOUGHT THIS WAS A FITTING PLACE FOR IT.
IT?
WHAT'S IN THAT CABIN. WHA I BROUGHT YOU HERE TO SEE.
I WANT TO TAKE THOSE RESTRAINTS OFF, LOGAN. BUT I NEED YOUR WORD THAT YOU'LL BEHAVE.
YOUR WORD, LOGAN.

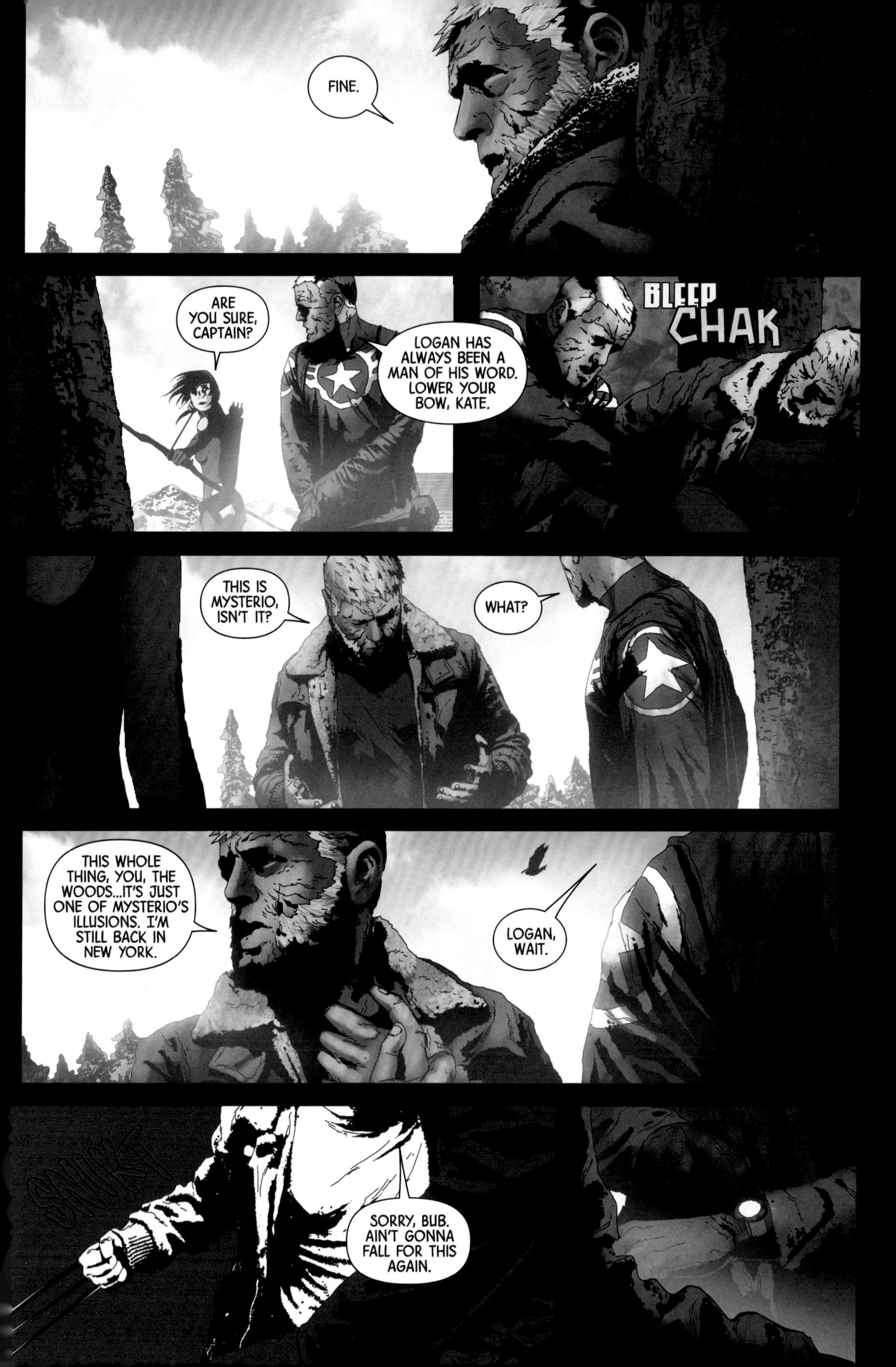
FINE.
ARE YOU SURE, CAPTAIN?
LOGAN HAS ALWAYS BEEN A MAN OF HIS WORD. LOWER YOUR BOW, KATE.
BLEEP
CHAK
THIS IS MYSTERIO, ISN'T IT?
WHAT?
THIS WHOLE THING, YOU, THE WOODS...IT'S JUST ONE OF MYSTERIO'S ILLUSIONS. I'M STILL BACK IN NEW YORK.
LOGAN, WAIT.
SNIKT
SORRY, BUB. AIN'T GONNA FALL FOR THIS AGAIN.

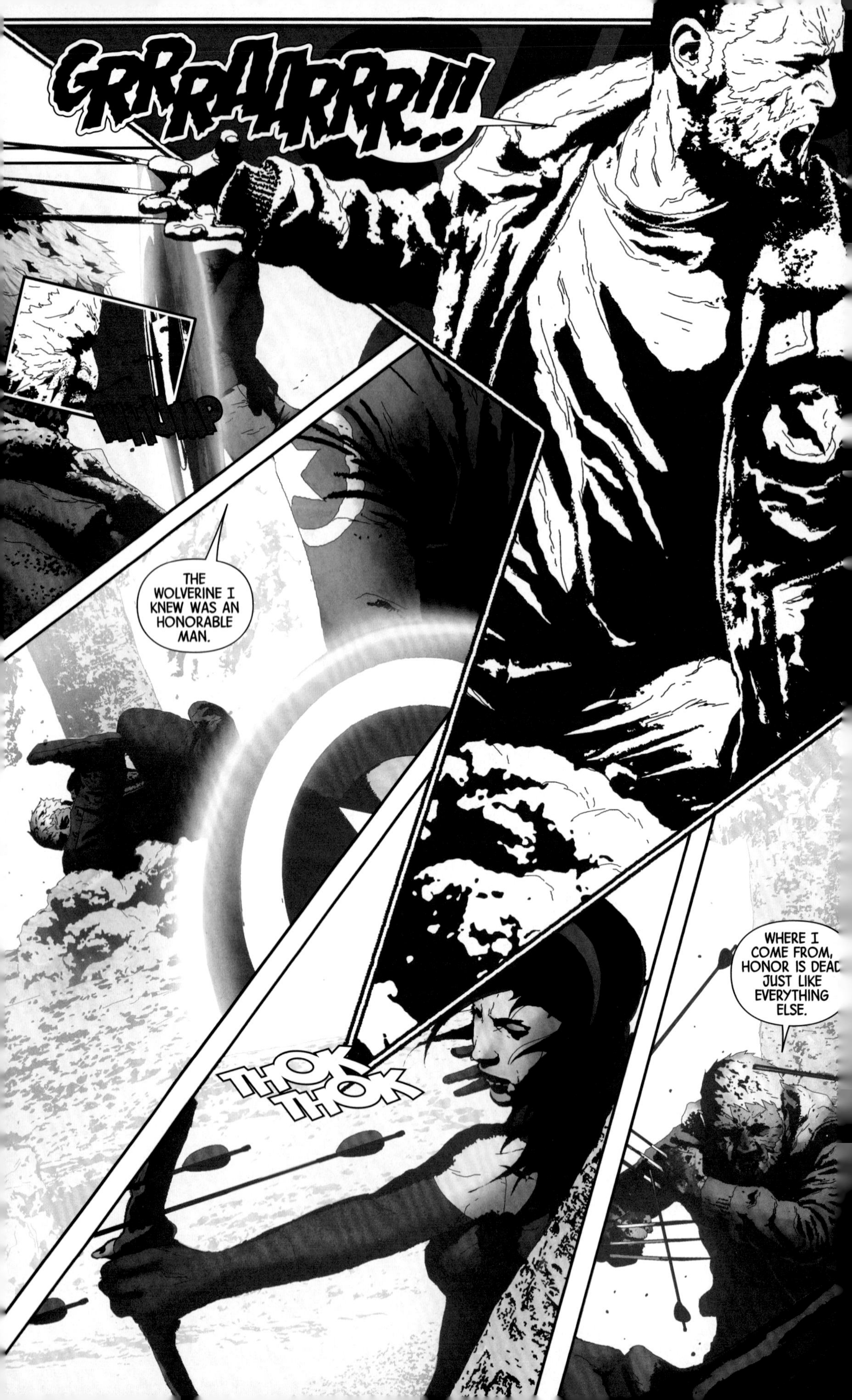

GRRRAARRR!!!...
WHUMP
THE WOLVERINE I KNEW WAS AN HONORABLE MAN.
THOK THOK
WHERE I COME FROM, HONOR IS DEAD JUST LIKE EVERYTHING ELSE.

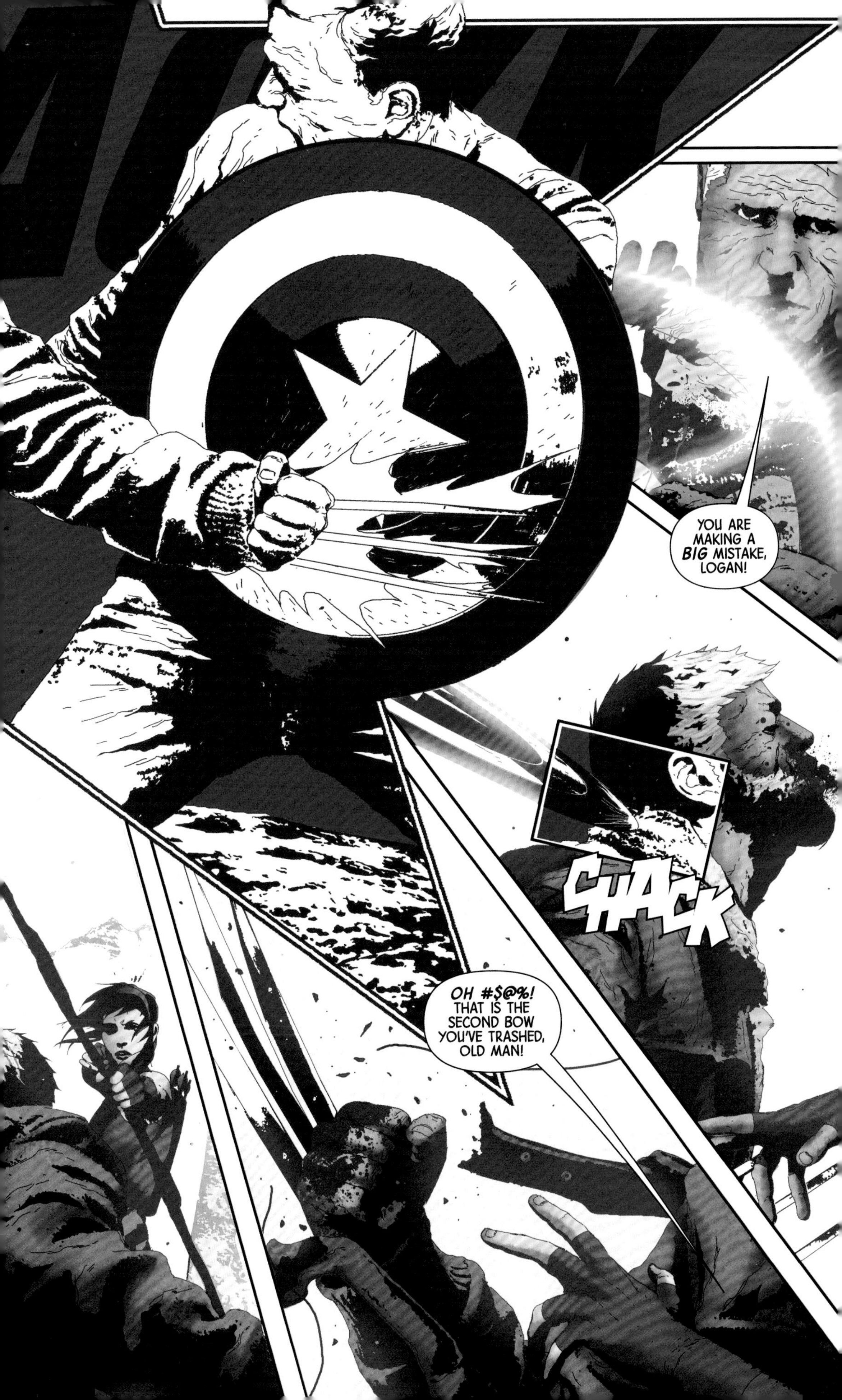
YOU ARE MAKING A BIG MISTAKE, LOGAN!
CHACK
OH #$@%! THAT IS THE SECOND BOW YOU'VE TRASHED, OLD MAN!

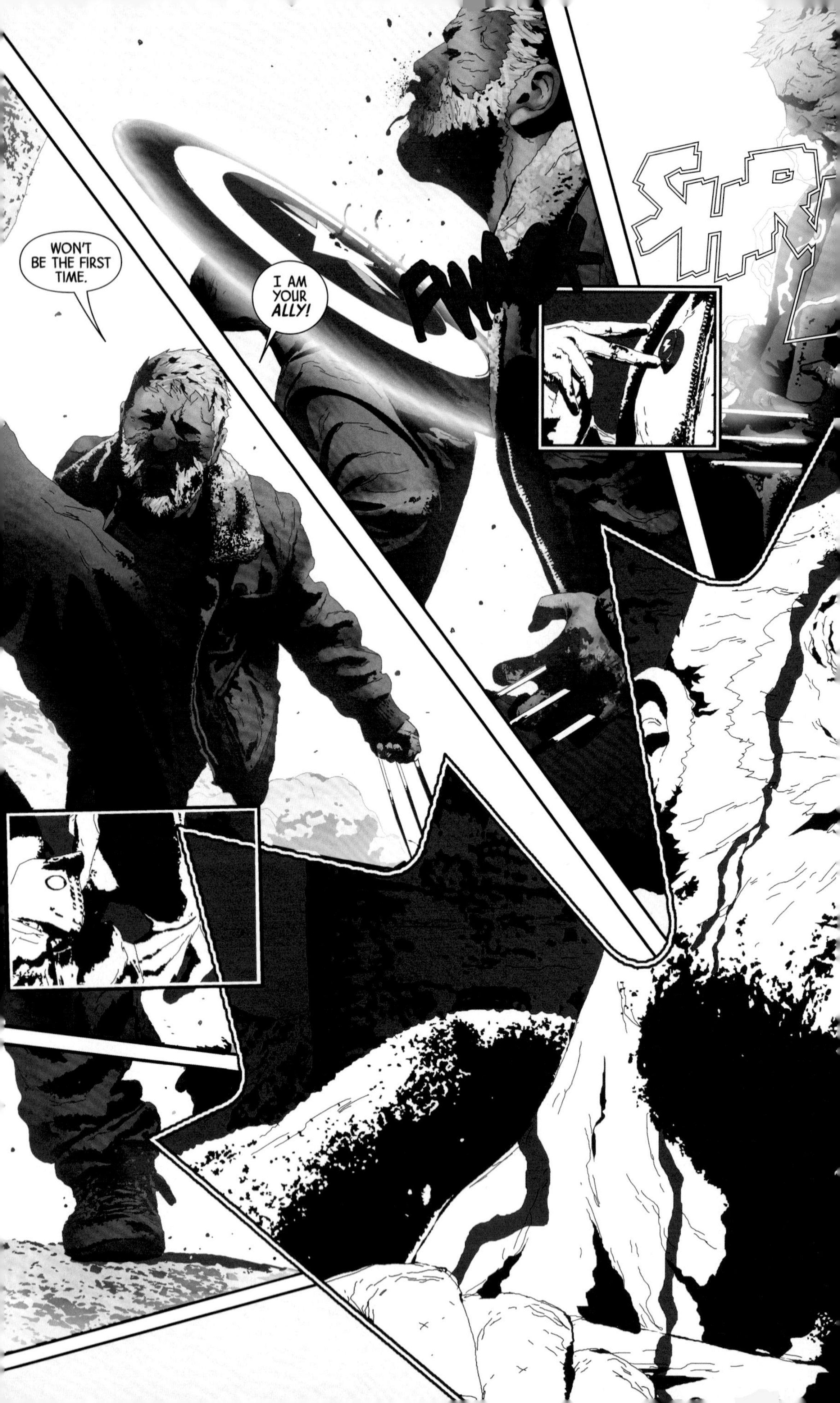
WON'T BE THE FIRST TIME.
I AM YOUR ALLY!
FWAK
SNIKT

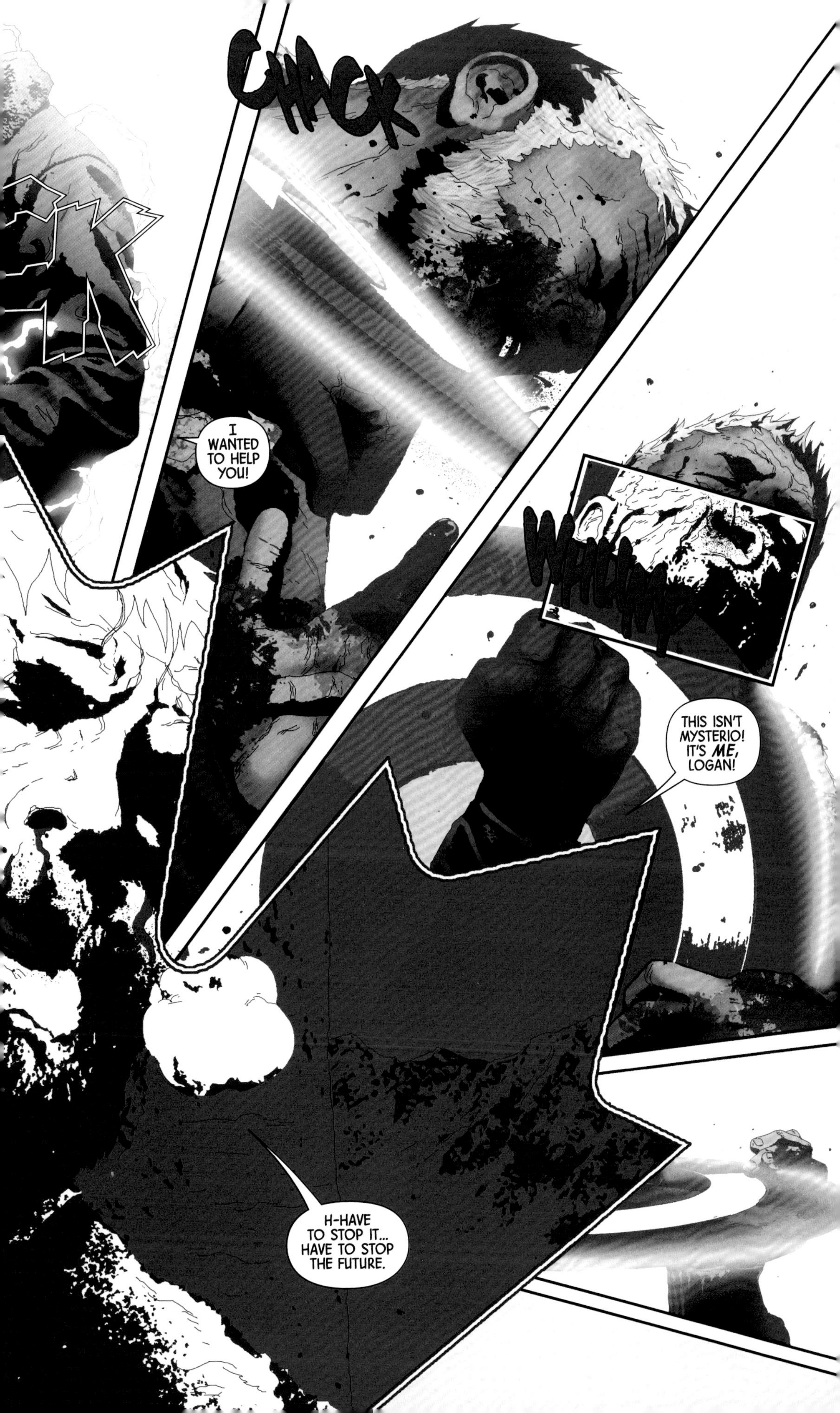
CHACK
I WANTED TO HELP YOU!
THIS ISN'T MYSTERIO! IT'S *ME*, LOGAN!
H-HAVE TO STOP IT... HAVE TO STOP THE FUTURE.

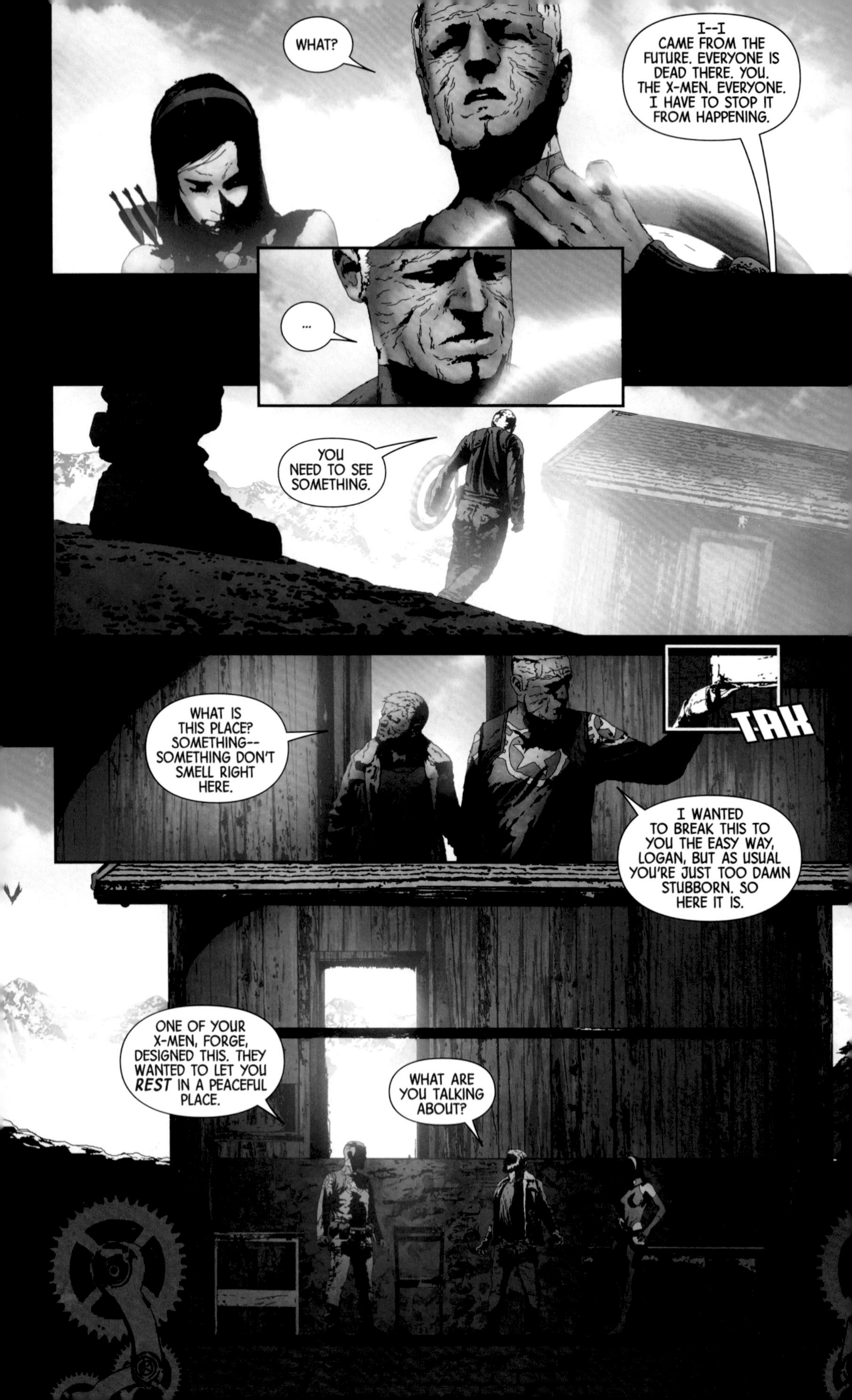
WHAT?
I--I CAME FROM THE FUTURE. EVERYONE IS DEAD THERE. YOU. THE X-MEN. EVERYONE. I HAVE TO STOP IT FROM HAPPENING.
...
YOU NEED TO SEE SOMETHING.
TAK
WHAT IS THIS PLACE? SOMETHING-- SOMETHING DON'T SMELL RIGHT HERE.
I WANTED TO BREAK THIS TO YOU THE EASY WAY, LOGAN, BUT AS USUAL YOU'RE JUST TOO DAMN STUBBORN. SO HERE IT IS.
ONE OF YOUR X-MEN, FORGE, DESIGNED THIS. THEY WANTED TO LET YOU REST IN A PEACEFUL PLACE.
WHAT ARE YOU TALKING ABOUT?

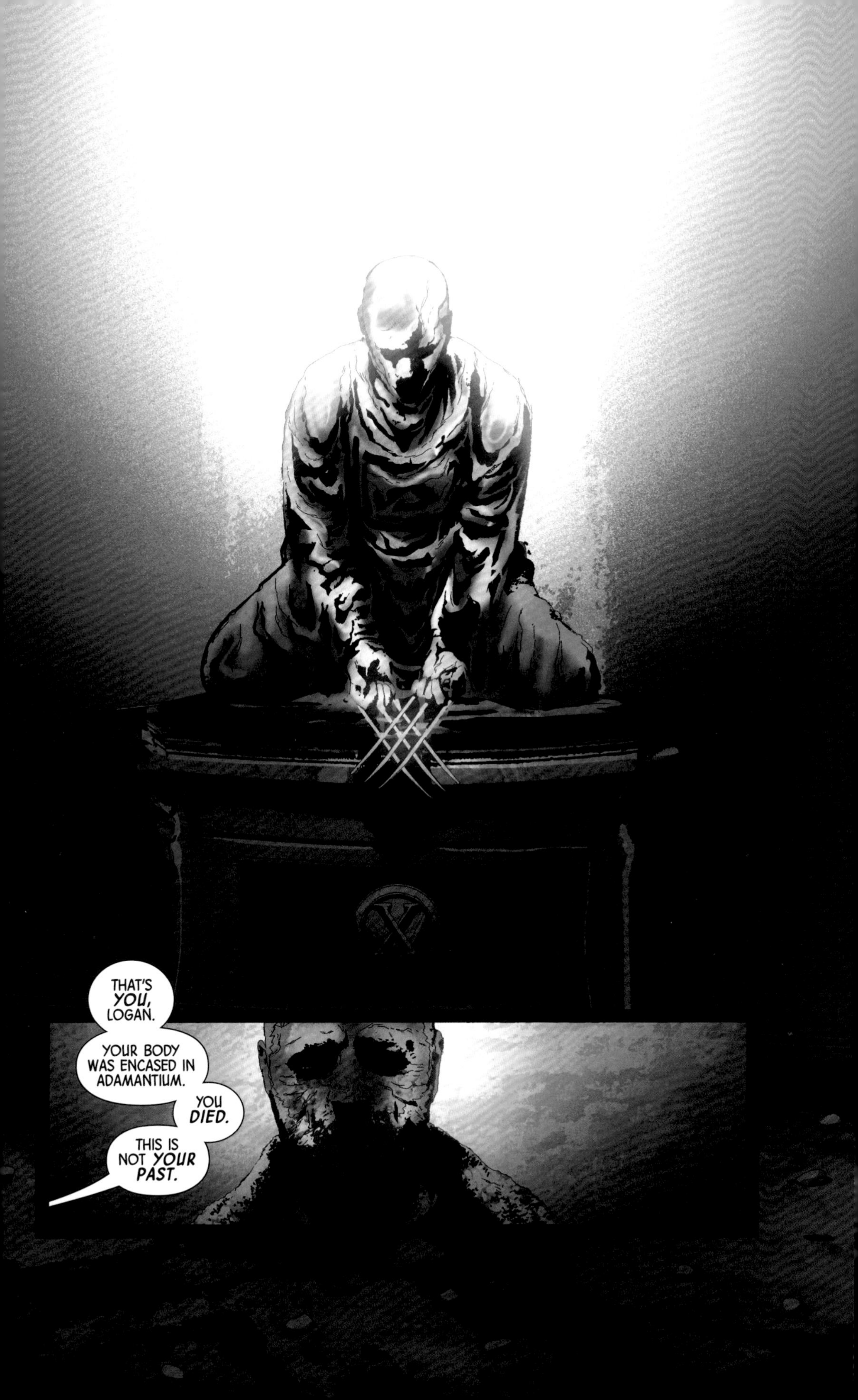
THAT'S *YOU,* LOGAN.
YOUR BODY WAS ENCASED IN ADAMANTIUM.
YOU *DIED.*
THIS IS NOT *YOUR PAST.*

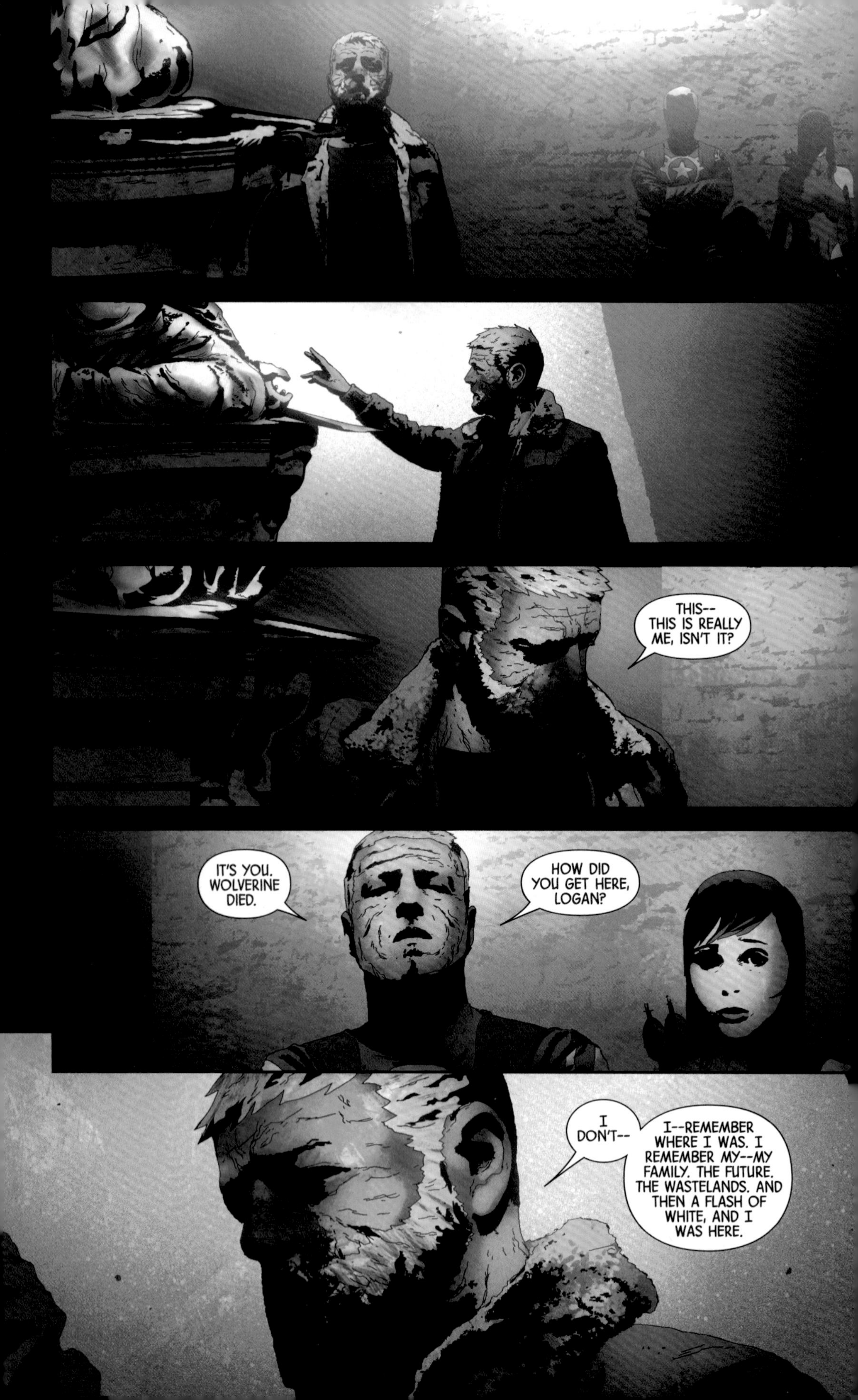
THIS-- THIS IS REALLY ME, ISN'T IT?
IT'S YOU. WOLVERINE DIED.
HOW DID YOU GET HERE, LOGAN?
I DON'T--
I--REMEMBER WHERE I WAS. I REMEMBER MY--MY FAMILY. THE FUTURE. THE WASTELANDS. AND THEN A FLASH OF WHITE, AND I WAS HERE.

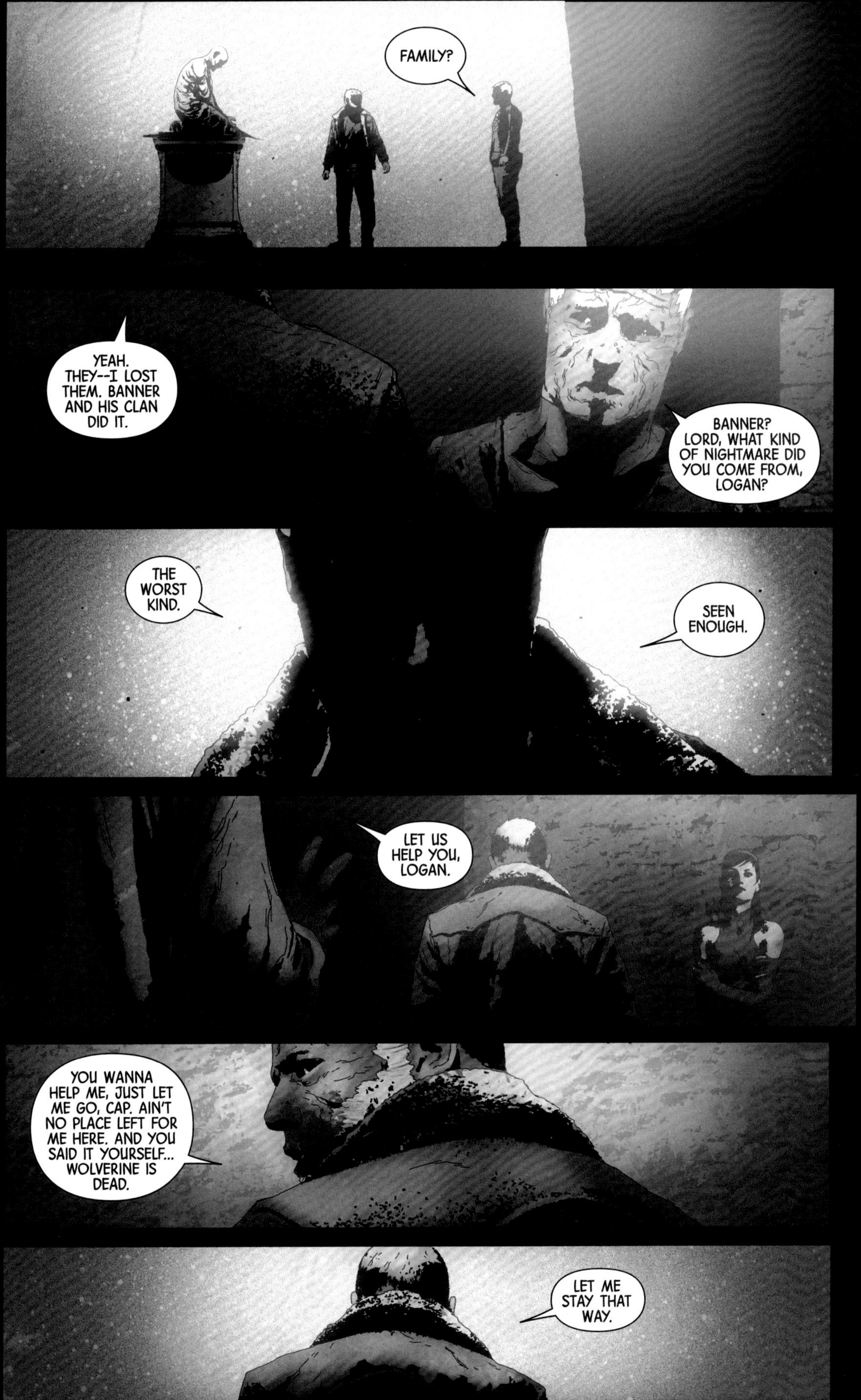
FAMILY?
YEAH. THEY--I LOST THEM. BANNER AND HIS CLAN DID IT.
BANNER? LORD, WHAT KIND OF NIGHTMARE DID YOU COME FROM, LOGAN?
THE WORST KIND.
SEEN ENOUGH.
LET US HELP YOU, LOGAN.
YOU WANNA HELP ME, JUST LET ME GO, CAP. AIN'T NO PLACE LEFT FOR ME HERE. AND YOU SAID IT YOURSELF... WOLVERINE IS DEAD.
LET ME STAY THAT WAY.

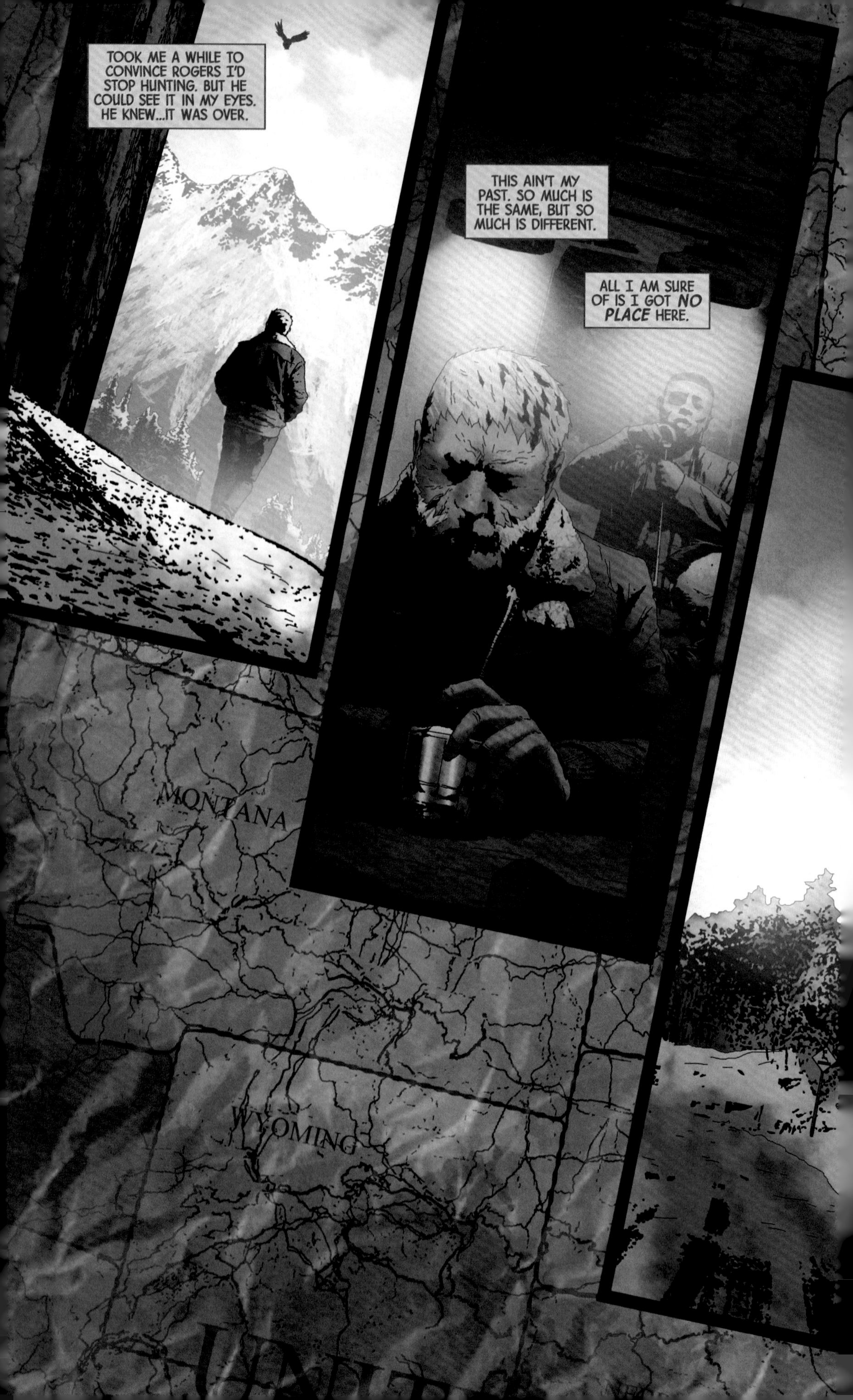
TOOK ME A WHILE TO CONVINCE ROGERS I'D STOP HUNTING. BUT HE COULD SEE IT IN MY EYES. HE KNEW...IT WAS OVER.
THIS AIN'T MY PAST. SO MUCH IS THE SAME, BUT SO MUCH IS DIFFERENT.
ALL I AM SURE OF IS I GOT *NO PLACE* HERE.
MONTANA
WYOMING

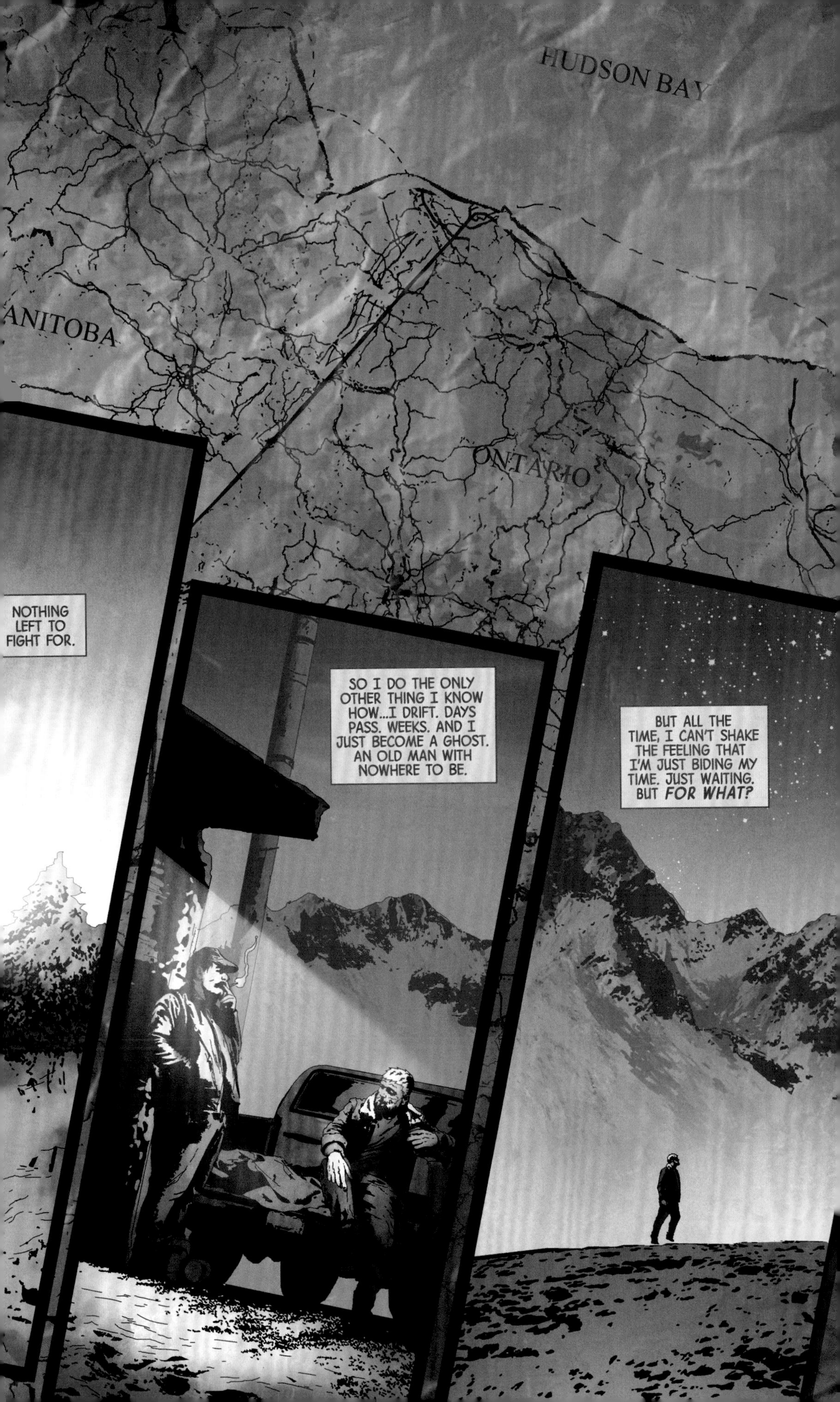
HUDSON BAY
ANITOBA
ONTARIO
NOTHING LEFT TO FIGHT FOR.
SO I DO THE ONLY OTHER THING I KNOW HOW...I DRIFT. DAYS PASS. WEEKS. AND I JUST BECOME A GHOST. AN OLD MAN WITH NOWHERE TO BE.
BUT ALL THE TIME, I CAN'T SHAKE THE FEELING THAT I'M JUST BIDING MY TIME. JUST WAITING. BUT FOR WHAT?

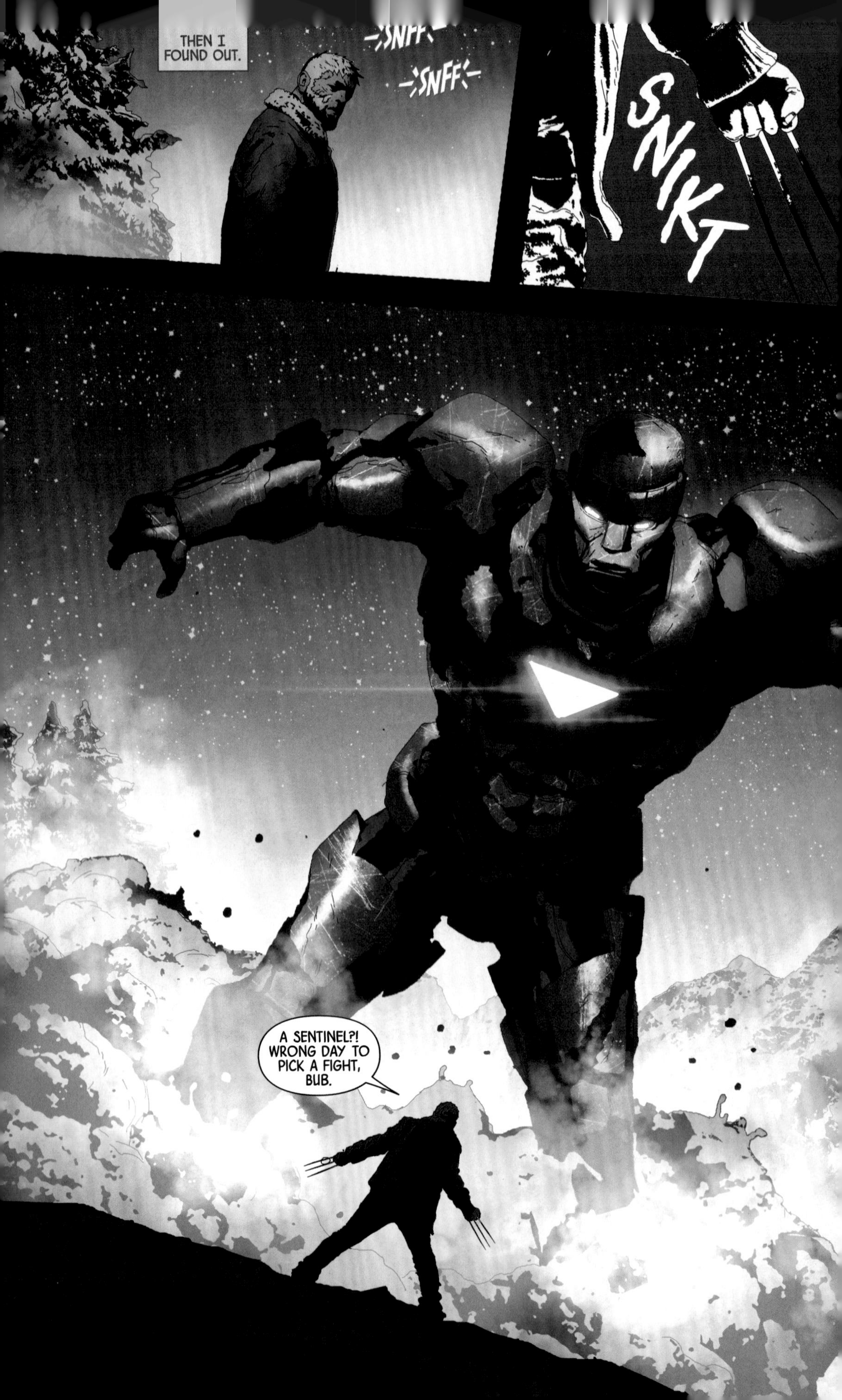

THEN I FOUND OUT.
SNFF
SNFF
SNIKT
A SENTINEL?! WRONG DAY TO PICK A FIGHT, BUB.

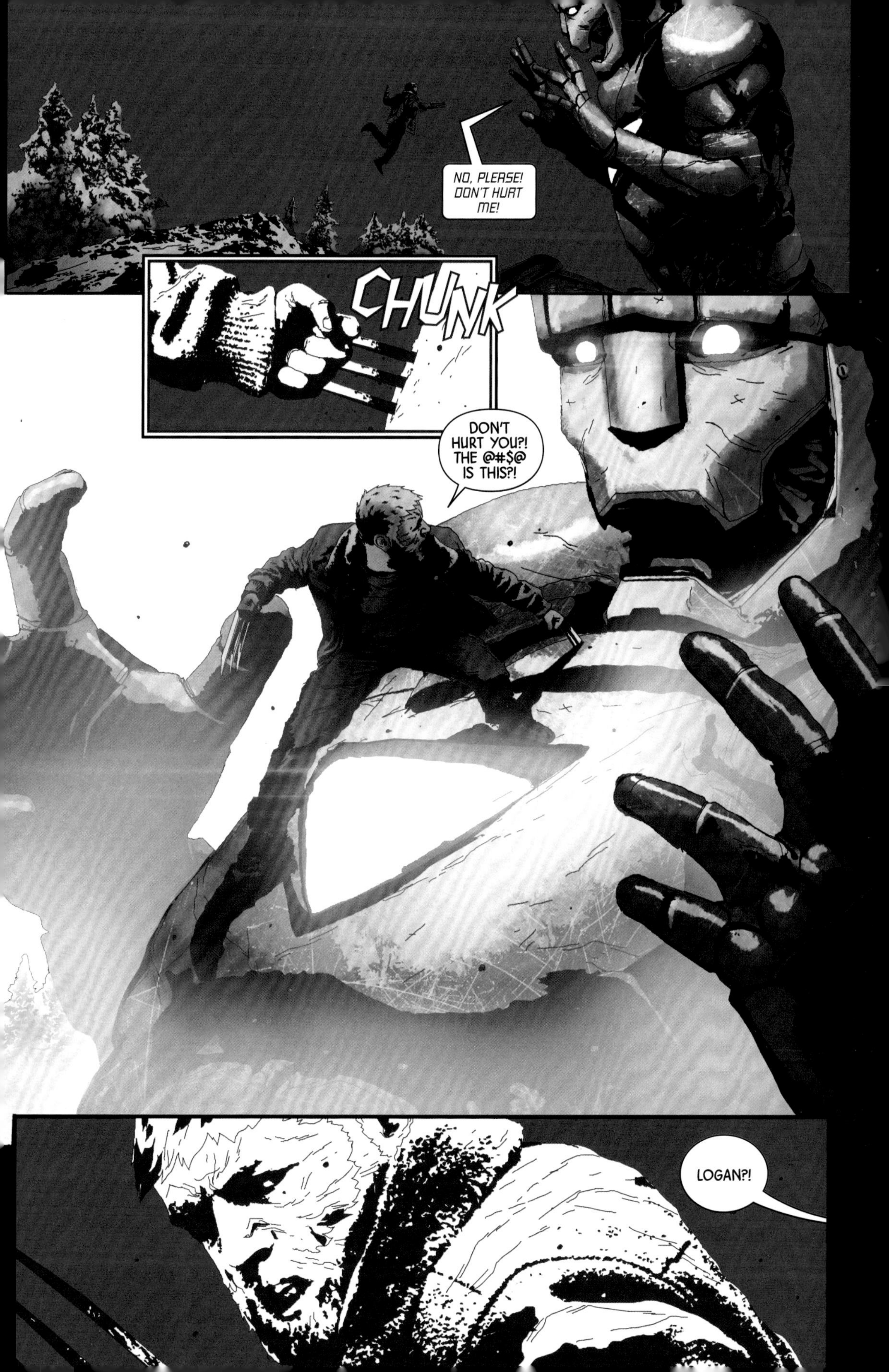
NO, PLEASE! DON'T HURT ME!
CHUNK
DON'T HURT YOU?! THE @#$@ IS THIS?!
LOGAN?!

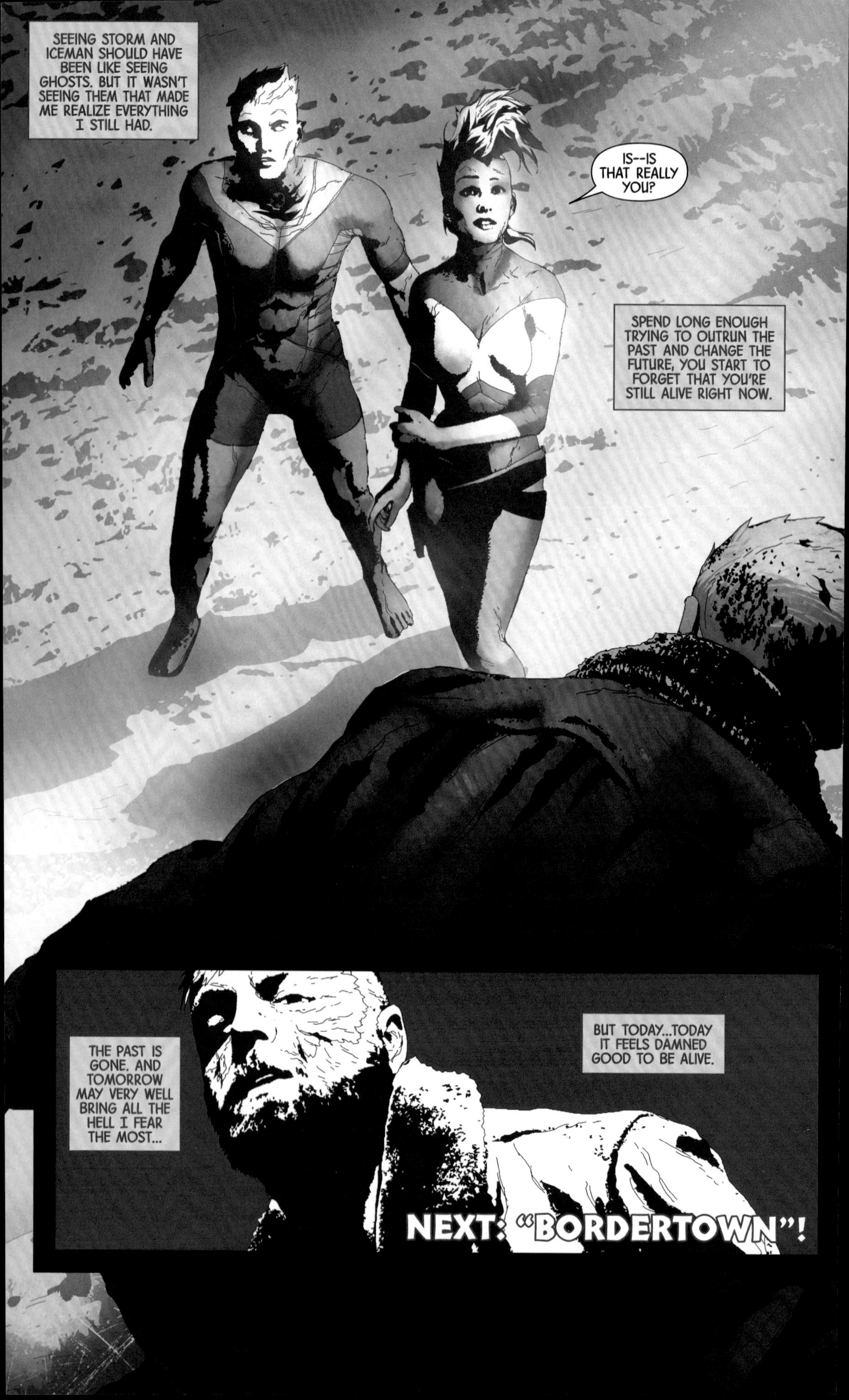
SEEING STORM AND ICEMAN SHOULD HAVE BEEN LIKE SEEING GHOSTS. BUT IT WASN'T SEEING THEM THAT MADE ME REALIZE EVERYTHING I STILL HAD.
IS--IS THAT REALLY YOU?
SPEND LONG ENOUGH TRYING TO OUTRUN THE PAST AND CHANGE THE FUTURE, YOU START TO FORGET THAT YOU'RE STILL ALIVE RIGHT NOW.
THE PAST IS GONE. AND TOMORROW MAY VERY WELL BRING ALL THE HELL I FEAR THE MOST...
BUT TODAY...TODAY IT FEELS DAMNED GOOD TO BE ALIVE.
NEXT: "BORDERTOWN"!

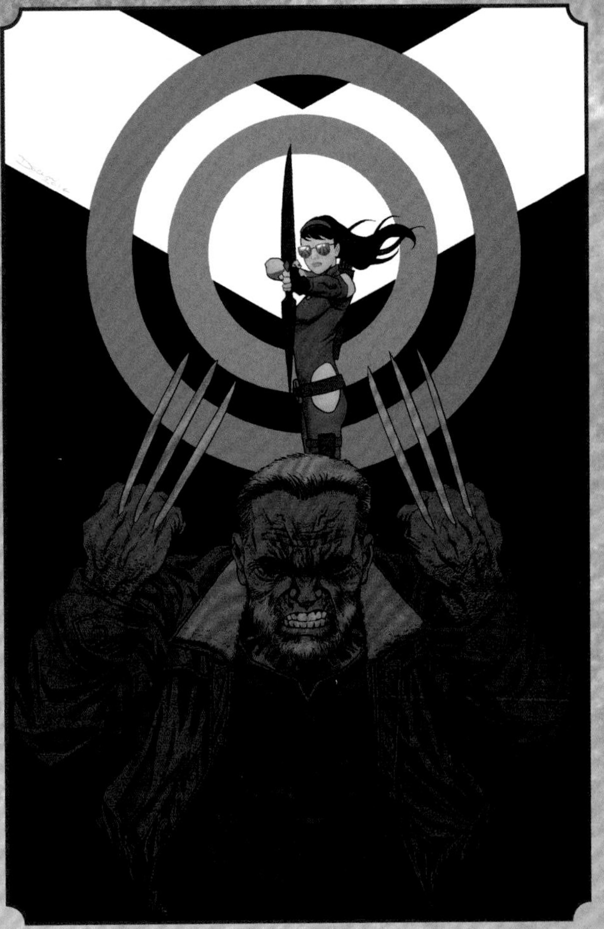

#3 VARIANT BY DECLAN SHALVEY & JORDIE BELLAIRE

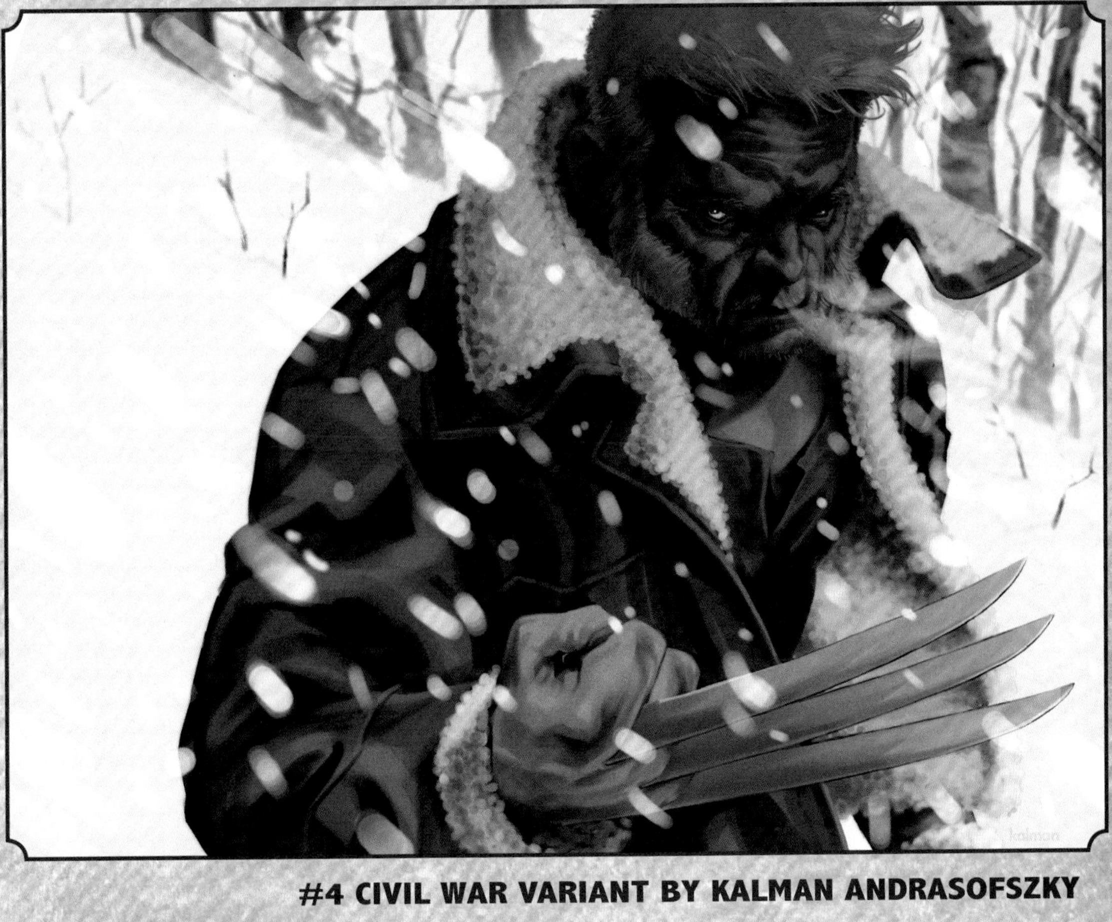

#4 CIVIL WAR VARIANT BY KALMAN ANDRASOFSZKY

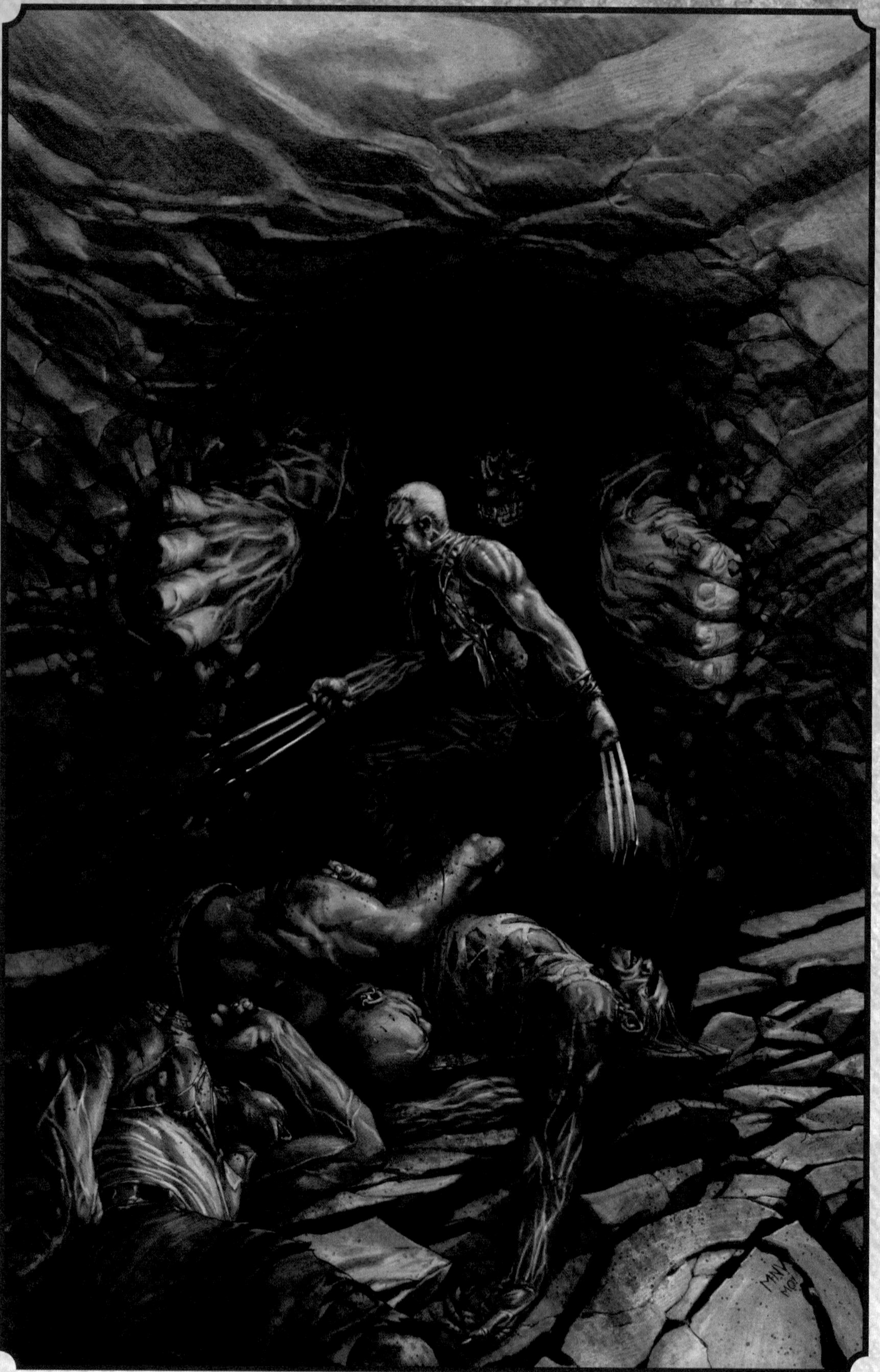

WOLVERINE:

OLD MAN LOGAN GIANT-SIZE #1

WRITER **MARK MILLAR**

PENCILER **STEVE McNIVEN**

INKERS **DEXTER VINES & MARK MORALES**

COLOR ARTIST **MORRY HOLLOWELL**

LETTERER **VC's CORY PETIT**

COVER ARTISTS **STEVE McNIVEN, DEXTER VINES & MORRY HOLLOWELL**

ASSISTANT EDITOR **JODY LEHEUP**

EDITORS **JEANINE SCHAEFER & JOHN BARBER**

GROUP EDITOR **AXEL ALONSO**

It's been fifty years since the heroes fell. Fifty years since super villains carved America amongst themselves and created a lawless empire. Only a handful of people know what really happened that day and Old Man Logan is one of them. But Logan, once known as the feral mutant Wolverine, doesn't want to remember. In that final battle, Logan suffered a terrible trauma and hasn't popped his claws since.

Now taking root in Sacramento, Logan is content with raising a family. But Logan's peaceful world is threatened by the Hulk Gang—the descendants of Bruce Banner—and they want their rent money...money the poor mutant farmer doesn't have.

Clint Barton, the now-blind former Avenger called Hawkeye, offers to pay Logan if he accompanies him on a cross-country journey to New Babylon where Clint must deliver a case of Super-Soldier serum to rebels hoping to start a new Avengers team. Logan reluctantly agrees to go on the condition that he will not be a party to violence...

Escaping danger after danger—from Moloids to cloned dinosaurs to alien symbiotes—the duo travel, and finally, they reach their destination. But Clint's contacts reveal themselves to be undercover S.H.I.E.L.D. agents working for the president—also known as the Red Skull. The agents then gun Logan down...and execute Hawkeye...

Logan then infiltrates the White House and after a brutal battle, kills the Red Skull. With his friend's death avenged, Logan dons Tony Stark's old Iron Man suit and flies home at top speed, carrying with him a case of money with which he intends to pay off the Hulk Gang. But he arrives too late. The Hulk Gang came calling earlier than they said they would, and massacred Old Man Logan's entire family...

Now...finally...the claws are out...and Wolverine has returned.

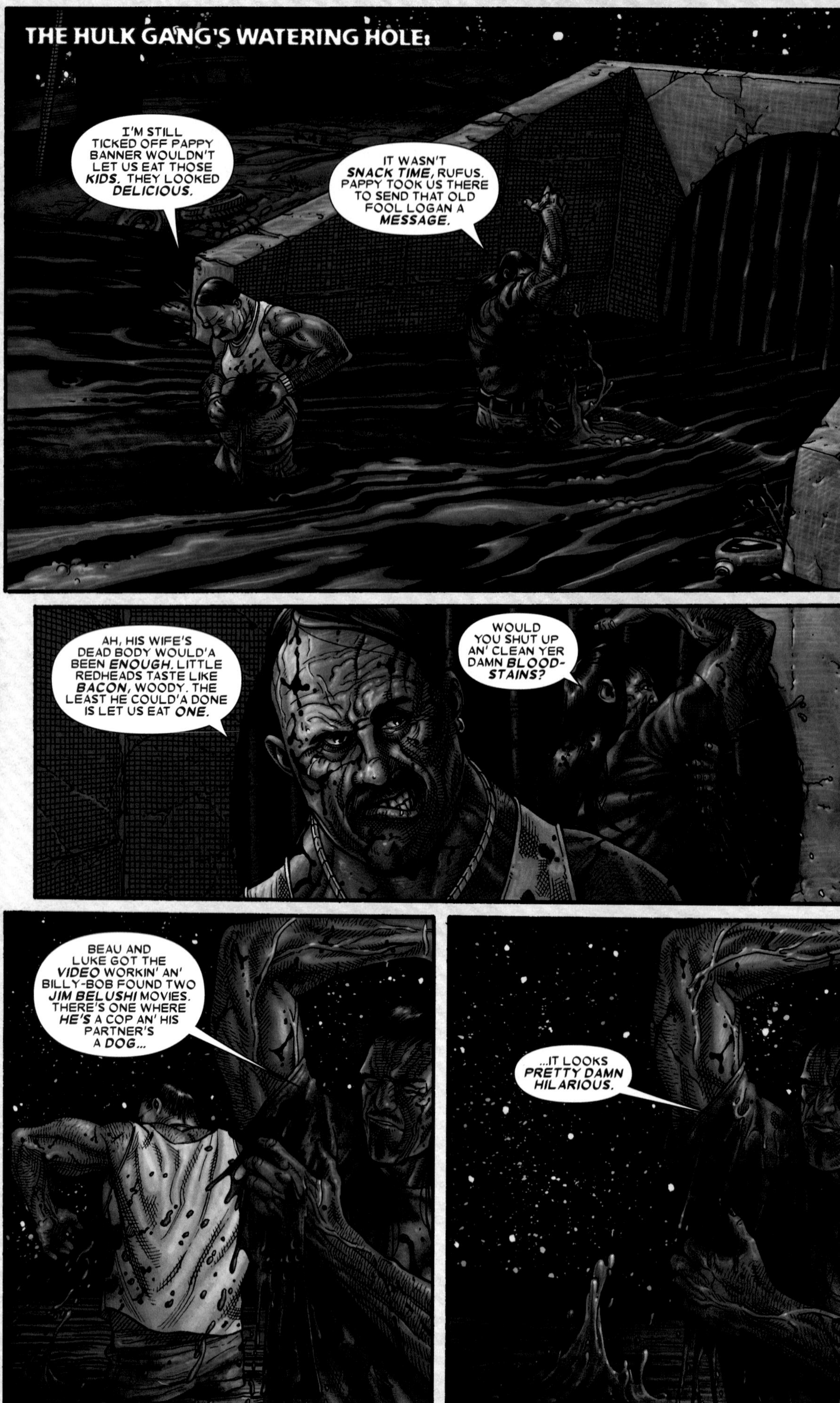
THE HULK GANG'S WATERING HOLE:
I'M STILL TICKED OFF PAPPY BANNER WOULDN'T LET US EAT THOSE KIDS. THEY LOOKED DELICIOUS.
IT WASN'T SNACK TIME, RUFUS. PAPPY TOOK US THERE TO SEND THAT OLD FOOL LOGAN A MESSAGE.
AH, HIS WIFE'S DEAD BODY WOULD'A BEEN ENOUGH. LITTLE REDHEADS TASTE LIKE BACON, WOODY. THE LEAST HE COULD'A DONE IS LET US EAT ONE.
WOULD YOU SHUT UP AN' CLEAN YER DAMN BLOOD-STAINS?
BEAU AND LUKE GOT THE VIDEO WORKIN' AN' BILLY-BOB FOUND TWO JIM BELUSHI MOVIES. THERE'S ONE WHERE HE'S A COP AN' HIS PARTNER'S A DOG...
...IT LOOKS PRETTY DAMN HILARIOUS.

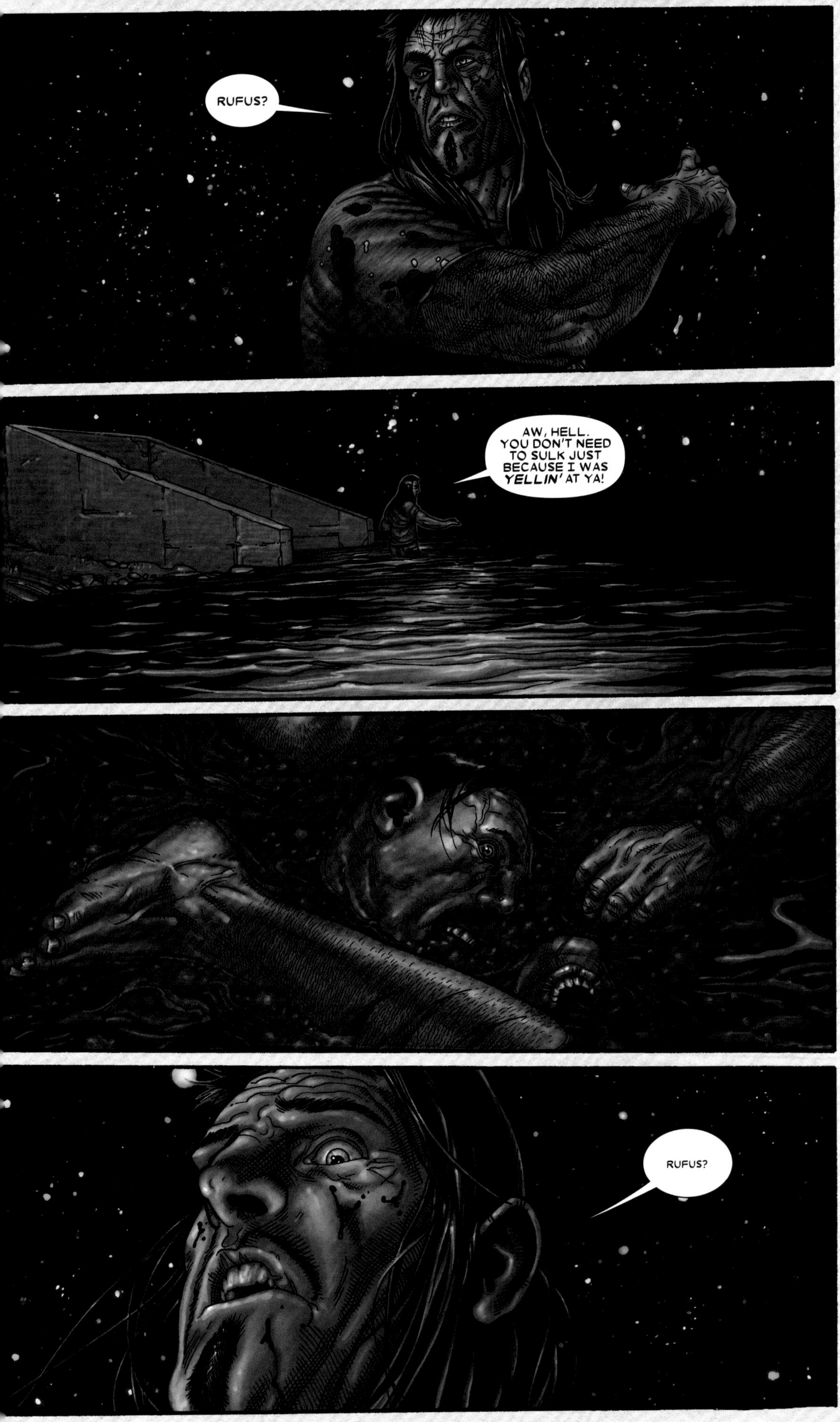
RUFUS?
AW, HELL. YOU DON'T NEED TO SULK JUST BECAUSE I WAS *YELLIN'* AT YA!
RUFUS?

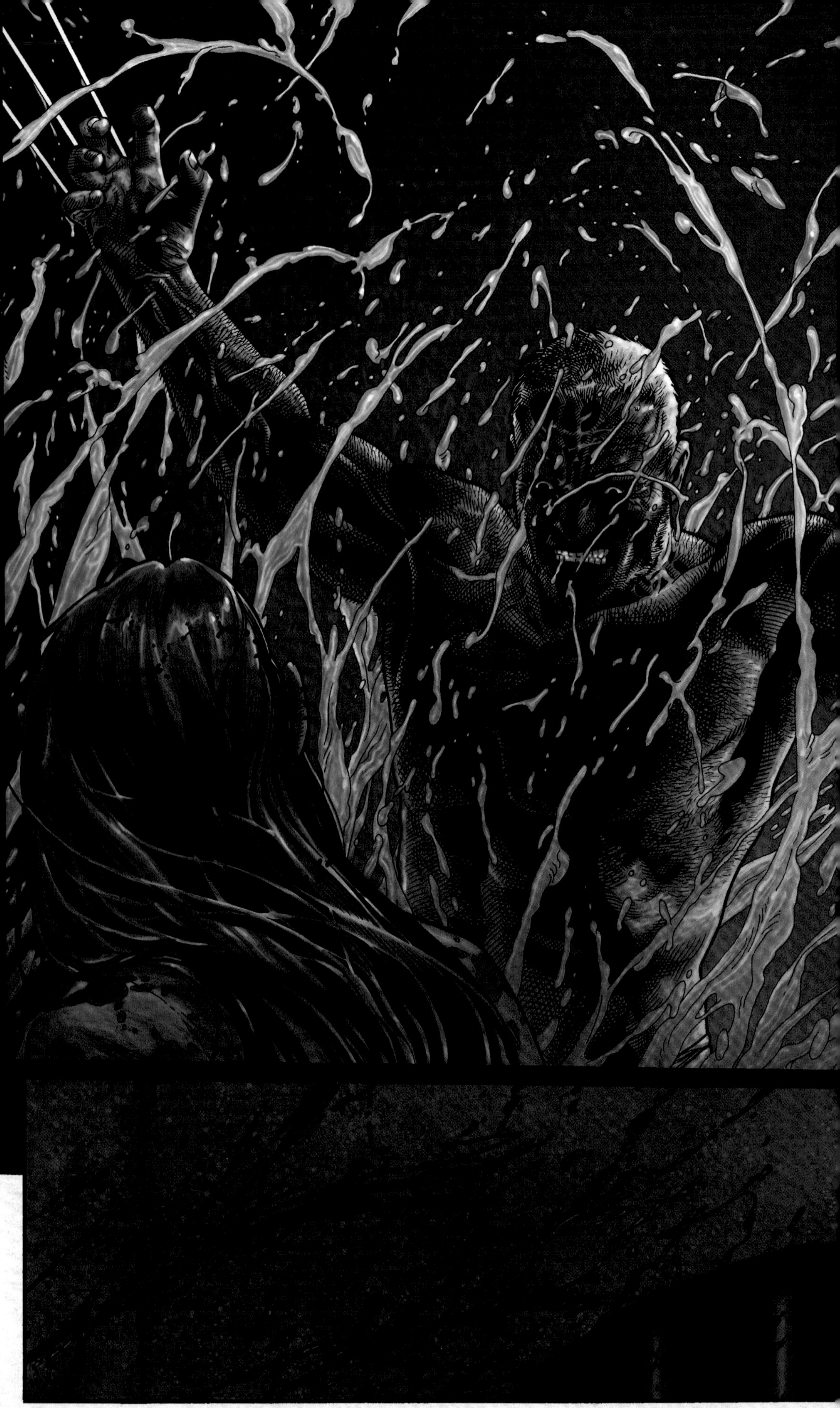

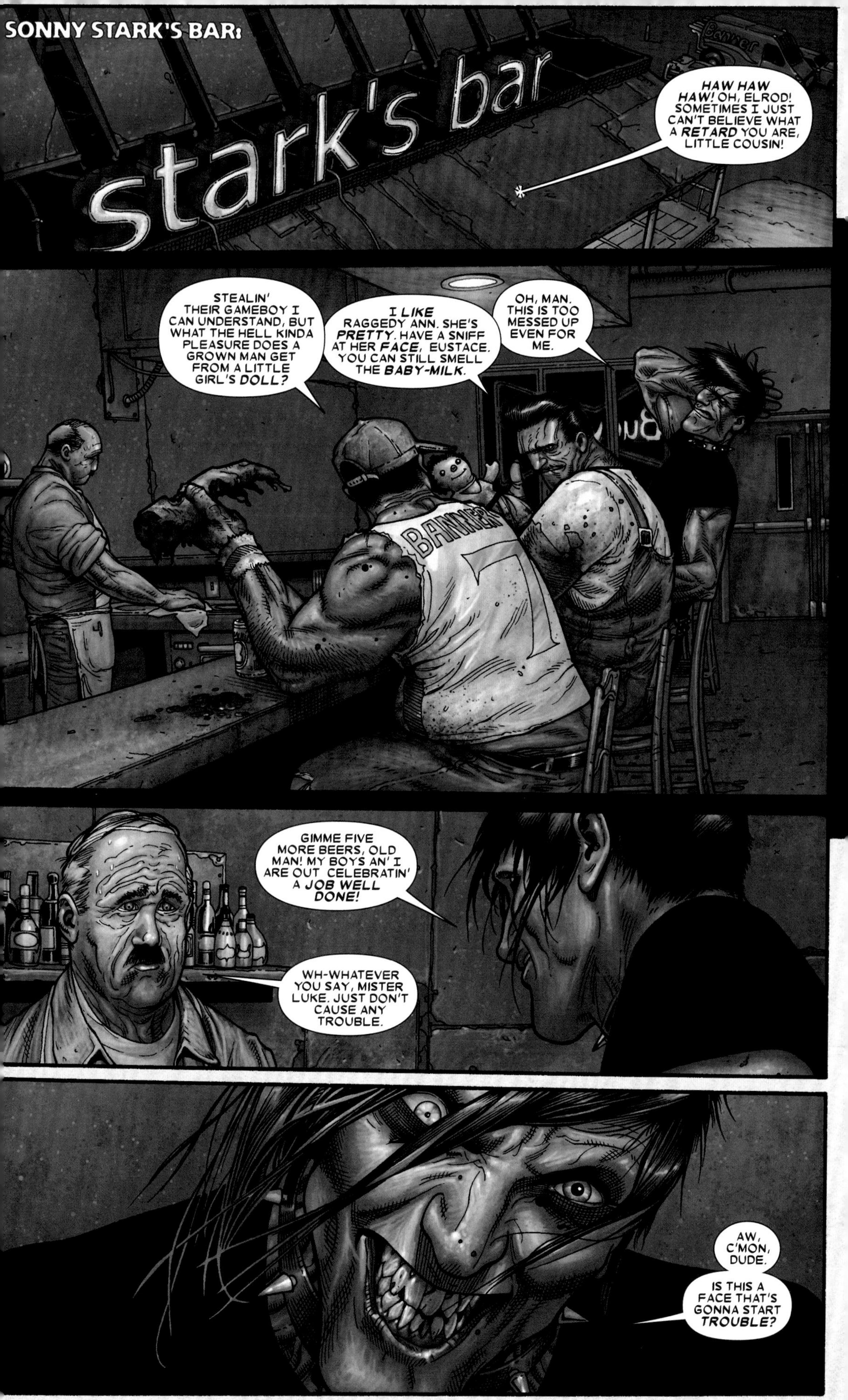
SONNY STARK'S BAR:
stark's bar
HAW HAW HAW! OH, ELROD! SOMETIMES I JUST CAN'T BELIEVE WHAT A RETARD YOU ARE, LITTLE COUSIN!
STEALIN' THEIR GAMEBOY I CAN UNDERSTAND, BUT WHAT THE HELL KINDA PLEASURE DOES A GROWN MAN GET FROM A LITTLE GIRL'S DOLL?
I LIKE RAGGEDY ANN. SHE'S PRETTY. HAVE A SNIFF AT HER FACE, EUSTACE. YOU CAN STILL SMELL THE BABY-MILK.
OH, MAN. THIS IS TOO MESSED UP EVEN FOR ME.
BANNER 7
GIMME FIVE MORE BEERS, OLD MAN! MY BOYS AN' I ARE OUT CELEBRATIN' A JOB WELL DONE!
WH-WHATEVER YOU SAY, MISTER LUKE. JUST DON'T CAUSE ANY TROUBLE.
AW, C'MON, DUDE.
IS THIS A FACE THAT'S GONNA START TROUBLE?

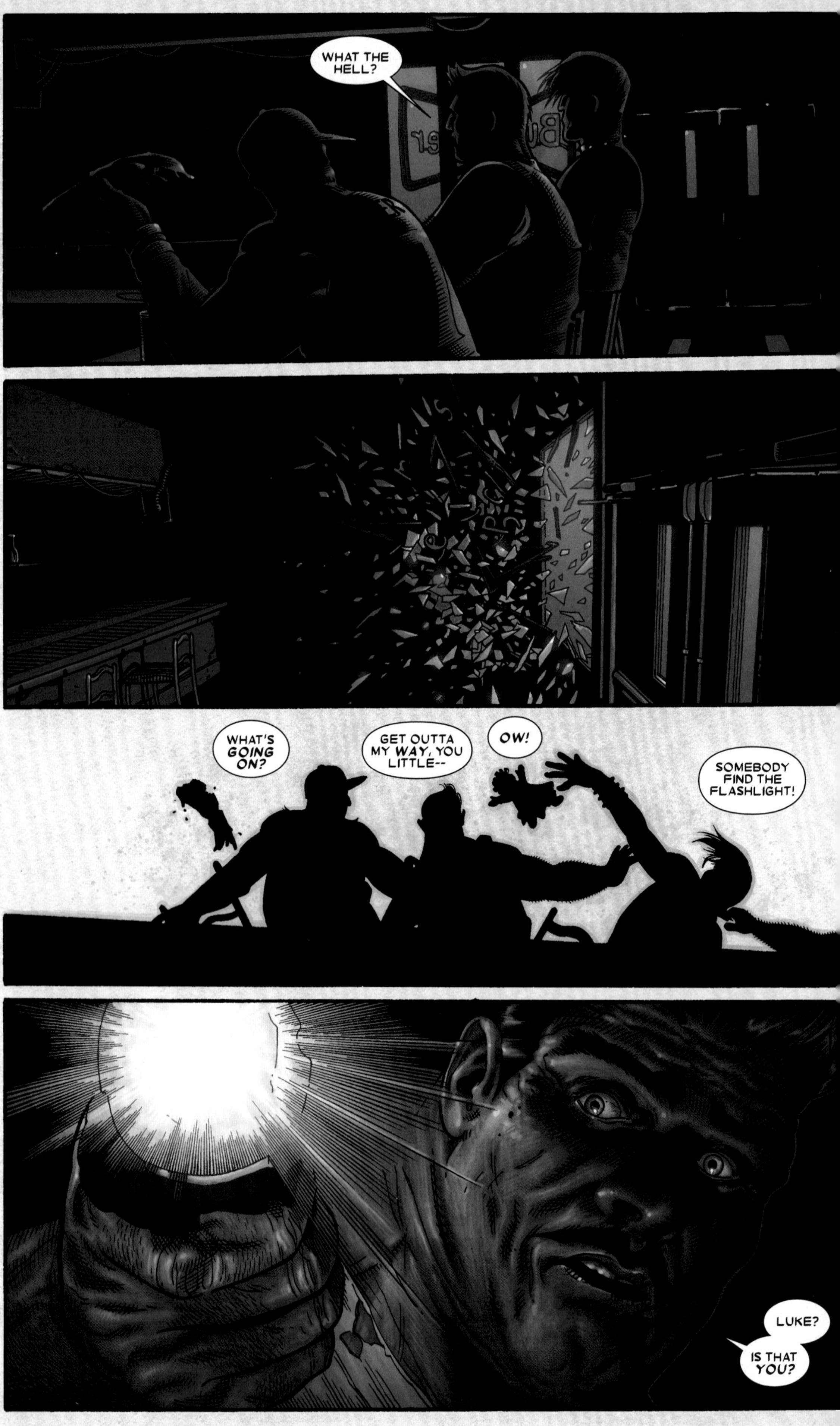
WHAT THE HELL?
WHAT'S GOING ON?
GET OUTTA MY WAY, YOU LITTLE--
OW!
SOMEBODY FIND THE FLASHLIGHT!
LUKE?
IS THAT YOU?

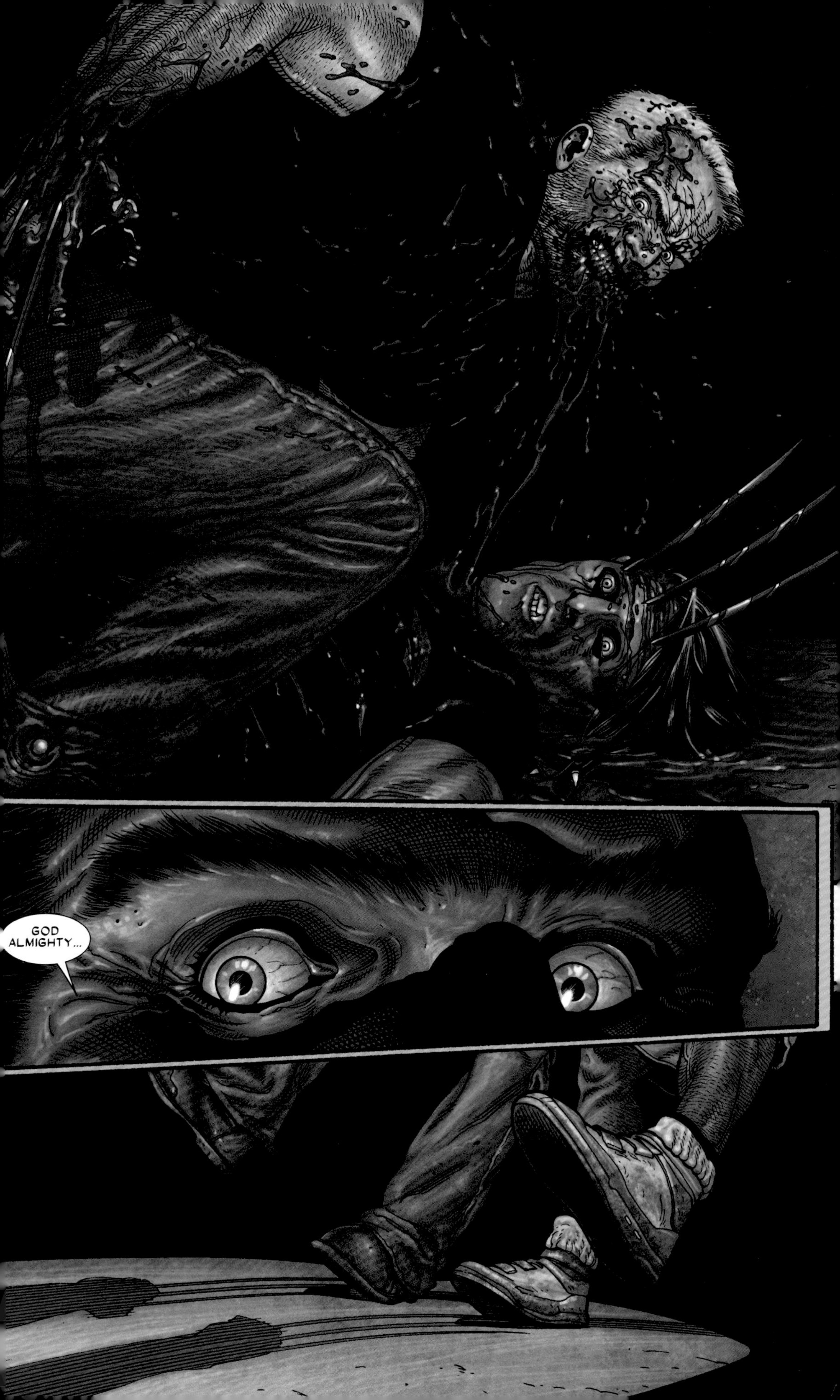
GOD ALMIGHTY...

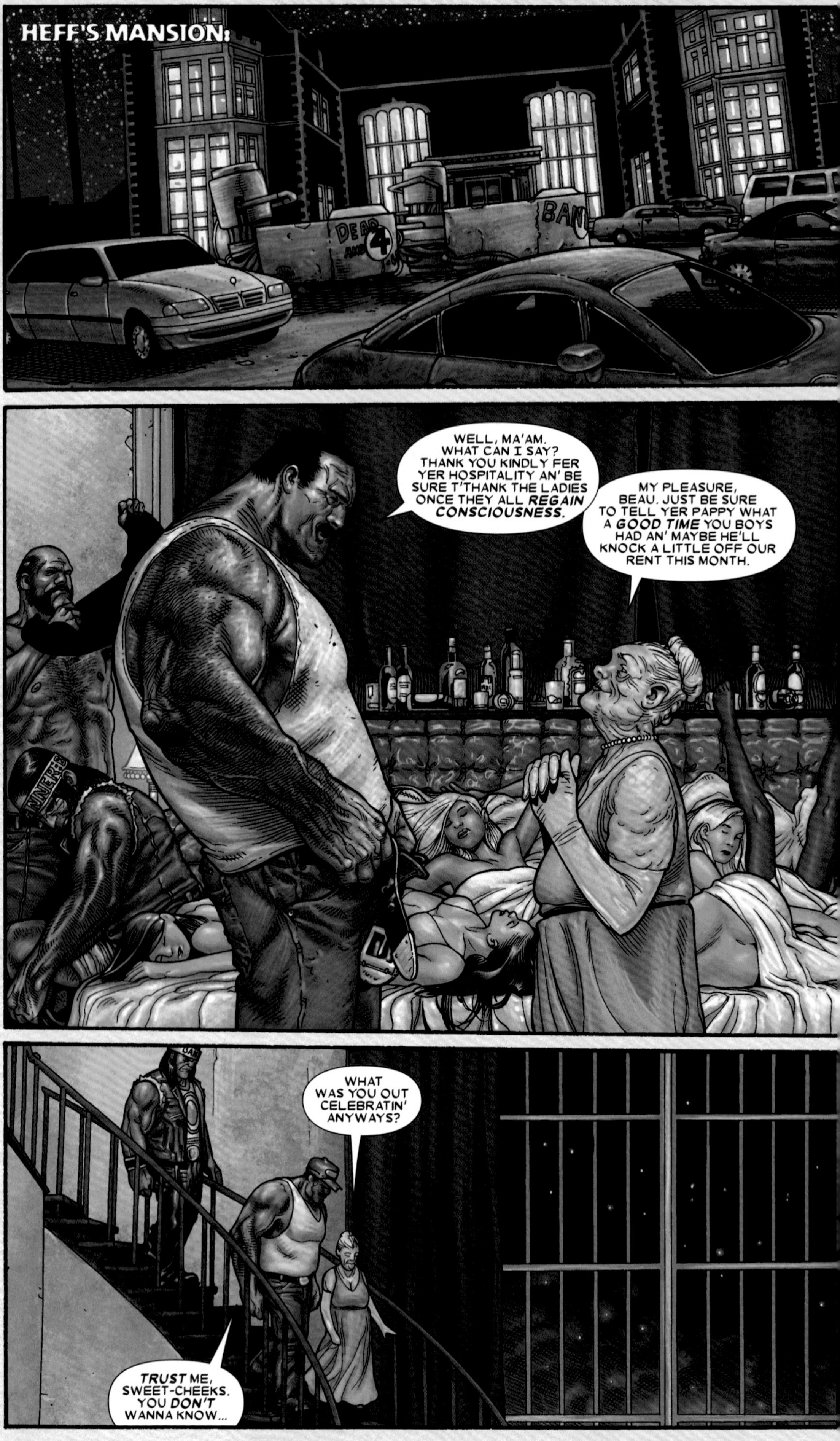
HEFF'S MANSION:
DEAD AND 4
BAN
WELL, MA'AM. WHAT CAN I SAY? THANK YOU KINDLY FER YER HOSPITALITY AN' BE SURE T'THANK THE LADIES ONCE THEY ALL *REGAIN CONSCIOUSNESS.*
MY PLEASURE, BEAU. JUST BE SURE TO TELL YER PAPPY WHAT A *GOOD TIME* YOU BOYS HAD AN' MAYBE HE'LL KNOCK A LITTLE OFF OUR RENT THIS MONTH.
WHAT WAS YOU OUT CELEBRATIN' ANYWAYS?
TRUST ME, SWEET-CHEEKS. YOU *DON'T* WANNA KNOW...

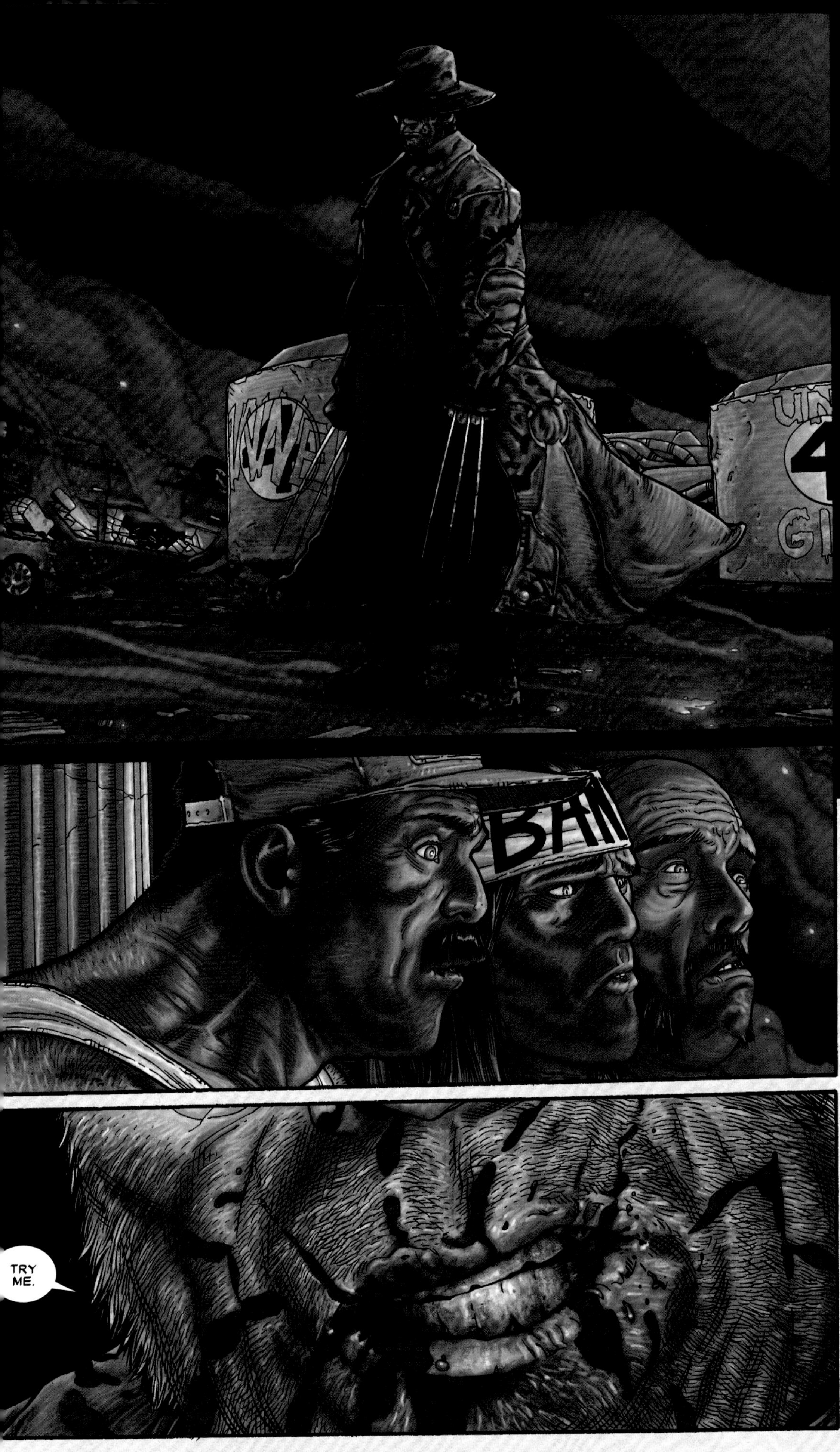
TRY ME.

BANNER'S LAIR:

YOU THINK HE'S GONNA *COME HERE*, PAPPY?

EVEN THOUGH THERE'S *SO MANY* OF US? YOU THINK HE'S GONNA COME HERE LOOKIN' FOR *REVENGE?*

WE KILLED HIS *WIFE AND CHILDREN*, BOBBI-JO. LAID THEM OUT LIKE THEY WAS A DAMN *FINGER-BUFFET.*

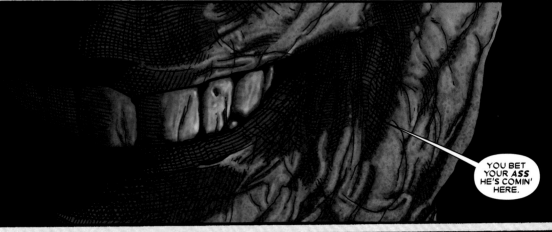

YOU BET YOUR *ASS* HE'S COMIN' HERE.

SWEET *JEEZUS...*

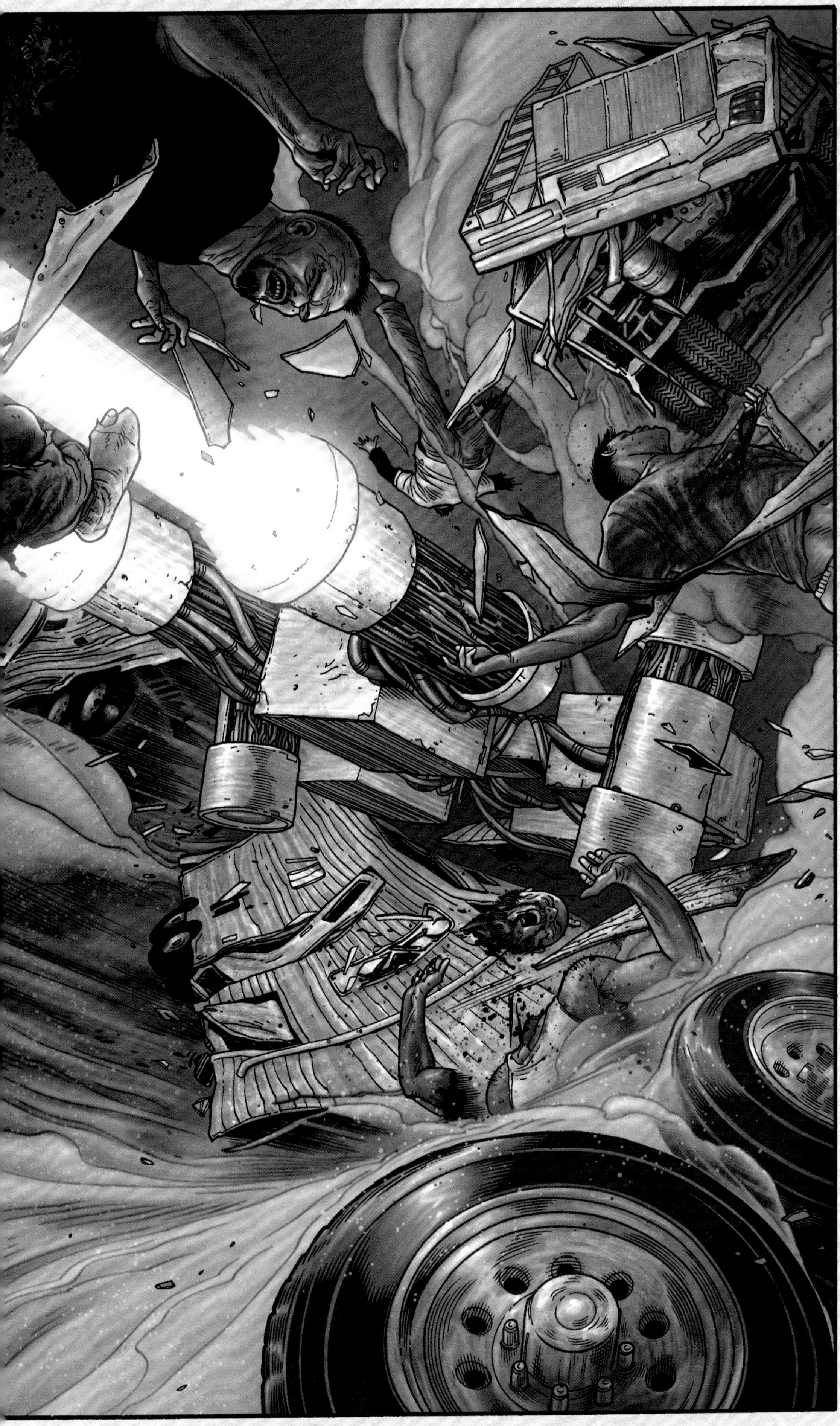

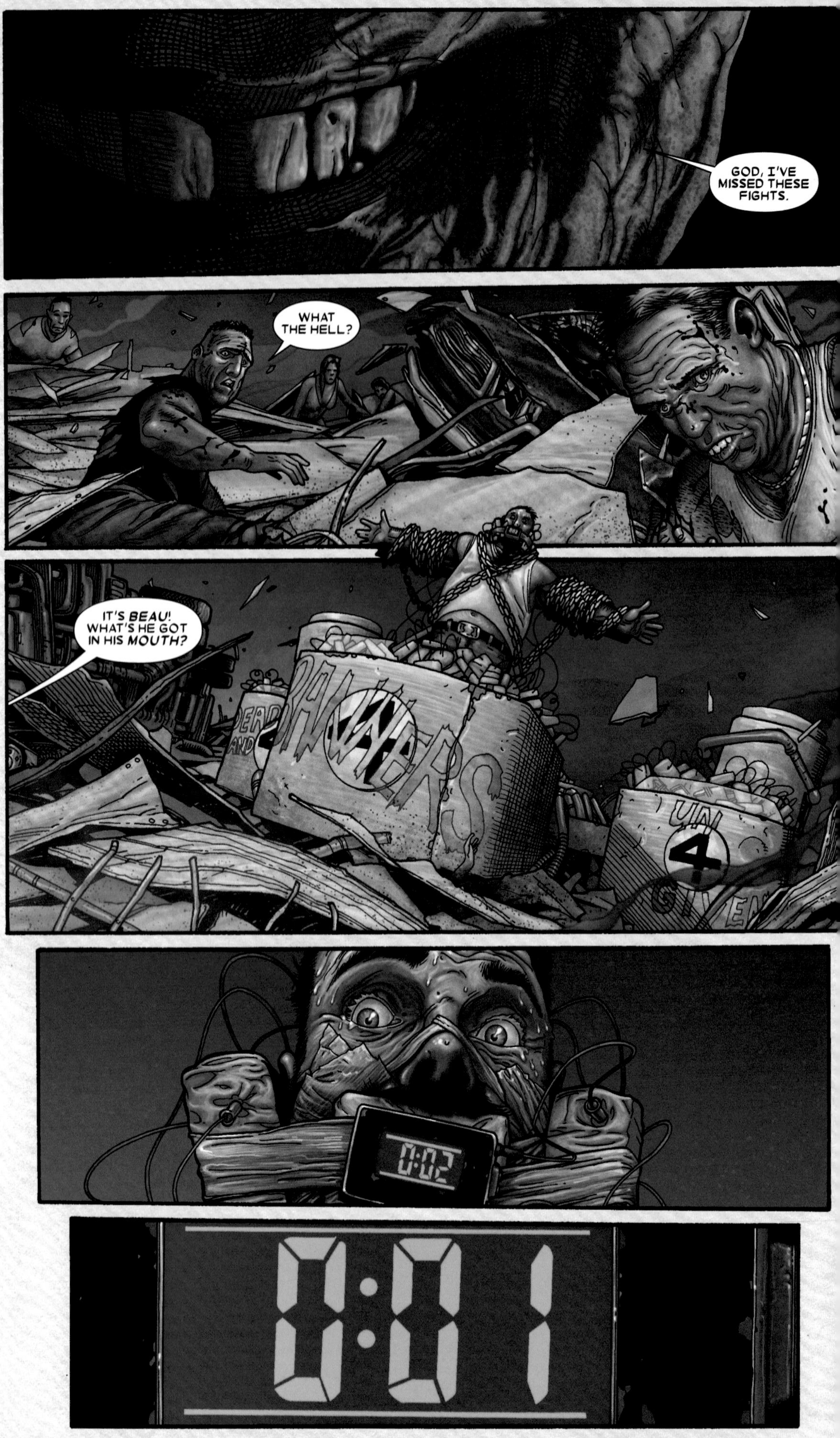
GOD, I'VE MISSED THESE FIGHTS.
WHAT THE HELL?
IT'S BEAU! WHAT'S HE GOT IN HIS MOUTH?
0:02
0:01

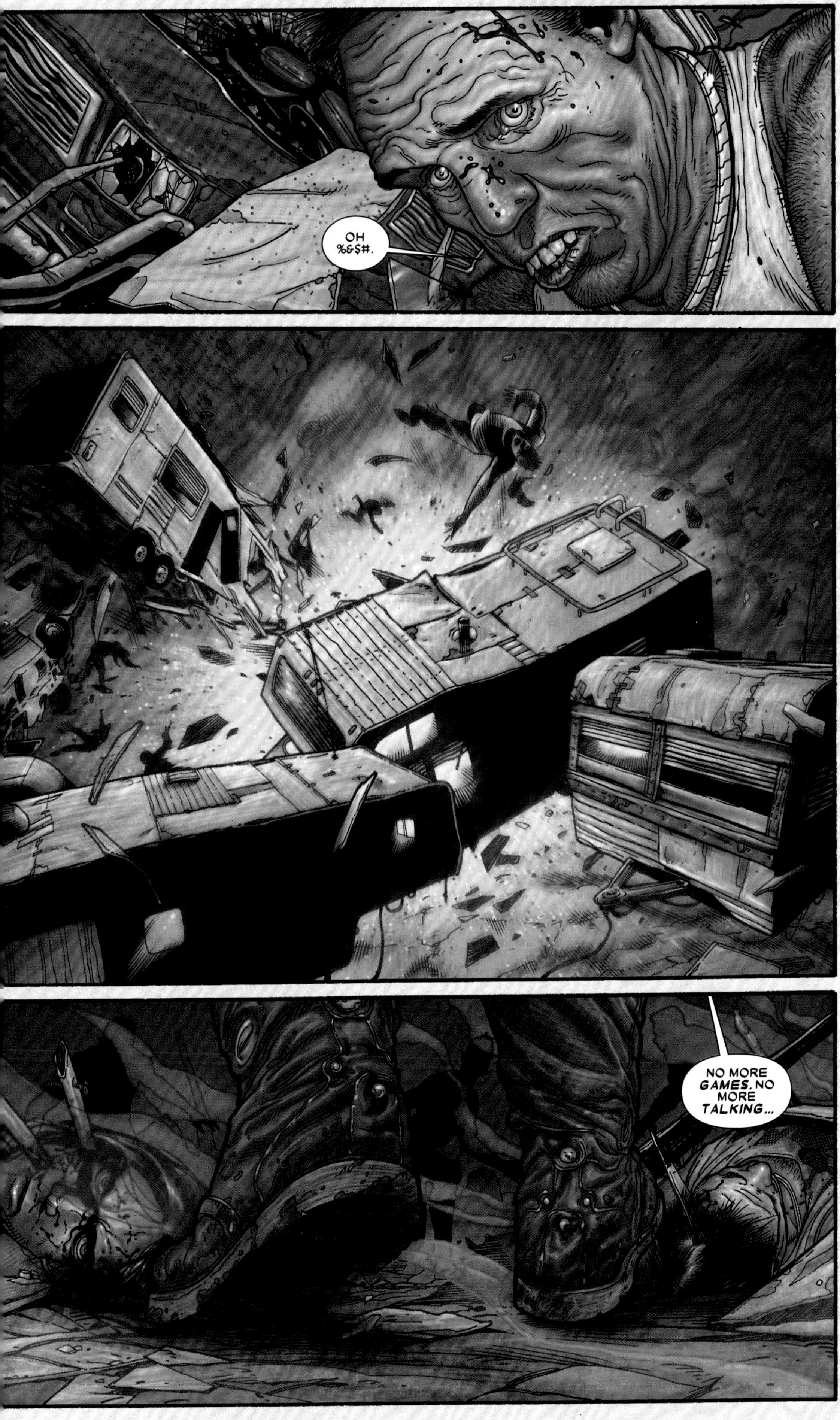
OH %&$#.
NO MORE GAMES. NO MORE TALKING...

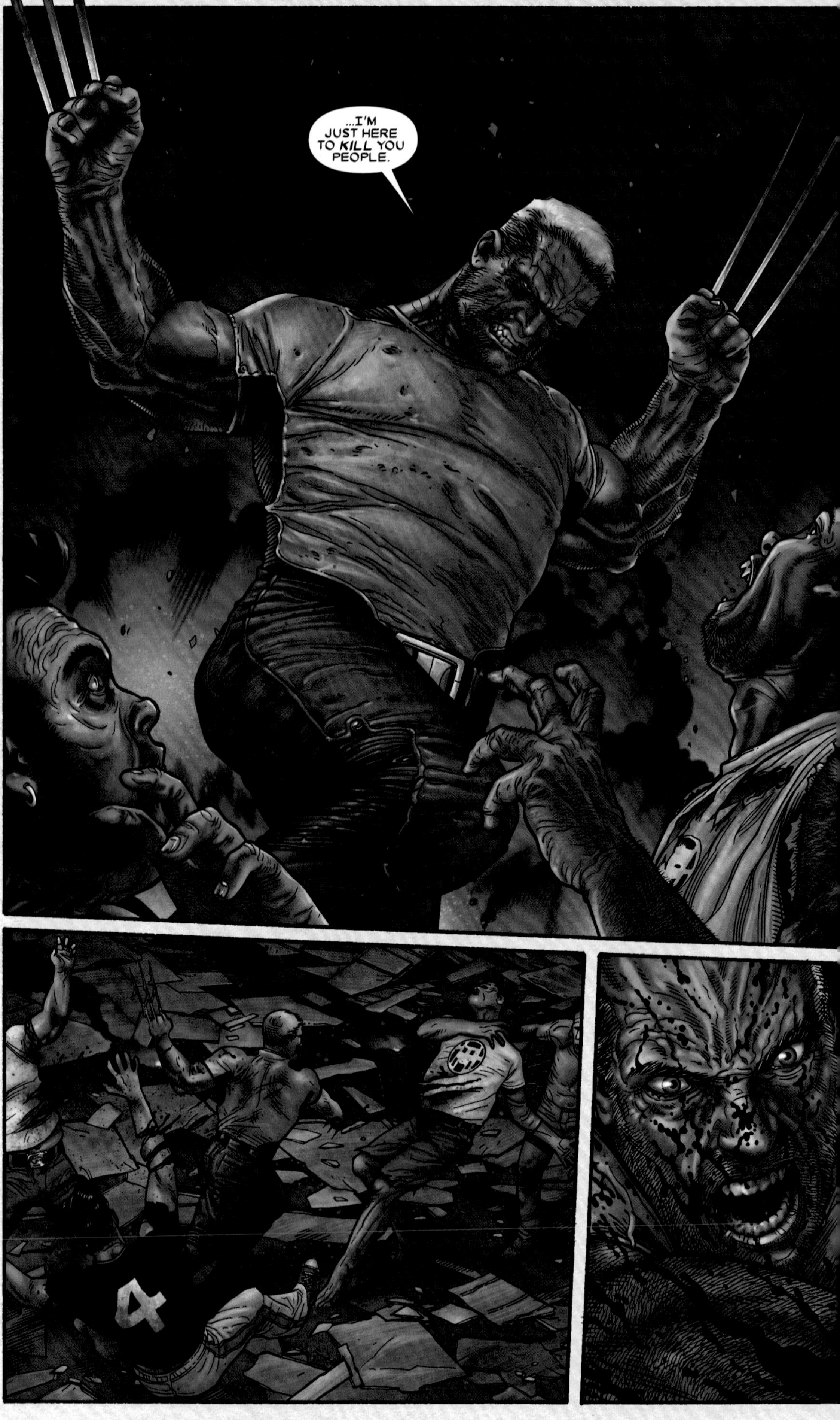
...I'M JUST HERE TO KILL YOU PEOPLE.

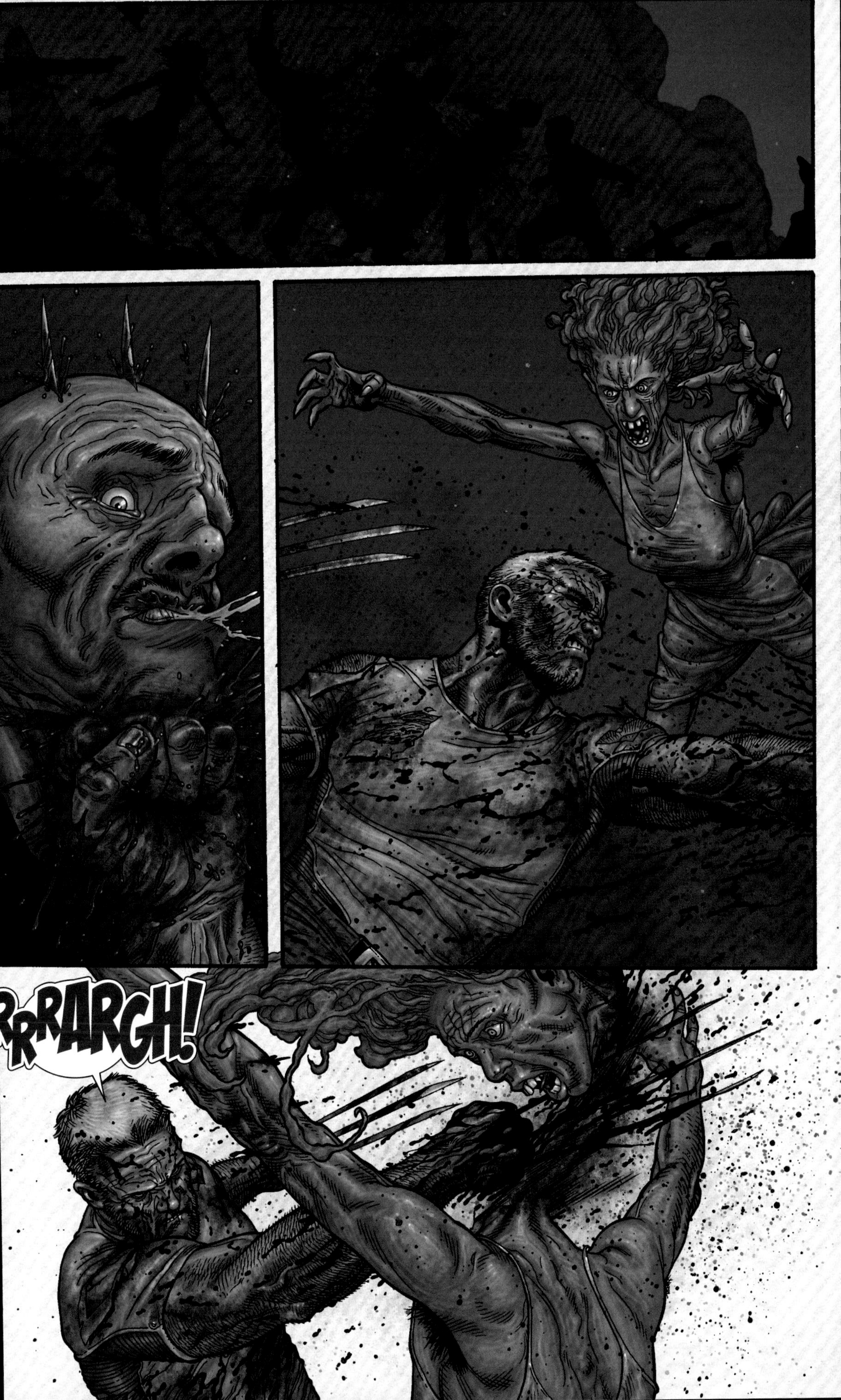
RRRARGH!

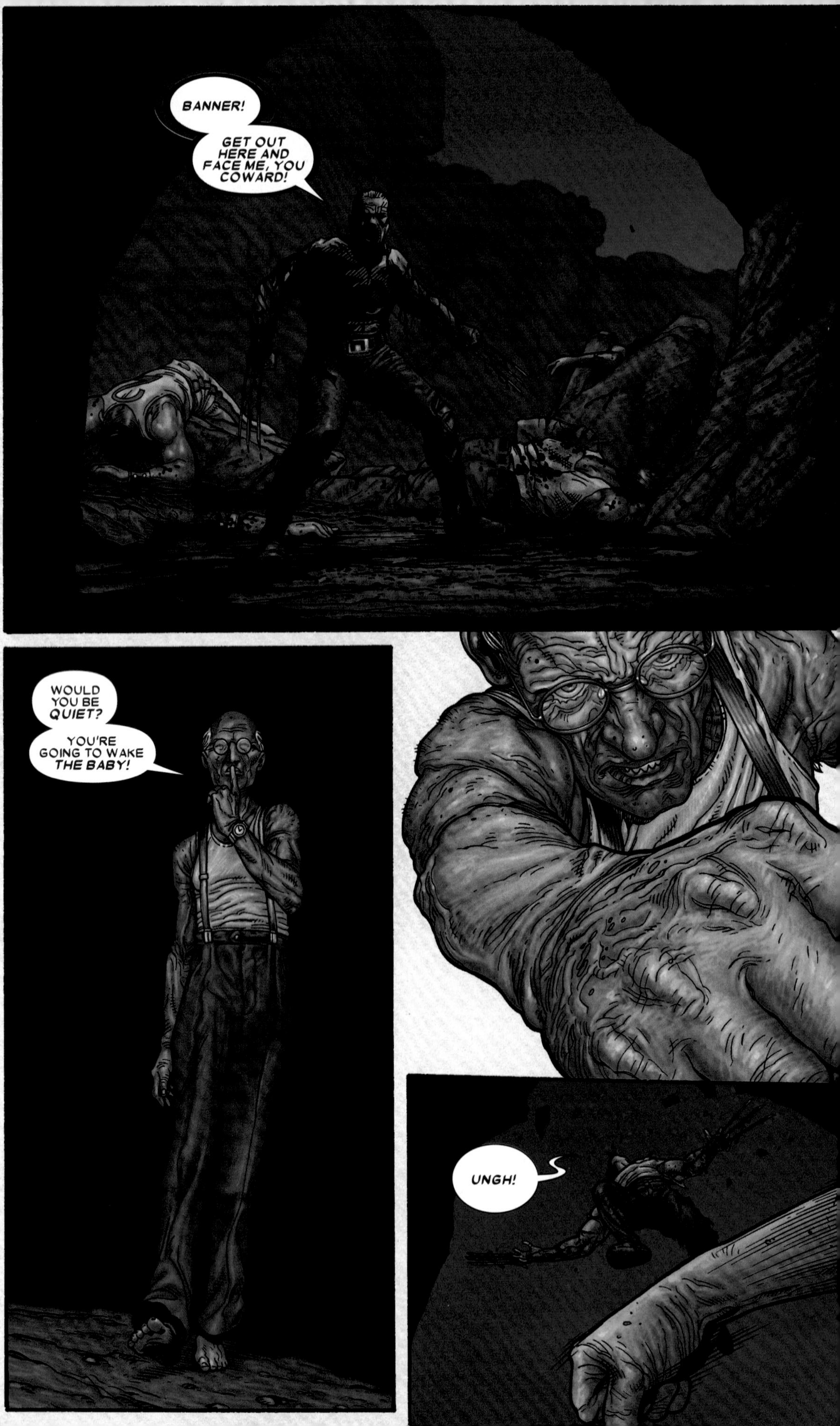
BANNER!
GET OUT HERE AND FACE ME, YOU COWARD!
WOULD YOU BE QUIET?
YOU'RE GOING TO WAKE THE BABY!
UNGH!

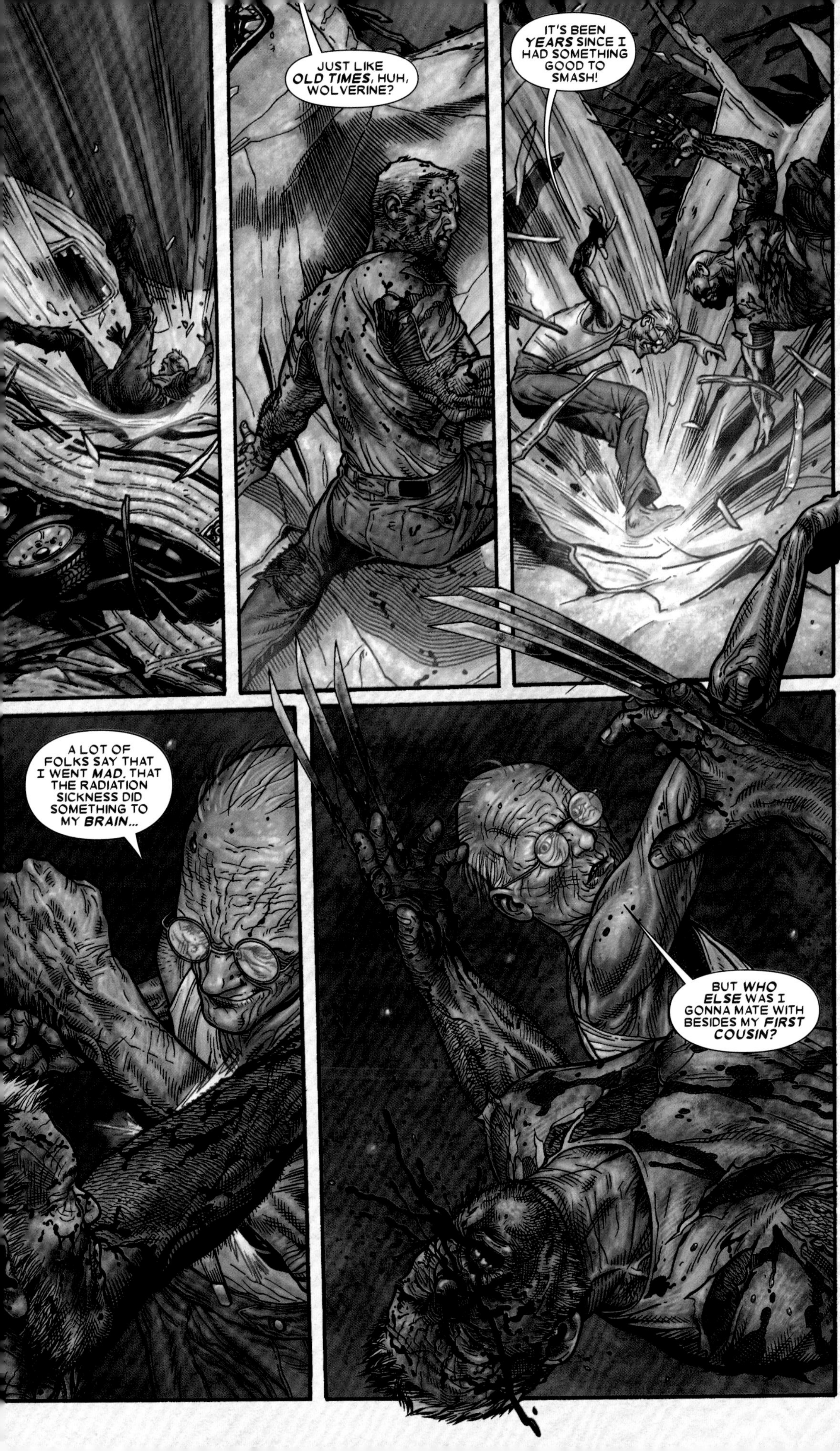

JUST LIKE OLD TIMES, HUH, WOLVERINE?
IT'S BEEN YEARS SINCE I HAD SOMETHING GOOD TO SMASH!
A LOT OF FOLKS SAY THAT I WENT MAD. THAT THE RADIATION SICKNESS DID SOMETHING TO MY BRAIN...
BUT WHO ELSE WAS I GONNA MATE WITH BESIDES MY FIRST COUSIN?

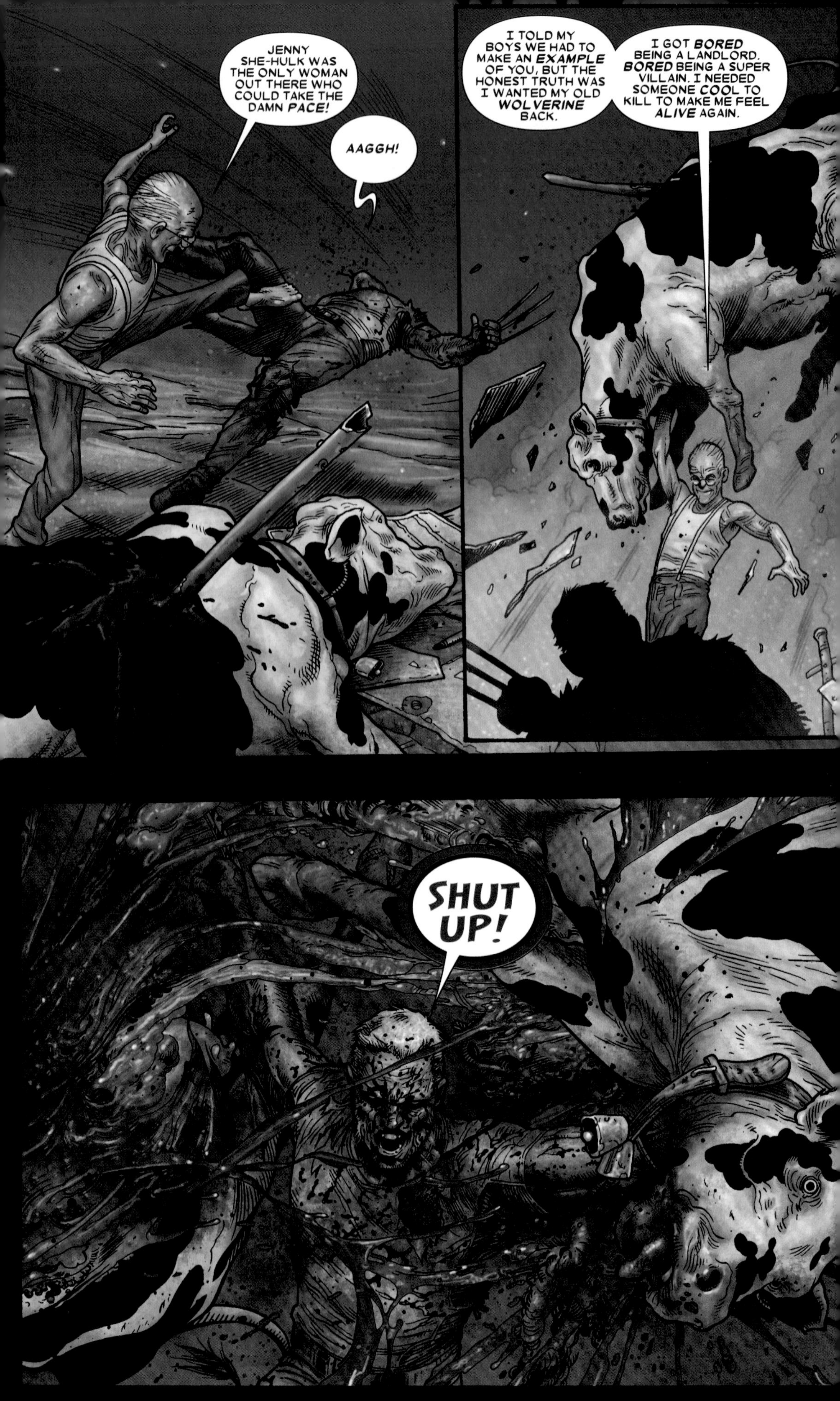

JENNY SHE-HULK WAS THE ONLY WOMAN OUT THERE WHO COULD TAKE THE DAMN PACE!
AAGGH!
I TOLD MY BOYS WE HAD TO MAKE AN EXAMPLE OF YOU, BUT THE HONEST TRUTH WAS I WANTED MY OLD WOLVERINE BACK.
I GOT BORED BEING A LANDLORD. BORED BEING A SUPER VILLAIN. I NEEDED SOMEONE COOL TO KILL TO MAKE ME FEEL ALIVE AGAIN.
SHUT UP!

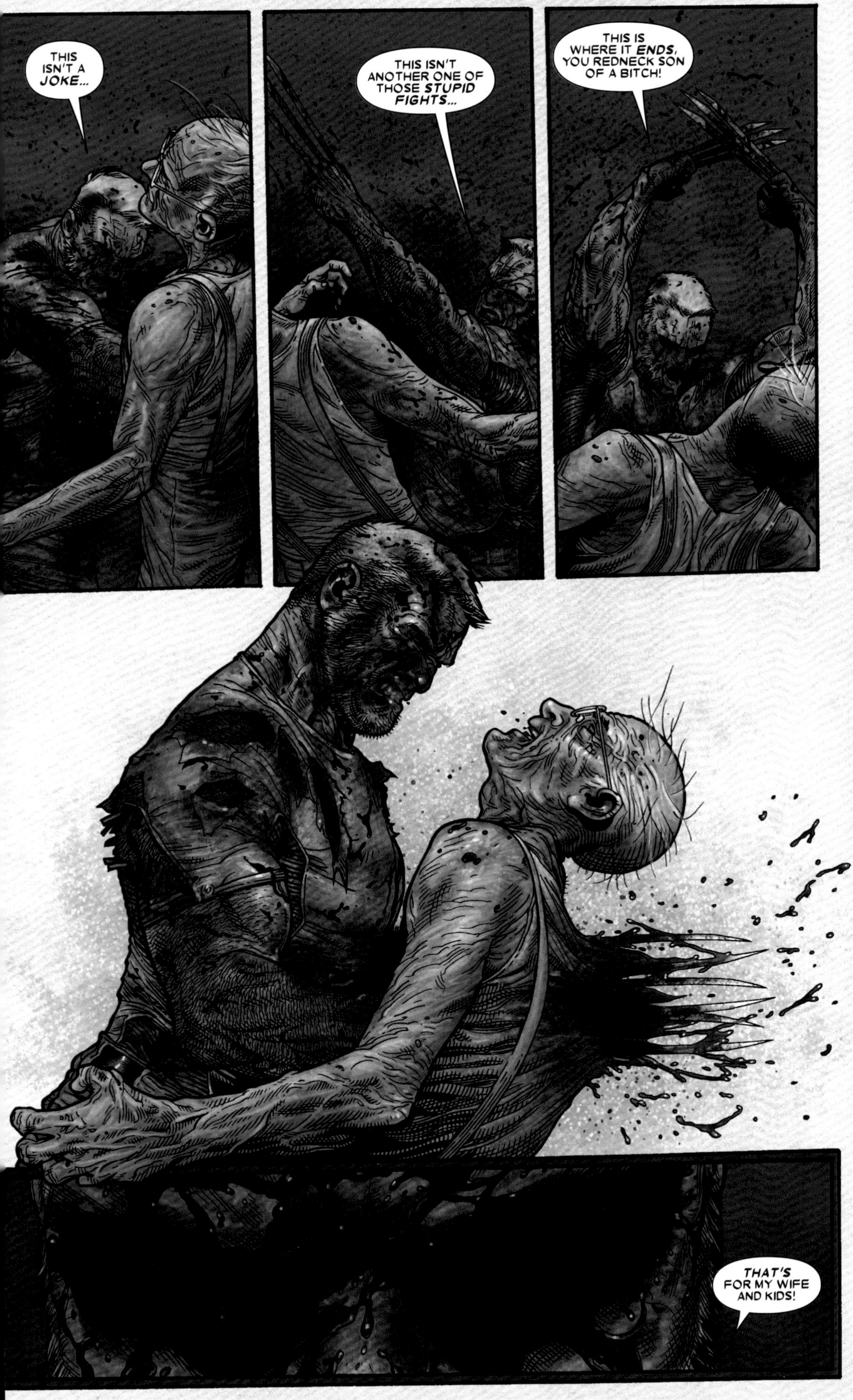
THIS ISN'T A JOKE...
THIS ISN'T ANOTHER ONE OF THOSE STUPID FIGHTS...
THIS IS WHERE IT ENDS, YOU REDNECK SON OF A BITCH!
THAT'S FOR MY WIFE AND KIDS!

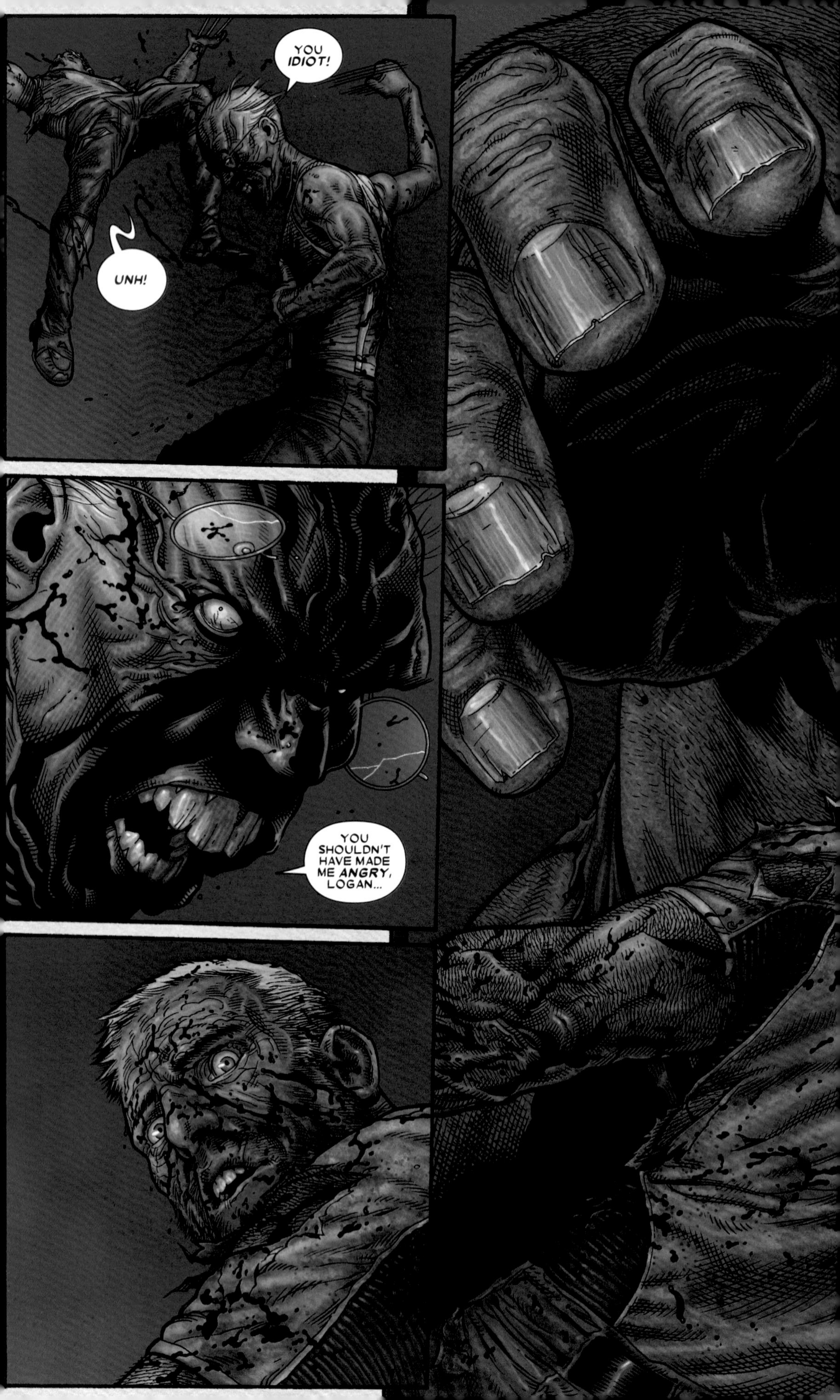
YOU IDIOT!
UNH!
YOU SHOULDN'T HAVE MADE ME ANGRY, LOGAN...

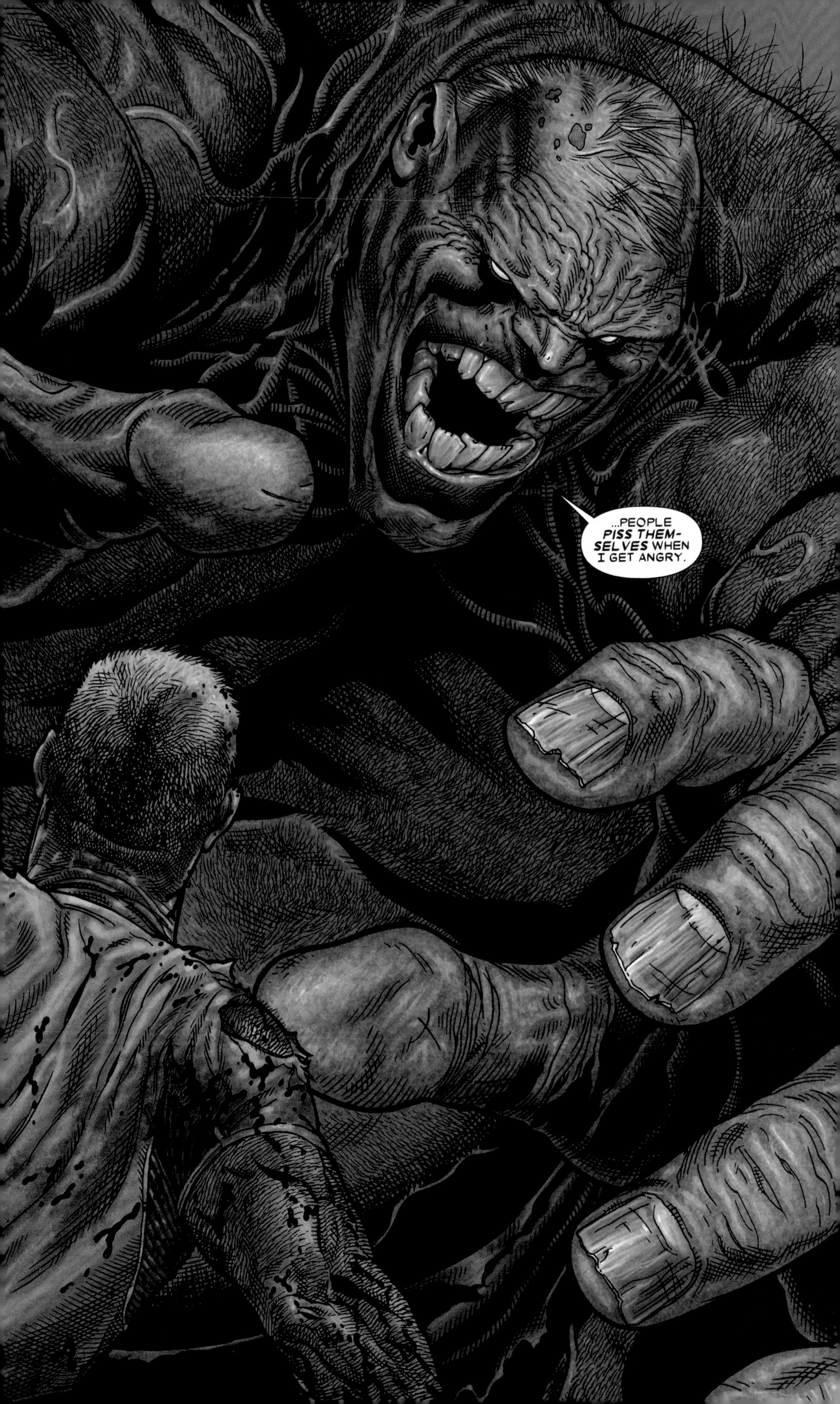
...PEOPLE PISS THEM-SELVES WHEN I GET ANGRY.

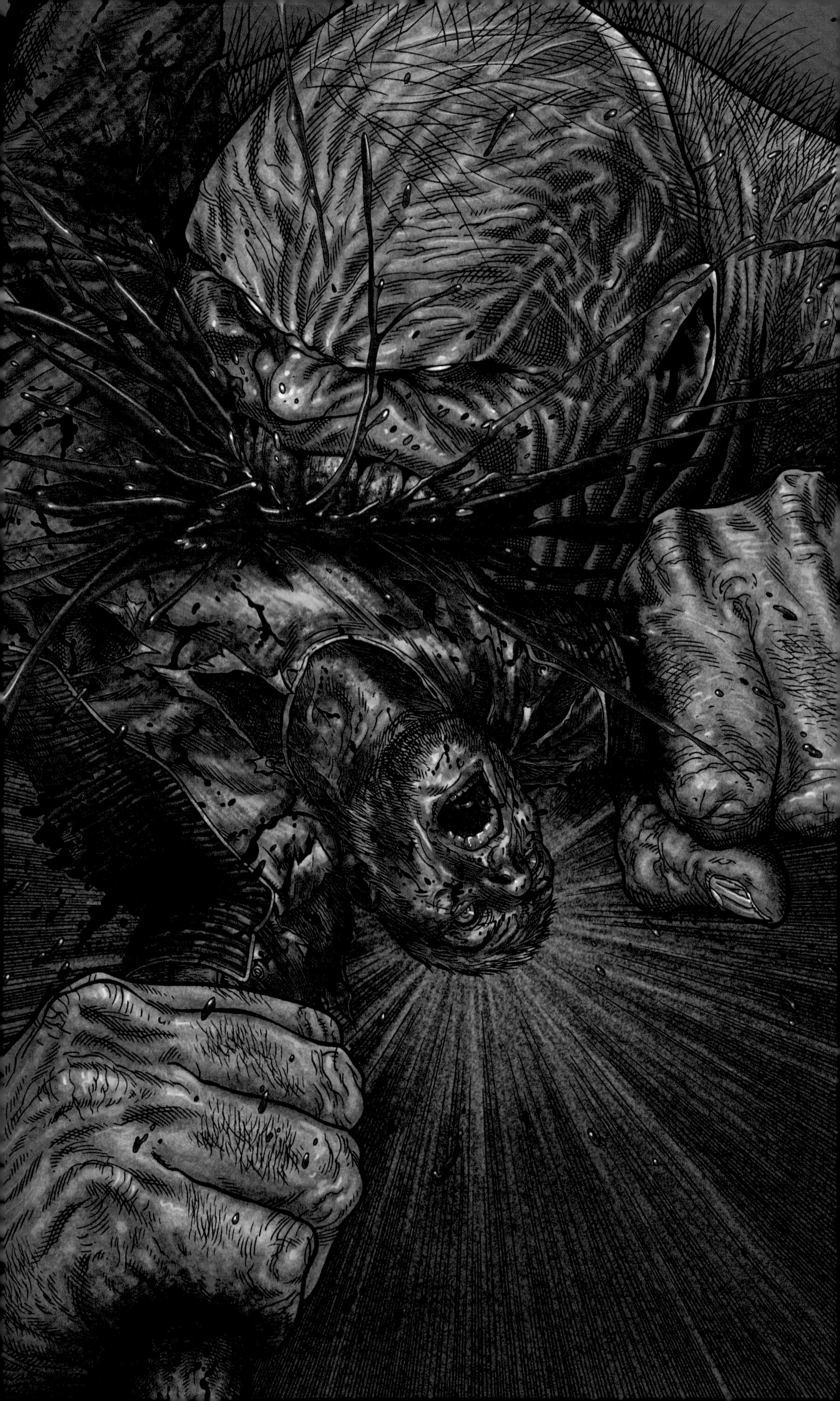

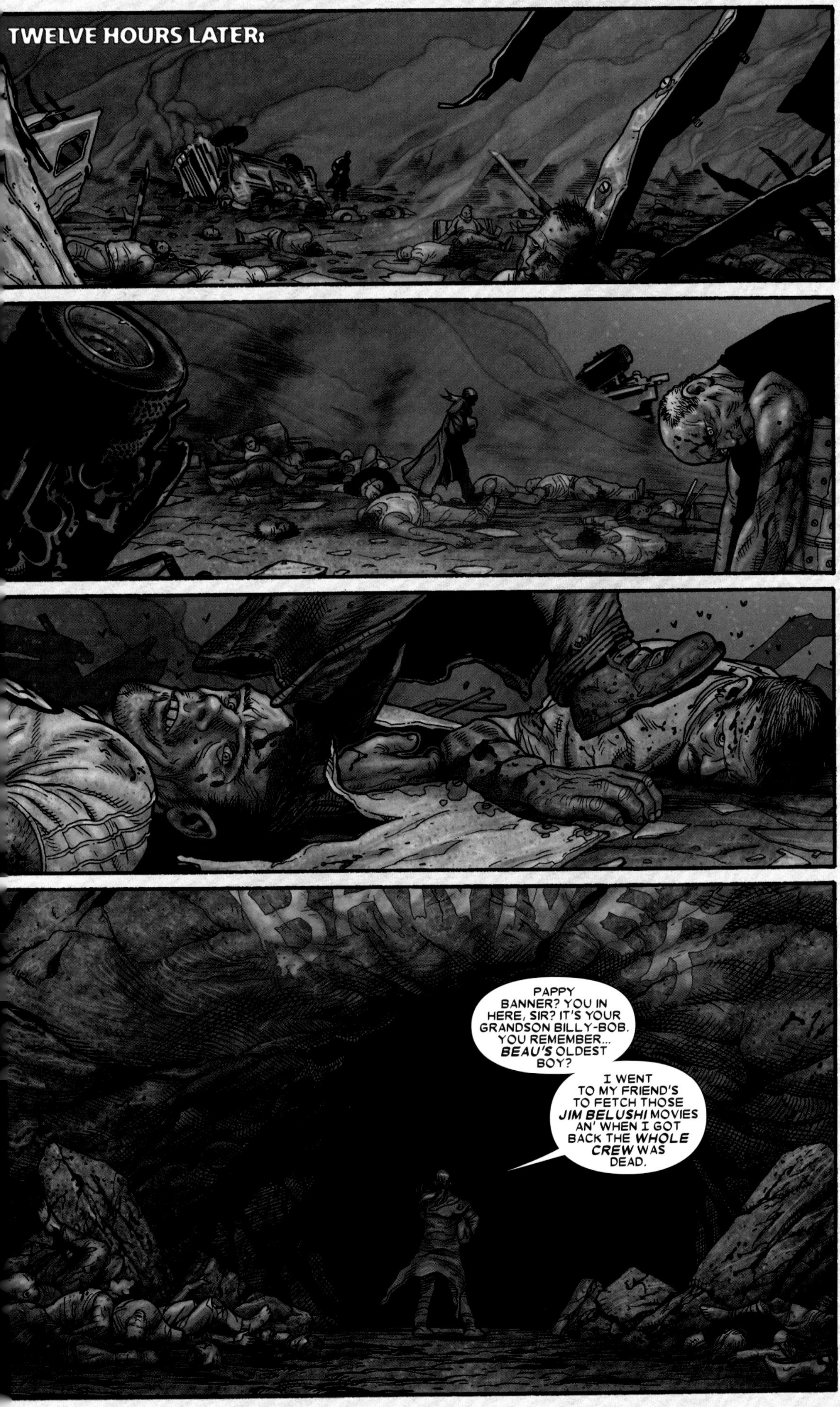
TWELVE HOURS LATER:
PAPPY BANNER? YOU IN HERE, SIR? IT'S YOUR GRANDSON BILLY-BOB. YOU REMEMBER... BEAU'S OLDEST BOY?
I WENT TO MY FRIEND'S TO FETCH THOSE JIM BELUSHI MOVIES AN' WHEN I GOT BACK THE WHOLE CREW WAS DEAD.

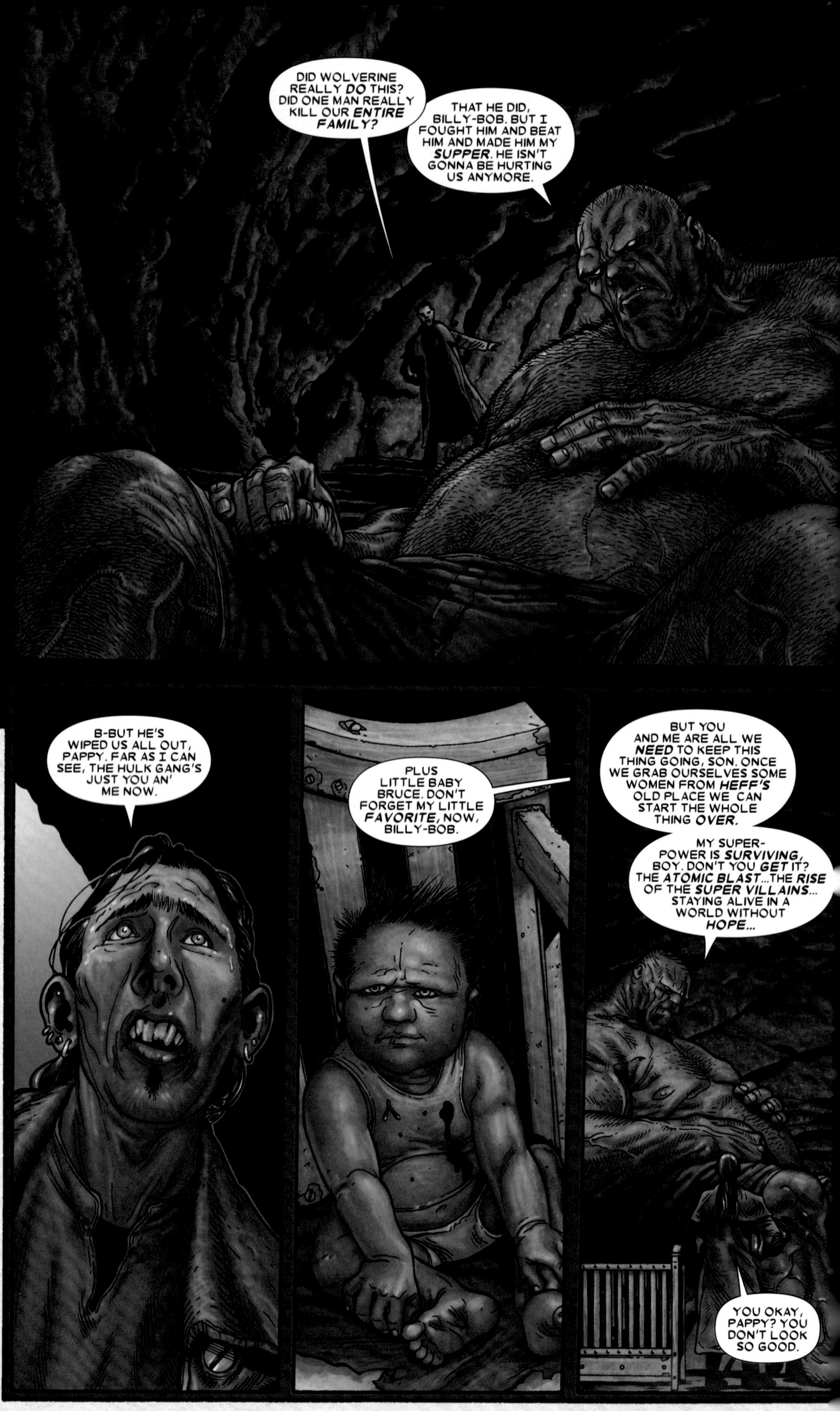
DID WOLVERINE REALLY DO THIS? DID ONE MAN REALLY KILL OUR ENTIRE FAMILY?
THAT HE DID, BILLY-BOB. BUT I FOUGHT HIM AND BEAT HIM AND MADE HIM MY SUPPER. HE ISN'T GONNA BE HURTING US ANYMORE.
B-BUT HE'S WIPED US ALL OUT, PAPPY. FAR AS I CAN SEE, THE HULK GANG'S JUST YOU AN' ME NOW.
PLUS LITTLE BABY BRUCE. DON'T FORGET MY LITTLE FAVORITE, NOW, BILLY-BOB.
BUT YOU AND ME ARE ALL WE NEED TO KEEP THIS THING GOING, SON. ONCE WE GRAB OURSELVES SOME WOMEN FROM HEFF'S OLD PLACE WE CAN START THE WHOLE THING OVER.
MY SUPER-POWER IS SURVIVING, BOY. DON'T YOU GET IT? THE ATOMIC BLAST...THE RISE OF THE SUPER VILLAINS... STAYING ALIVE IN A WORLD WITHOUT HOPE...
YOU OKAY, PAPPY? YOU DON'T LOOK SO GOOD.

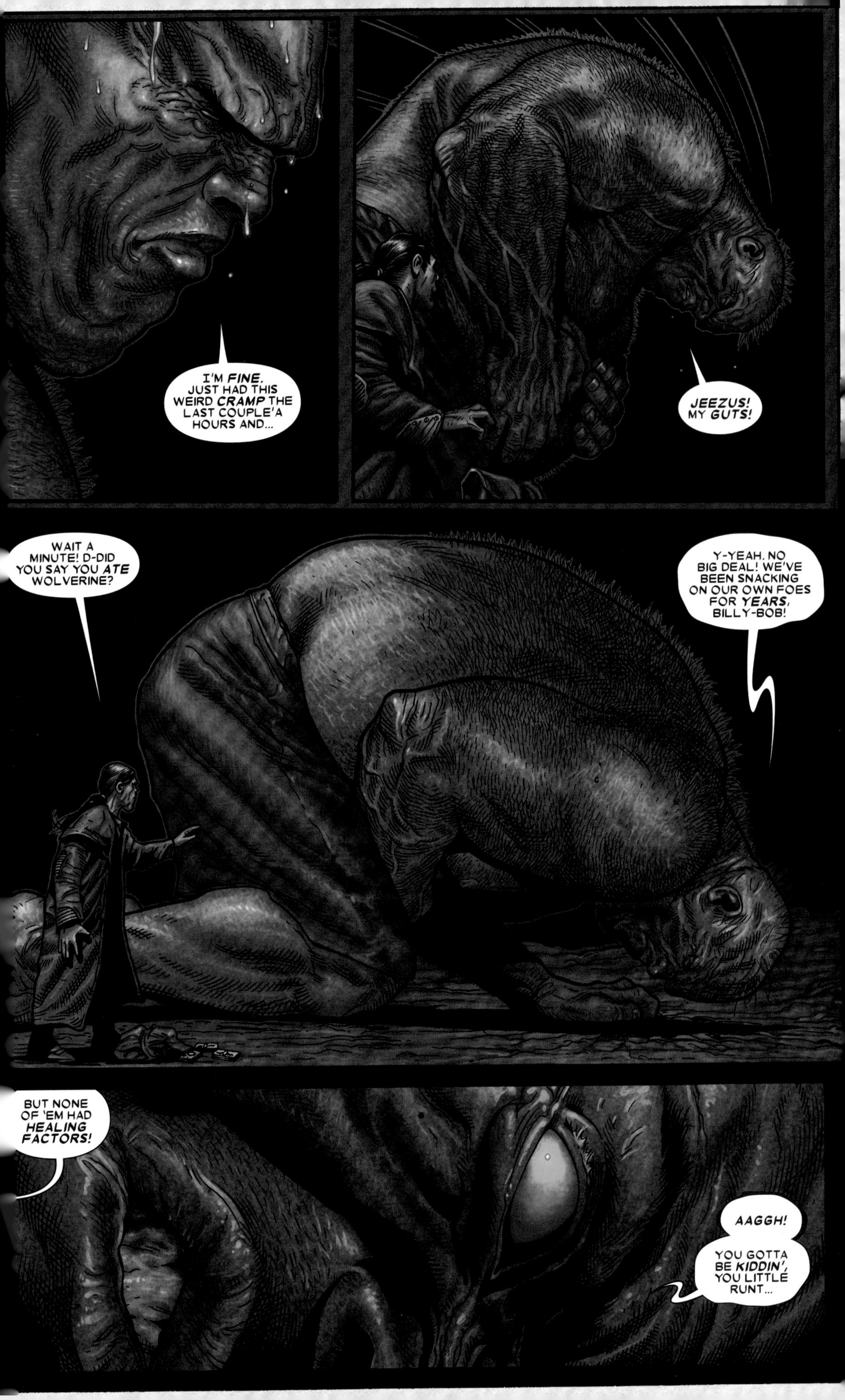
I'M FINE. JUST HAD THIS WEIRD CRAMP THE LAST COUPLE'A HOURS AND...
JEEZUS! MY GUTS!
WAIT A MINUTE! D-DID YOU SAY YOU ATE WOLVERINE?
Y-YEAH. NO BIG DEAL! WE'VE BEEN SNACKING ON OUR OWN FOES FOR YEARS, BILLY-BOB!
BUT NONE OF 'EM HAD HEALING FACTORS!
AAGGH!
YOU GOTTA BE KIDDIN', YOU LITTLE RUNT...

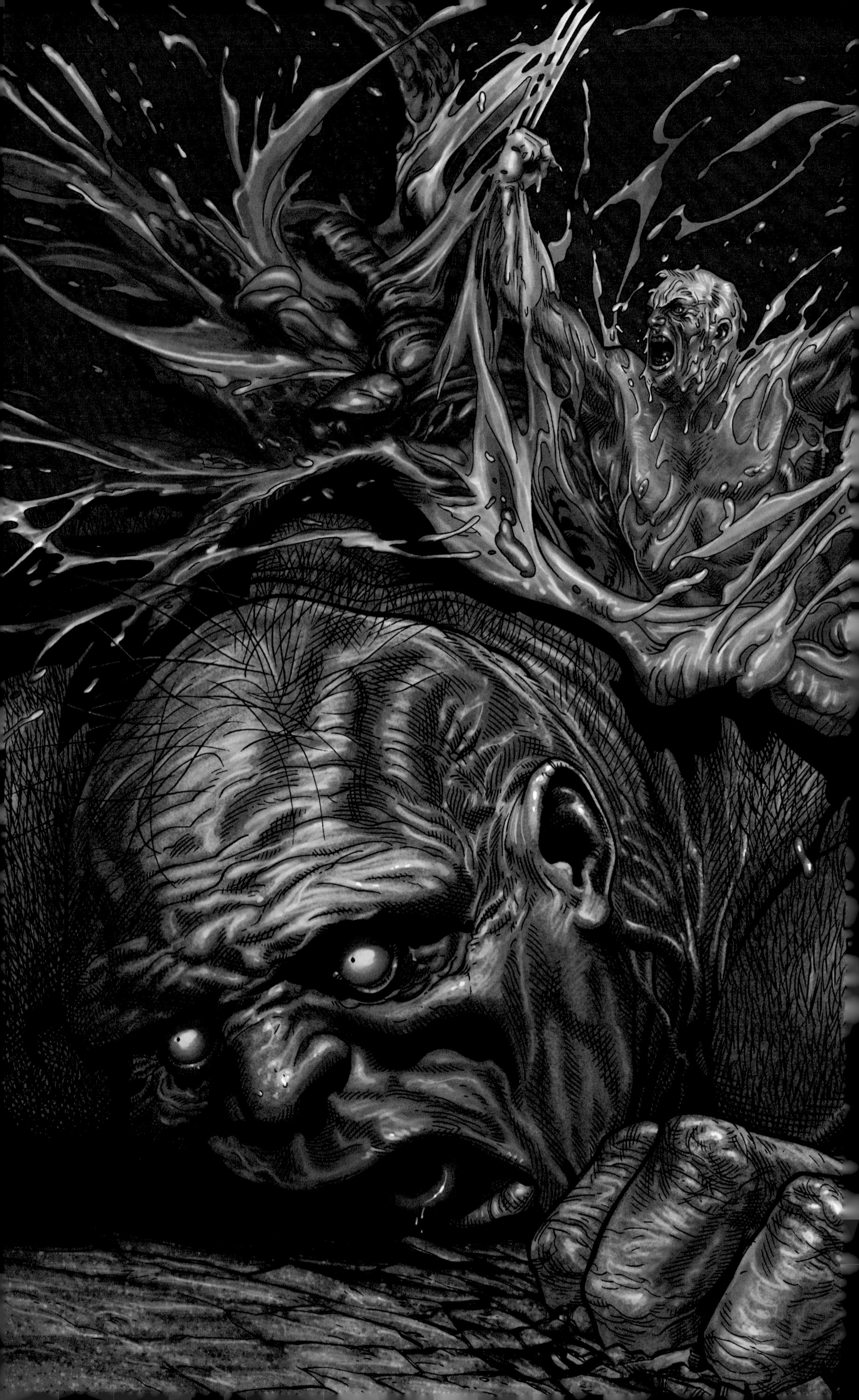

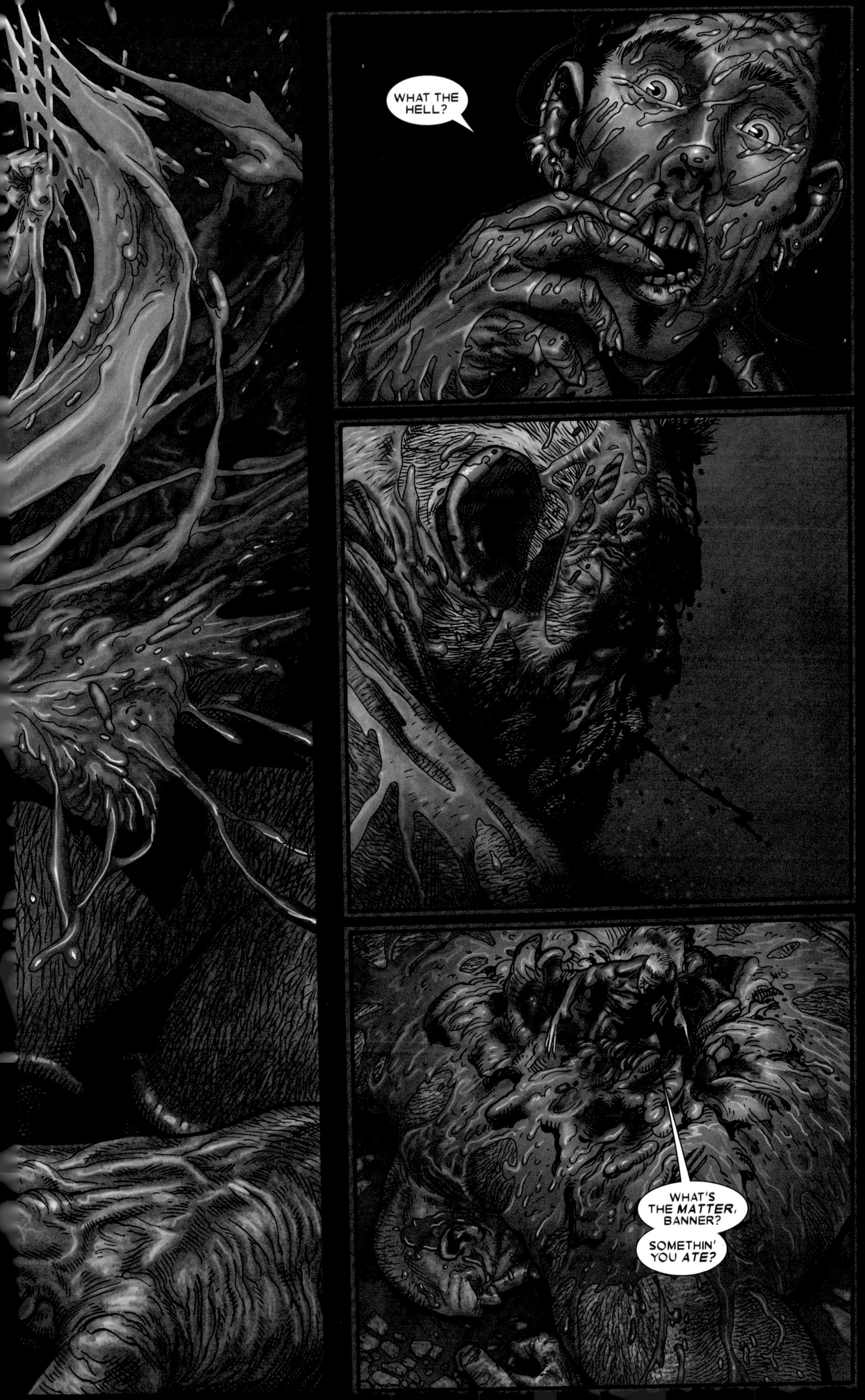
WHAT THE HELL?
WHAT'S THE *MATTER,* BANNER?
SOMETHIN' YOU *ATE?*

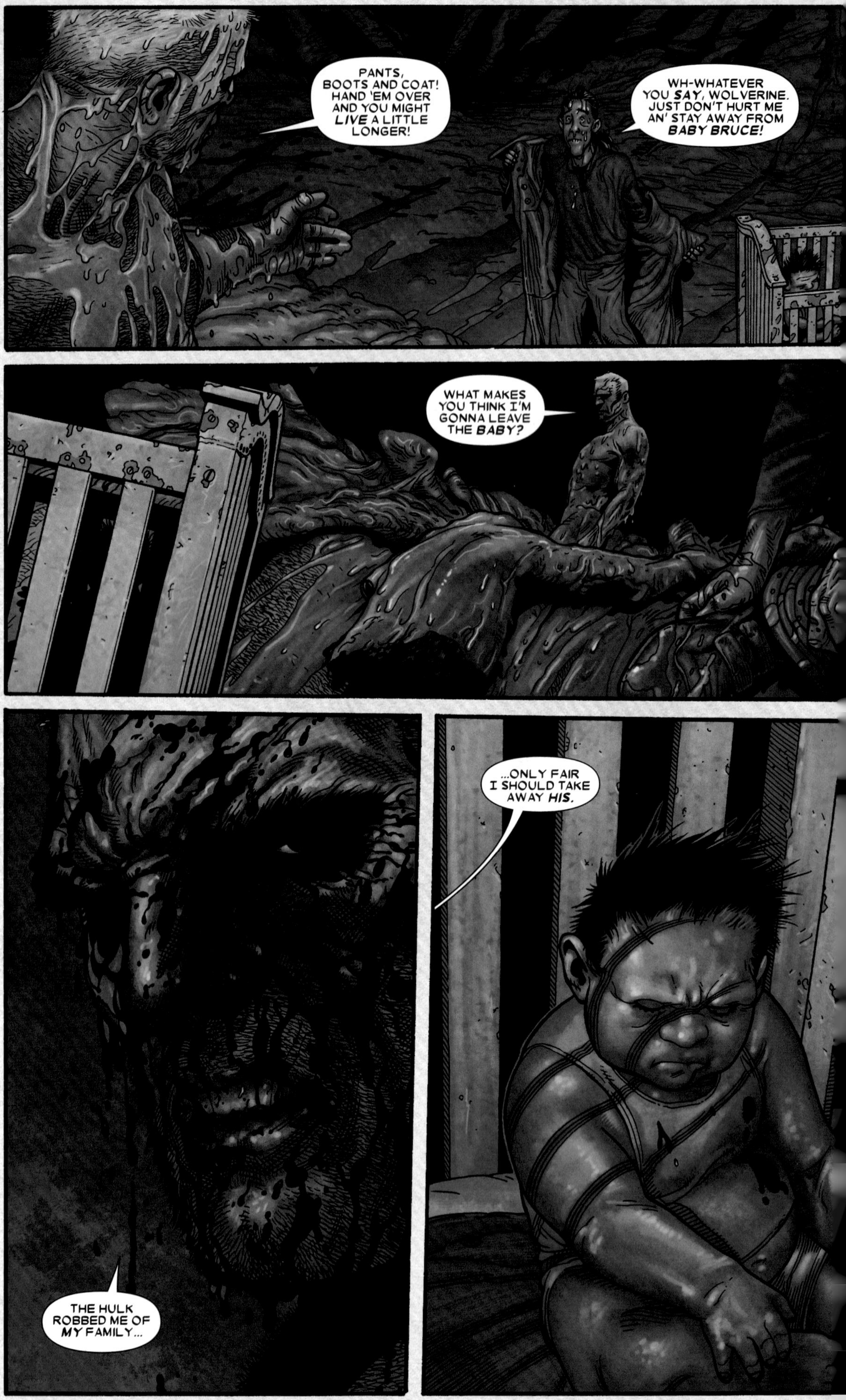
PANTS, BOOTS AND COAT! HAND 'EM OVER AND YOU MIGHT *LIVE* A LITTLE LONGER!
WH-WHATEVER YOU *SAY*, WOLVERINE. JUST DON'T HURT ME AN' STAY AWAY FROM *BABY BRUCE!*
WHAT MAKES YOU THINK I'M GONNA LEAVE THE *BABY?*
THE HULK ROBBED ME OF *MY* FAMILY...
...ONLY FAIR I SHOULD TAKE AWAY *HIS.*

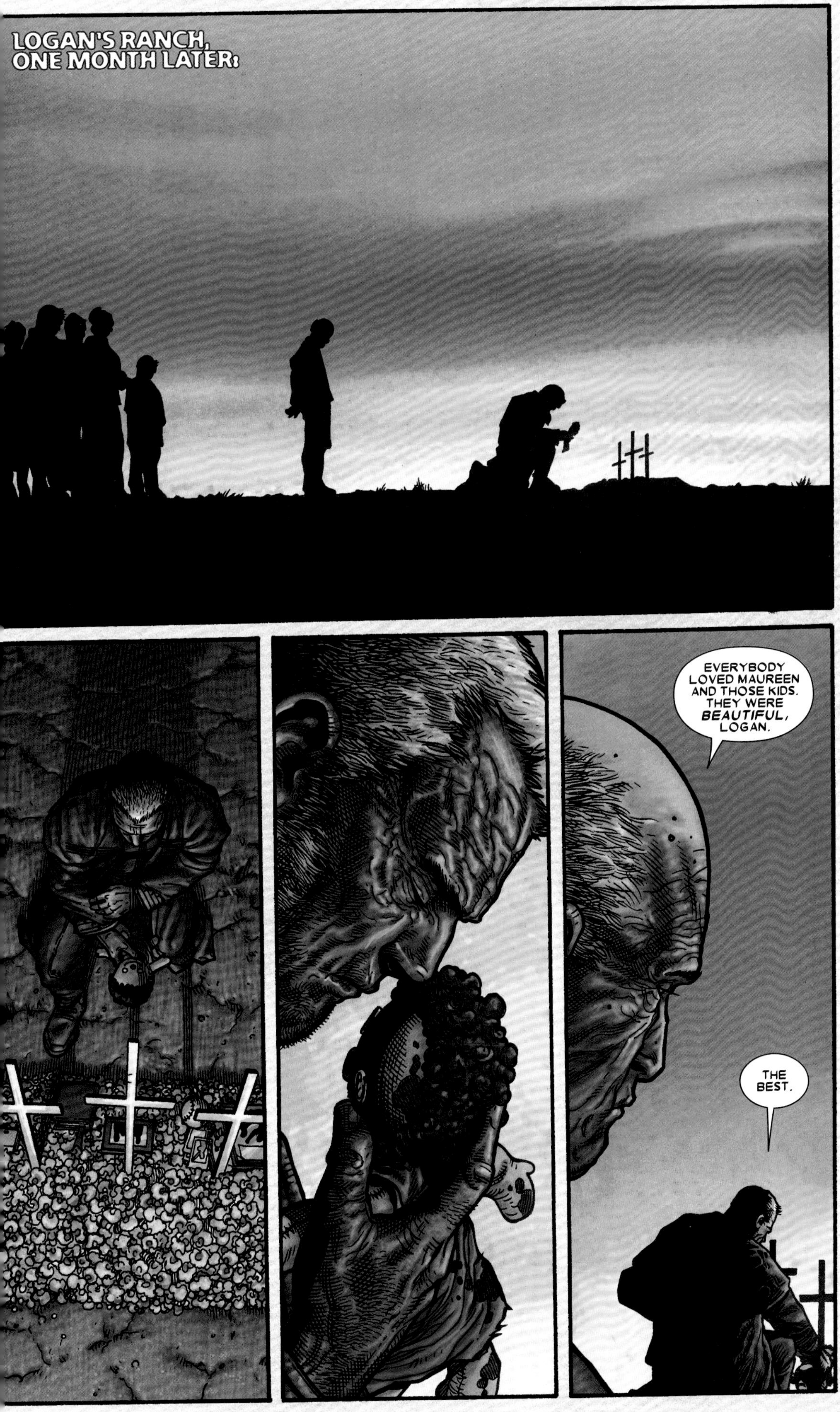
LOGAN'S RANCH, ONE MONTH LATER:
EVERYBODY LOVED MAUREEN AND THOSE KIDS. THEY WERE *BEAUTIFUL*, LOGAN.
THE BEST.

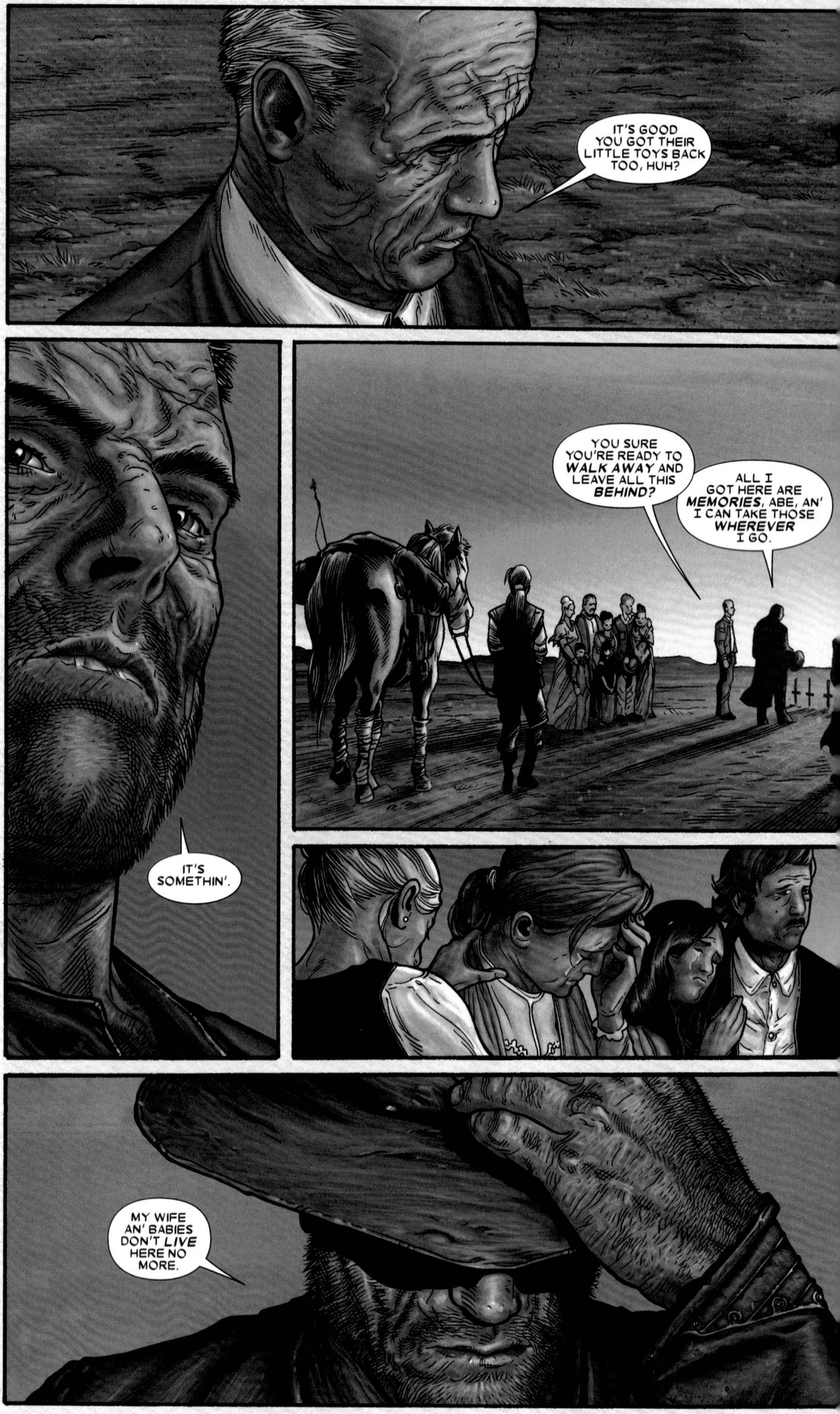
IT'S GOOD YOU GOT THEIR LITTLE TOYS BACK TOO, HUH?
IT'S SOMETHIN'.
YOU SURE YOU'RE READY TO WALK AWAY AND LEAVE ALL THIS BEHIND?
ALL I GOT HERE ARE MEMORIES, ABE, AN' I CAN TAKE THOSE WHEREVER I GO.
MY WIFE AN' BABIES DON'T LIVE HERE NO MORE.

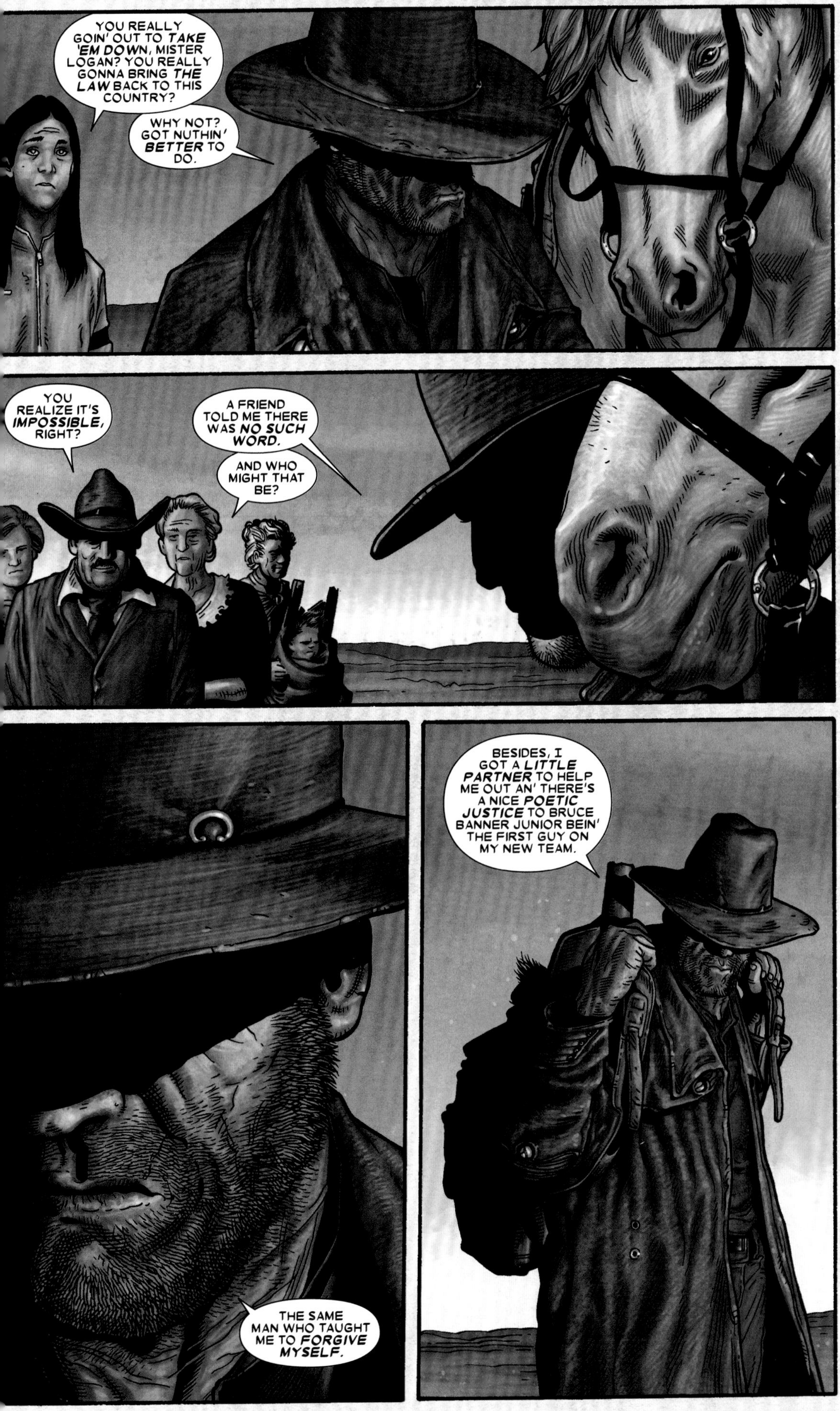

YOU REALLY GOIN' OUT TO TAKE 'EM DOWN, MISTER LOGAN? YOU REALLY GONNA BRING THE LAW BACK TO THIS COUNTRY?
WHY NOT? GOT NUTHIN' BETTER TO DO.
YOU REALIZE IT'S IMPOSSIBLE, RIGHT?
A FRIEND TOLD ME THERE WAS NO SUCH WORD.
AND WHO MIGHT THAT BE?
THE SAME MAN WHO TAUGHT ME TO FORGIVE MYSELF.
BESIDES, I GOT A LITTLE PARTNER TO HELP ME OUT AN' THERE'S A NICE POETIC JUSTICE TO BRUCE BANNER JUNIOR BEIN' THE FIRST GUY ON MY NEW TEAM.

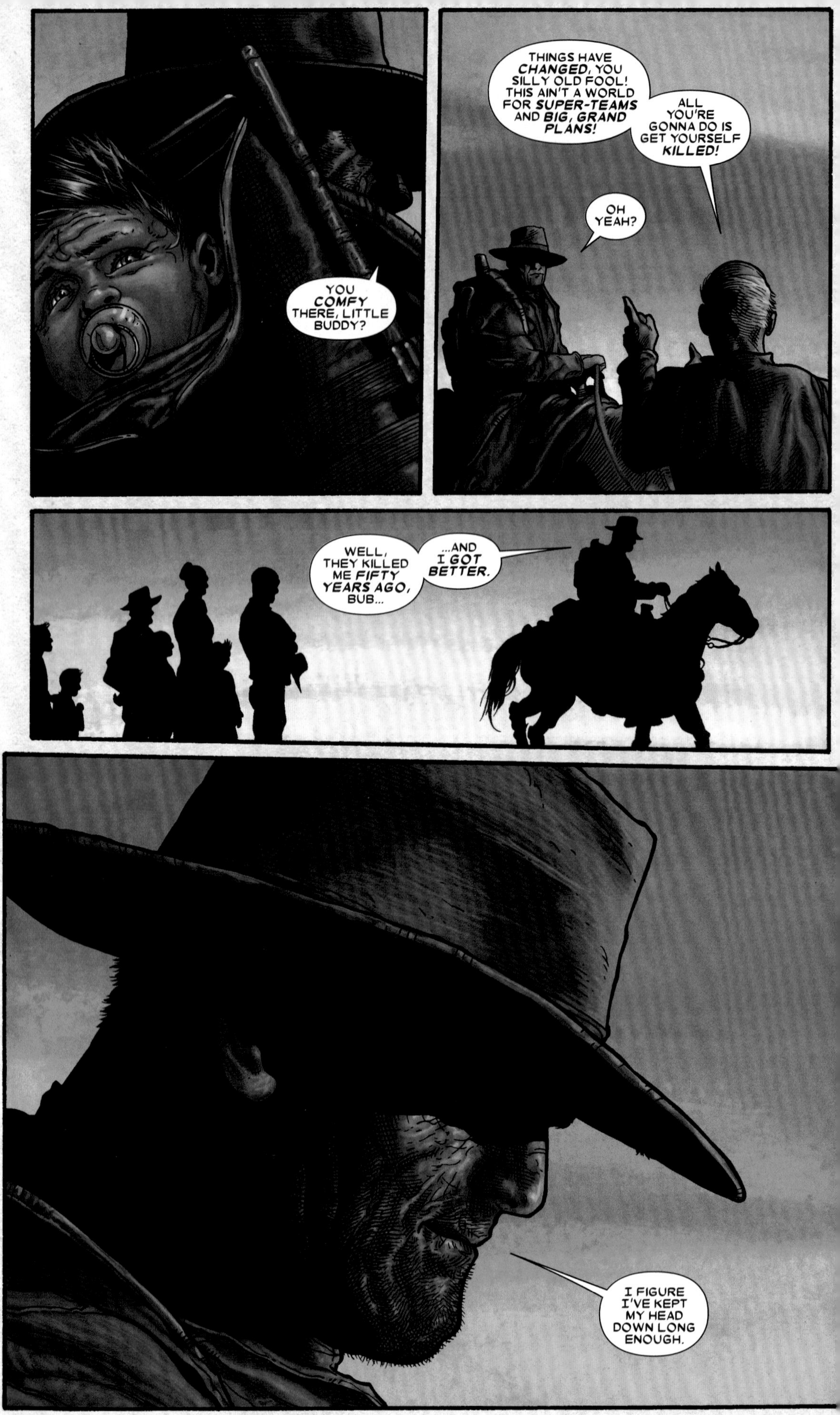
YOU COMFY THERE, LITTLE BUDDY?
THINGS HAVE CHANGED, YOU SILLY OLD FOOL! THIS AIN'T A WORLD FOR SUPER-TEAMS AND BIG, GRAND PLANS!
ALL YOU'RE GONNA DO IS GET YOURSELF KILLED!
OH YEAH?
WELL, THEY KILLED ME FIFTY YEARS AGO, BUB...
...AND I GOT BETTER.
I FIGURE I'VE KEPT MY HEAD DOWN LONG ENOUGH.

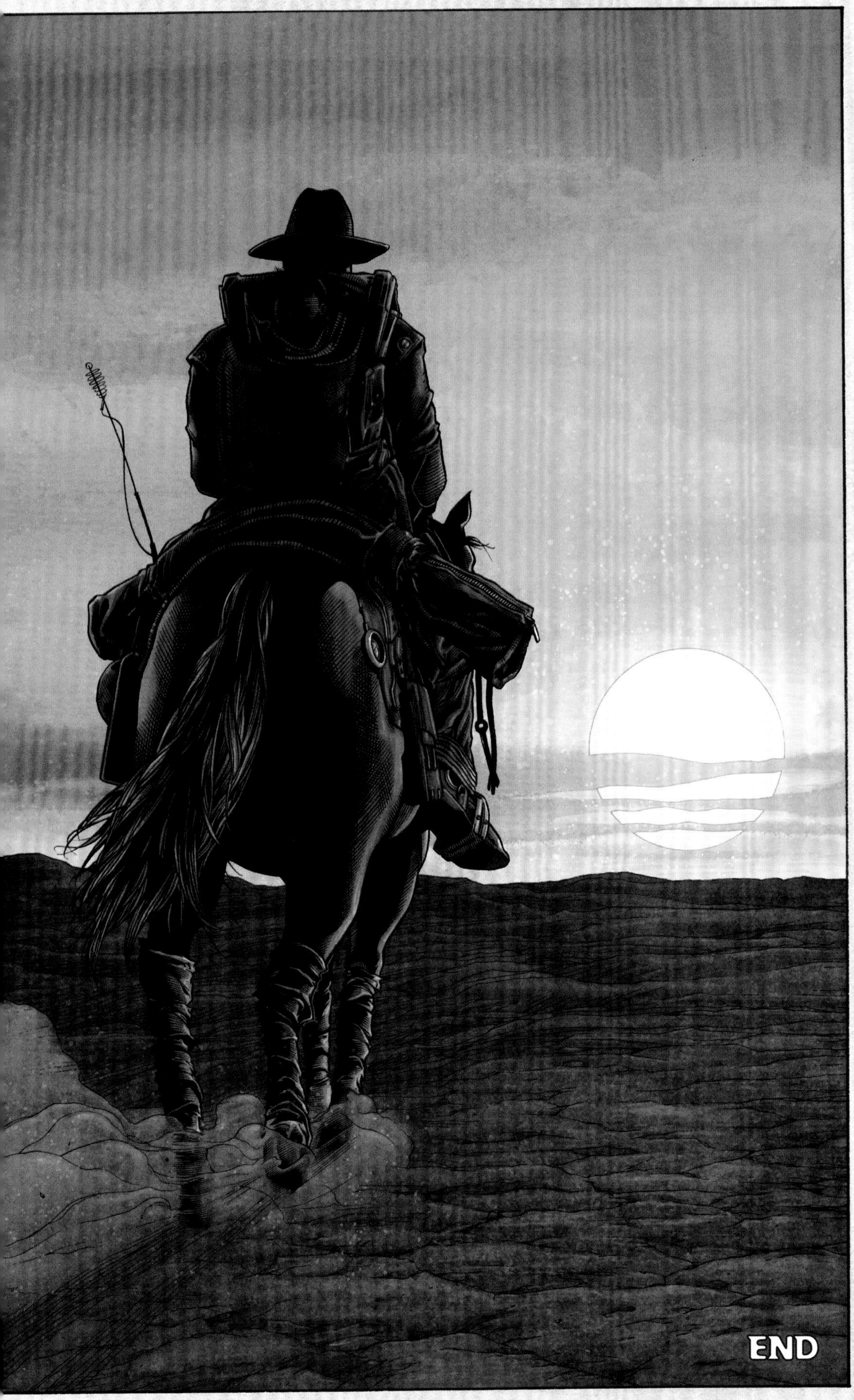
END

WOLVERINE: OLD MAN LOGAN GIANT-SIZE #1 VARIANT BY ED MCGUINNESS & CHRIS SOTOMAYOR

WOLVERINE: OLD MAN LOGAN GIANT-SIZE #1 VARIANT BY PAOLO RIVERA